Typesetting Tables with LaTeX

Typesetting Tables with LATEX

Herbert Voss

UIT
CAMBRIDGE, ENGLAND

Published by
UIT Cambridge Ltd.
PO Box 145
Cambridge
CB4 1GQ
England

Tel: +44 1223 302 041
Web: www.uit.co.uk

ISBN 978-1-906860-25-7

This book was previously published in German by
Lehmanns Media (**www.lehmanns.de**) in 2009.

10 9 8 7 6 5 4 3 2

Contents

Preface

You might be surprised that we've dedicated a whole book to typesetting tables in LaTeX but a quick glance at the volume of questions and contributions online about this topic highlights the need for a publication of this kind. The *LaTeX Companion* [42] offers only a short introduction to the basics of tables and the use of the most widely known packages in its 40-page chapter on the subject. More useful was the tabsatz [50] document created by Axel Reichert just over a decade ago, providing a general reference for problems with tables; we've included all of Axel's examples or adaptations of them in this publication.

Time has moved on since tabsatz was published, however, and more and more packages have been developed that support creating tables in many different ways. This book introduces all existing packages to you, though sometimes the scope of this publication limited the coverage we could give each package, especially for the datatool package by Nicola Talbot.

In principle, TeX does not distinguish between a table and a matrix (array). Nevertheless, this book only deals with tables containing normal text. If you want to find out more about typesetting tables containing mathematical elements, look in *Mathematics with LaTeX* [56].

You can download all the examples as complete LaTeX documents at CTAN (Comprehensive TeX Archive Network – http://www.ctan.org) in the directory CTAN://info/examples/Tabellen/. Only use them for experimenting; often loading packages or general code has been moved into the non-visible preamble in the examples for space reasons; for example loading the package eurosym when using the € symbol. The omitted parts are never important to understand the examples though. Some of the examples use non-standard packages or further external programs; they are available in the same CTAN directory.

If nothing else has been specified, the packages from TeX Live 2007 or the packages from CTAN from the end of 2007 are used. Newer versions of TeX Live should not cause any problems unless individual packages have made extreme changes to the syntax. Sometimes explanations of different packages will seem similar; we decided it would be better to restate them instead of referring the reader to the appropriate explanation given for a different package. It is always difficult to evaluate which individual packages are best, but loading the `array`, `booktabs`, `tabularx`, and (for external data) `datatool` packages should always be a sensible default. Identifying preferences between the other packages is left to the reader.

Conventions used in this book:

- Names of commands, environments, packages etc. when referred to in the text are set in a monospace font, like `longtable`.
- Throughout the book we have referred to mathematics as math.
- Optional symbols or parameters are signified in syntax by being set against a grey background. For environments, this applies especially to the starred variant (*).
- In some cases parts of a preamble have been moved to the non-visible part of an example's coding to save space. There is always a note in the text where this has been done. This will not limit the user's understanding; the entire source code of all the examples can be downloaded from CTAN at any time (`http://mirror.CTAN.org/info/examples/Tabulars-E/`).

CTAN

- The symbol in the margin indicates an issue that the user should bear in mind as it can cause a problem.

My thanks, as always, go to Klaus Höppner, Lutz Ihlenburg, Christoph Kaeder, Rolf Niepraschk, Uwe Ziegenhagen, and especially Volker RW Schaa, who kindly looked over the manuscript, pointed out errors, and gave valuable feedback. And last but not least a big thank you to Lars Kotthoff, who translated this English version from the German original and to Catherine Jagger for her excellent job of proof reading.

Berlin, November 2010 Herbert Voß

Chapter 1

Introduction

When you display information in a table, the typography you choose is very important; tables containing the same information can be typeset in many different ways, but some layouts will be much clearer than others. It's difficult (and subjective) to define conventions that will always result in a table that is easily understood, but the following points are good guidelines:

- no vertical lines
- no double lines
- rows not too narrow
- columns not too far apart
- rows left- and right-aligned with horizontal lines
- horizontal lines of different widths

This first chapter looks at the two environments supported in standard LaTeX for typesetting tables: the `tabular` environment and the `tabbing` environment. Chapters 2–4 introduce all the additional packages that provide support for typesetting tables, with chapter 3 focusing on the use of colour and chapter 4 on multi-page tables. Chapters 5 and 7 cover some general points that are not package specific, while chapter 6 provides a large and useful set of examples to help the reader.

1.1 The tabular environment

The default `tabular` environment corresponds to the mathematical `array` environment (not to be confused with the `array` package cf. Section 2.1 on page 21). The syntax of the `tabular` environment and its alternative starred version are:

```
\begin{tabular} [position] {column definition}
...&...&...\\
...&...&...\\
...
\end{tabular}

\begin{tabular*}{width} [position] {column definition}
...&...&...\\
...&...&...\\
...
\end{tabular*}
```

Valid notations for the *column definition* are:

`l`	left-aligned column (without line break!).
`c`	centred column (without line break!).
`r`	right-aligned column (without line break!).
`p{`*length*`}`	corresponds to the definition `\parbox[`*c*`]{`*length*`}`; it is always typeset justified and with line breaks.
`@{`*column separator*`}`	inserts `@{`*column separator*`}` before and after each column; by default, this uses the `\tabcolsep` space (cf. Table 1.1 for further explanation).
|	vertical line, can be extended arbitrarily to || ...

TEX can measure the width of a table exactly, as shown in the following example, which means you can predetermine the exact width of a table. Table 1.1 has a column definition of `{|l|r|p{3cm}|}` and is followed by a list of the widths of each component of the table.

Table 1.1: This example illustrates the use of the `\tabcolsep` space; the lighter block marks the left side of a column and the darker block the right.

left	right	p{3cm}
left	right	p{3cm}

width	*value*
\tabcolsep	6.0pt
\widthof{left}	13.36996pt
2\tabcolsep	12.0pt
\widthof{right}	19.96996pt
2\tabcolsep	12.0pt
p{3cm}	85.35826pt
\tabcolsep	6.0pt
full width	154.69818pt

01-01-1

If the whole table is put into a box, the resulting width is 156.29816pt when using the `array` package at the same time; this corresponds to a difference of 1.59998pt, or rounded 1.6pt. This is the sum of the width of the four vertical lines in Table 1.1, which is given by the width of `\arrayrulewidth`=0.4pt. If these vertical lines are omitted, or the `array` package is not used, the width of the box is 154.69818pt. All of the lengths specified here were measured by TEX and output with `\the\<length>` to ensure that the calculation was correct.

Being able to determine the exact width of a table is especially useful when you want a table to span several pages, using the whole width of each page. However, actually achieving this is only possible through reading an external file or using other packages, as shown in Section 4.3 on page 141. Without any extension package, there are only two special symbols that you can use for extended column definitions, * and @:

*{*number*}{*column type*}, where *number* is the repetition factor and *column type* an arbitrary code sequence.

01-01-2

l	l	l	r	r	r	r
L	L	L	R	R	R	R

```
\usepackage{array}

\begin{tabular}
 {|*{3}{l}|*{4}{r|}}\cline{1-3}
l&l&l&r&r&r&r\\ L&L&L&R&R&R&R\\\cline{1-3}
\end{tabular}
```

@{...}, where "..." stands for an arbitrary code sequence that is now inserted on each line *instead* of the column spacing. There is no space to the left and right between two columns. In the following example, firstly a colon and then an arrow are inserted instead of the column space.

01-01-3

left	right:centred→box
l	r: c →p{1.5cm}

```
\begin{tabular}%
   {@{}l|r@{:}c@{$\rightarrow$}p{1.5cm}@{}}
left & right & centred & box\\\cline{2-4}
l & r & c & p\{1.5cm\}\\\cline{1-1}
\end{tabular}
```

Using the starred version of the tabular environment lets you specify a certain table width; however, LaTeX only adapts the width of the last column to achieve the specification. The following example shows this clearly; the last column of the second table is right-aligned, but this has no effect as the space that follows remains the same as in the first table.

01-01-4

1	2	3
A	B	left

1	2	3
A	B	right

```
\begin{tabular*}{\linewidth}{lll}
1 & 2 & 3 \\\hline A & B & left \\\hline
\end{tabular*}\par\bigskip
\begin{tabular*}{\linewidth}{llr}
1 & 2 & 3 \\\hline A & B & right \\\hline
\end{tabular*}
```

This doesn't usually produce a satisfactory result, but if you also use the @ operator and the \extracolsep command, an even distribution of the "column widths" can be achieved. The syntax of the \extracolsep command is:

```
\extracolsep{length}
```

To achieve an even distribution of columns, you have to pass the dynamic length \fill as the {*length*} or column distance. The difference between enlarging the column width and the spacing between columns (\tabcolsep) becomes visible when using vertical lines; the following examples clearly illustrate that the tabular* environment only changes the spacing between columns.

1	2	3
A	B	C

1	2	3
A	B	C

```
\begin{tabular*}{\linewidth}%
   {|l@{\extracolsep{\fill}}|l|l|}
1 & 2 & 3 \\\hline A & B & C \\\hline
\end{tabular*}\par\bigskip
\begin{tabular*}{\linewidth}%
   {|l|l|@{\extracolsep{\fill}}r|}
1 & 2 & 3 \\\hline A & B & C \\\hline
\end{tabular*}
```

01-01-5

As the first table above showed, inserting `@{\extracolsep{\fill}}` *after* the first table column distributes the additional column spacing evenly. Alternatively you can insert it before the first column if you don't want a `\tabcolsep` space at the left-aligned border, as shown below.

1	2	3
A	B	C

1	2	3
left	left	right

```
\begin{tabular*}{\linewidth}%
   {|@{\extracolsep{\fill}}l|l|l@{}|}
1 & 2 & 3 \\\hline A & B & C \\\hline
\end{tabular*}\par\bigskip
\begin{tabular*}{\linewidth}%
   {|@{\extracolsep{\fill}}l|l|r@{}|}
1 & 2 & 3 \\\hline
left & left & right \\\hline
\end{tabular*}
```

01-01-6

To achieve better results, you should use the `tabularx` environment from the package of the same name when creating tables of a certain width; corresponding examples can be found in Section 2.18 on page 87. Alternatively, the widths of the columns can be calculated manually, as shown already in Table 1.1 on page 4. The advantage of this is that it is the widths of the columns that are adapted to achieve the specified width and not the spacing between the columns.

tabularx

1.1.1 Lines

You should always bear in mind that lines usually do *not* improve the clarity of a table and using them is often counterproductive. This is especially true for vertical lines. Therefore, the following examples are explicitly not intended as a guide, but only as examples of how to create lines. Horizontal lines spanning the whole table width are created with `\hline`, or you can use `\cline` to add a horizontal line across a specified range of columns.

```
\hline
\cline{start column-end column}
```

You usually need to precede either of these commands with `\\` or `\tabularnewline`; the only exception is when you want to get a line above a table, in which case the relevant command is placed immediately after the column definition. If the values for *start column* and *end column* are the same, the line spans only this single column.

Horizontal lines always take precedence over vertical lines (particularly important to remember if you are using double lines). This results from the fact that TeX typesets the vertical lines line by line, only taking the line height into account. The following example shows how to use \hline to create borders and multiple lines:

01-01-7

left	p-column	right
A	Now this column has a fixed width and a \ creates a new row in this column	B
1	2	3

```
\begin{tabular}{|l||p{4cm}|r||}\hline
 left & p--column & right\\
    \hline\hline\hline
 A      &  Now this column has a fixed width
           and a \Lcs{\newline}\newline
           creates a new row in
           this column & B \\\hline\hline
     1 &  2          & 3 \\\hline\hline
\end{tabular}
```

The next example also uses the \cline command:

01-01-8

left	p-column	right
A	Now this column has a fixed width and a \ creates a new row in this column	B
1	2	3

```
\begin{tabular}{lp{4cm}r}
left & p--column & right\\
        \cline{1-2}\hline% see text below
 A      &  Now this column has a fixed width
           and a \Lcs{\newline}\newline
           creates a new row in this
           column & B \\\cline{2-2}
     1 &  2          & 3 \\\cline{2-3}
\end{tabular}
```

\cline{*2-2*} creates a line only below the second column and \cline{*2-3*} below the second and third columns. If a \cline command is preceded or followed by a \hline command, it has no effect as it is overwritten by \hline. \cline may occur several times in a row, but behaves like a single \cline without code modifications! However, you can use \cline several times in a row to achieve horizontal lines over various ranges of columns, as in Example 01-01-11 on the next page. To find out how to colour horizontal lines, see Section 3.3 on page 122.

Very thick lines can look bad as LaTeX can't join them neatly at the corners and doesn't take the width of the lines into account when determining the line spacing, as illustrated here: *thick lines*

01-01-9

```
\setlength\arrayrulewidth{5pt}
\begin{tabular}{|c|c|}\hline
A & B \\\cline{1-1}
C & D \\\hline
\end{tabular}
```

You can easily influence the height of an individual row by inserting a \rule command in one of its cells. Setting the width to null makes the inserted line invisible. Vertical lines are more problematic as their width does *not* affect the horizontal width of a table; the lines are drawn "on top" of the text. Bear this in mind especially for thick vertical lines. The array package (cf. Section 2.1 on page 21) fixes the corner connections and produces better results with thick vertical lines (cf. Section 2.1.1 on page 26). This example uses both the array package and the \rule command to produce a better result: *vertical lines*

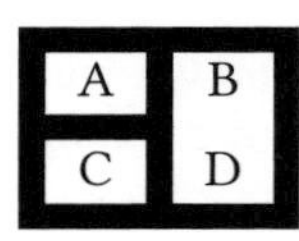

```
\usepackage{array}

\setlength\arrayrulewidth{5pt}
\begin{tabular}{|c|c|}\hline
A & B \\\cline{1-1}
\rule{0pt}{3.2ex}C & D \\\hline
\end{tabular}
```

01-01-10

1.1.2 Cells covering several columns

The `\multicolumn` command allows you to merge *several* cells within a row into *one* cell with an independent column definition, including the possibility of adding vertical lines that are only valid for this cell. It can also be used for an individual cell to change the column type. The syntax is:

`\multicolumn{`*number of columns*`}{`*column definition*`}{`*content*`}`

For the *column definition*, you can use any of the notations valid for the standard `tabular` environment. More options are available when using the `array` package, (cf. Section 2.1 on page 21).

```
\begin{tabular}{@{}cccc@{}}\hline
\multicolumn{2}{|@{}c}{\textbf{people}} &
   \multicolumn{2}{@{}c|}{\textbf{profession}}\\\hline
number& sex  & employed & freelance\\\hline
222   &  m   &    160   & 62        \\
  2   &  n   &\textbf{1}& 2         \\[5pt]
97    &  w   &    70    & 27        \\\hline
\multicolumn{4}{c}{sums}            \\\cline{1-1}
\multicolumn{1}{@{}|c|@{}}{319} & & 230 & 89 \\\cline{1-1}\cline{3-4}
      &      & \multicolumn{2}{|c|}{319}\\\cline{3-4}
\end{tabular}
```

people		**profession**	
number	sex	employed	freelance
222	m	160	62
2	n	**1**	2
97	w	70	27
sums			
319		230	89
		319	

01-01-11

Using the `\multicolumn` command is fairly straightforward, but you need to take a little care over vertical lines. The table's overall column definition, controlling each column's type and vertical lines, is ignored through `\multicolumn`, so part of a vertical line will be missing unless you remember to repeat the line definition within `\multicolumn`. Normally this only applies when a column followed by a vertical line is included in a `\multicolumn` command, but in the case where the first column is incorporated as well, any lefthand vertical line that borders the cell must also be redefined within the command. The following examples show the different effects of vertical line definitions when the `\multicolumn` command is used:

01-01-12

people		**profession**	
number	sex	employed	freelance
222	m	160	62
2	n	**1**	2
97	w	70	27
		sums	
319		230	89
		319	

```
\begin{tabular}{|cc|cc|}\hline
\multicolumn{2}{|c}{\textbf{people}} &
\multicolumn{2}{c|}{\textbf{profession}} \\\hline
\multicolumn{4}{c}{}\\% empty line without |
number& sex& employed& freelance\\\hline
222   &    m    &    160 & 62   \\
  2   &    n    &\textbf{1}&2   \\[5pt]
97    &    w    &     70  & 27   \\\hline
\multicolumn{4}{c}{sums}      \\\cline{1-1}
\multicolumn{1}{|c|}{319} & & 230 & 89
    \\\cline{1-1}\cline{3-4}
 & & \multicolumn{2}{c|}{319}\\\cline{3-4}
\end{tabular}
```

01-01-13

people		*profession*	
number	sex	employed	freelance
222	m	160	62
2	n	**1**	2
97	w	70	27
		sums	
319		230	89
		319	

```
\begin{tabular}{|cc|cc|}
\multicolumn{2}{|c|}{\emph{people}} &
\multicolumn{2}{c|}{\emph{profession}}\\[5pt]
number & sex & employed & freelance\\\hline
222      &    m     &    160   & 62   \\
  2      &    n     &\textbf{1}&  2 \\[5pt]
97       &    w     &     70    & 27   \\\hline
\multicolumn{4}{|c|}{sums}       \\\cline{1-1}
\multicolumn{1}{|c|}{319} & & 230 & 89
     \\\cline{1-1}\cline{3-4}
\multicolumn{1}{c}{}
  & &  \multicolumn{2}{c|}{319} \\\cline{3-4}
\end{tabular}
```

1.1.3 Nested tables

Tables can be nested arbitrarily. We recommend that you align the code clearly though, as nestings frequently make it harder to get an overview and errors are introduced more easily, which are then very hard to find. Nesting tables lets you typeset any complex arrangement without having to resort to using the `multirow` package (cf. Section 2.3 on page 30), which doesn't always produce the desired result. In the following example, the cells with lowercase characters are part of a nested table, which can be framed easily with the `\hline` or `\cline` command.

```
\begin{tabular}{ccccc}
A1 & A1 & A1 & A1 & A1\\\hline
A2 & \begin{tabular}{|c|}\hline
       a1\\a1\\a1\\\hline
     \end{tabular}
```

```
        & \begin{tabular}{c}a2\\a2\\a2\\\end{tabular}
             & A & \begin{tabular}{|c|}\hline
                     a3\\a3\\a4\\\hline
                   \end{tabular}\\
A3 & A3 & A3 & A3 & A3\\\cline{3-4}
A4 & A4 & \multicolumn{2}{|c|}{A4*} & A4\\\cline{3-4}
A5 & A5 & A5 & A5 & A5\\
\end{tabular}
```

A1	A1	A1	A1	A1
A2	a1 a1 a1	a2 a2 a2	A	a3 a3 a4
A3	A3	A3	A3	A3
A4	A4	A4*		A4
A5	A5	A5	A5	A5

01-01-14

The following example shows an unsatisfactory result, with the spacing between the columns much too large. This is caused by the \tabcolsep space that precedes every table, leading to additional space when a table is nested inside another table. According to Table 1.1 on page 4, in this example there is a space of 3\tabcolsep or 4\tabcolsep between any two columns.

co1 l1	co2 l1	co3 l1
co1 l2 co1 l3	co2 l2/3	co4 l2 co4 l3
co1 l4	co2 l4	co3 l4

```
\begin{tabular}{|ccc|}
 co1 l1 & co2 l1 & co3 l1\\
 \begin{tabular}{c}co1 l2\\co1 l3\end{tabular}
 & \begin{tabular}{|c|}\hline
    co2 l2/3\\\hline \end{tabular}
 & \begin{tabular}{c}co4 l2\\co4 l3\end{tabular}\\
  co1 l4 & co2 l4 & co3 l4
\end{tabular}
```

01-01-15

Using the @ column operator corrects these additional spaces, as shown in the following example. In this case the superordinate table uses a column definition of {|@{}c @{}c@{} c@{}|} to ensure that all the columns have no extra space (as can be seen on the outside of the external columns). Nevertheless, there is still a space of 2\tabcolsep between the inner columns, caused by the inner (nested) tables.

co1 l1	co2 l1	co3 l1
co1 l2 co1 l3	co2 l2/3	co4 l2 co4 l3
co1 l4	co2 l4	co3 l4

```
\begin{tabular}{|@{}c @{}c@{} c@{}|}
  co1 l1 & co2 l1 & co3 l1\\
  \begin{tabular}{c} co1 l2\\co1 l3 \end{tabular} &
  \begin{tabular}{|c|}\hline
    co2 l2/3\\\hline \end{tabular} &
  \begin{tabular}{c} co4 l2\\co4 l3 \end{tabular}\\
  co1 l4 & co2 l4 & co3 l4
\end{tabular}
```

01-01-16

|@{} and @{}| are different

The order of | and @{} has to be observed; at the start of a column definition you must specify first the vertical line, then no additional space. If you did the reverse, (@{} then |), @{}

would have no effect – it is cancelled by the vertical line, which is then followed by either the default \tabcolsep or whatever else is specified next.

You can take different approaches, depending on what structure of table and placement of lines you want to produce. For example inner tables can be typeset without spacing between the columns, or the frame of an inner table can be put around it from the outside, as illustrated in the following example.

01-01-17

co1 l1	co2 l1	co3 l1
co1 l2	co2 l2/3	co4 l2
co1 l3		co4 l3
co1 l4	co2 l4	co3 l4

```
\begin{tabular}{@{}c @{}c@{} c@{}}
  co1 l1 & co2 l1 & co3 l1\\\cline{2-2}
  \begin{tabular}{c|} co1 l2\\co1 l3 \end{tabular} &
  \begin{tabular}{c} co2 l2/3 \end{tabular} &
  \begin{tabular}{|c} co4 l2\\co4 l3 \end{tabular}
     \\\cline{2-2}
  co1 l4 & co2 l4 & co3 l4
\end{tabular}
```

It is also a good idea to define abbreviations to make your code clearer and therefore reduce the likelihood of errors with nested tables. For example we define:

```
\newcommand\Btab{}% make sure that it does not exist
\renewcommand\Btab[2][c]{\tabular[#1]{#2}}
\newcommand\Etab{}% ditto
\renewcommand\Etab{\endtabular}
```

We will define and use these commands in the following example. Also in this case the first line is extended upwards and the last line downwards to achieve a better placement of the frame; this is done using \rule.

01-01-18

co1 l1	co2 l1	co3 l1
co1 l2	co2 l2/3	co4 l2
co1 l3		co4 l3
co1 l4	co2 l4	co3 l4

```
\newcommand\Btab{}
\renewcommand\Btab[2][c]{\tabular[#1]{#2}}
\newcommand\Etab{}\renewcommand\Etab{\endtabular}

\Btab{|@{}c @{}c@{} c@{}|}\hline
  \rule{0pt}{3ex}% better spacing above
  co1 l1 & co2 l1 & co3 l1\\\cline{2-2}
  \Btab{c|} co1 l2\\co1 l3 \Etab &
  \Btab{c} co2 l2/3\\ \Etab &
    \Btab{|c} co4 l2\\co4 l3 \Etab \\\cline{2-2}
  \rule[-1.5ex]{0pt}{2ex}% better spacing below
  co1 l4 & co2 l4 & co3 l4\\\hline
\Etab
```

Further explanations on producing specific types of lines can be found in:

- ▷ Example 03-03-1 on page 122 for coloured lines.
- ▷ Section 2.2 on page 27 for dashed lines.
- ▷ Section 2.10 on page 64 for non-overlapping double (sub-)lines.

1.1.4 Footnotes

The `\footnote` command doesn't work as expected within a table as the text of the footnote doesn't display. Instead, there are packages that support footnotes in tables or you can use the `\footnotemark` and `\footnotetext` combination of commands. The latter works in virtually all cases where the `\footnote` command fails.

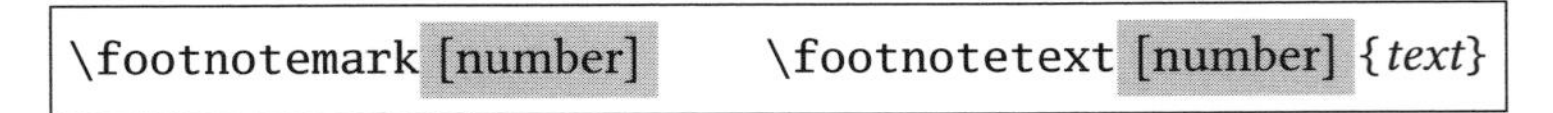

`\footnotemark` increments the footnote counter `footnote` and only typesets the number of the footnote, while `\footnotetext` only typesets the text of the footnote without changing the counter. If the optional argument is given, the footnote counter is not changed and *number* is taken as the footnote, where *number* must be a positive number.

L[1]	C	R
L	C	R
L	C[2]	R
L	C	R
L	C	R[3]

Normal line of text after the centred table with normal footnote[4].

[1] left-aligned
[2] centred
[3] right-aligned
[4] normal footnote

01-01-19

```
\begin{center}
\begin{tabular}{lcr}\hline
L\footnotemark & C & R\\
L & C & R\\
L & C\footnotemark & R\\
L & C & R\\
L & C & R\footnotemark\\\hline
\end{tabular}
\addtocounter{footnote}{-2}
\footnotetext{left-aligned}
\stepcounter{footnote}\footnotetext{centred}
\stepcounter{footnote}\footnotetext{right-aligned}
\end{center}
Normal line of text after the centred table with
normal footnote\footnote{normal footnote}.
```

1.2 The tabbing environment

Standard LaTeX's `tabbing` environment doesn't actually create a table, but allows for tabular alignments, so we are covering it here in conjunction with tables. Its major advantages are that it allows footnotes and page breaks. The name of the environment harks back to the old tabulator key present on even the earliest typewriters; the principle of this "tabulator key" has been preserved in the `tabbing` environment. Several short commands are defined for controlling the tabulators; these are summarized in Table 1.2 on the next page.

```
\begin{tabbing}
A \=example line... \kill \\
\>formatted lines\\
...
\end{tabbing}
```

Table 1.2: Summary of the tabulator commands for the `tabbing` environment.

command	*meaning*
`\=`	Puts a tab at the current position.
`\>`	Jumps to the next tab.
`\<`	Puts text to the left of the left margin without changing it.
`\+`	The left margin is moved one tab to the right.
`\-`	The left margin is moved one tab to the left.
`\'`	The text before the `\'` command is right-aligned and the text after it is left-aligned.
``\` ``	The text after the ``\` `` command is right-aligned on the line.
`\a`	To typeset accents within the `tabbing` environment; for example `\a'e` displays as é.
`\kill`	Deletes the current (example) line and keeps the tabs defined in it.
`\pushtabs`	Saves all current tabs.
`\poptabs`	Loads all last saved tabs.

01-02-1

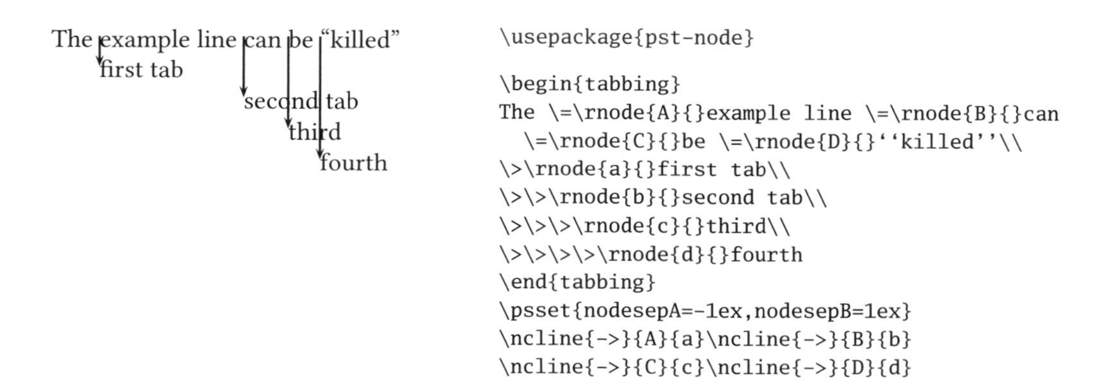


```
\usepackage{pst-node}

\begin{tabbing}
The \=\rnode{A}{}example line \=\rnode{B}{}can
  \=\rnode{C}{}be \=\rnode{D}{}``killed''\\
\>\rnode{a}{}first tab\\
\>\>\rnode{b}{}second tab\\
\>\>\>\rnode{c}{}third\\
\>\>\>\>\rnode{d}{}fourth
\end{tabbing}
\psset{nodesepA=-1ex,nodesepB=1ex}
\ncline{->}{A}{a}\ncline{->}{B}{b}
\ncline{->}{C}{c}\ncline{->}{D}{d}
```

The *example line* in conjunction with the `\kill` command lets you specify the individual tabs easily; `\kill` deletes the line, but not the positions specified through `\=`.

01-02-2

```
   first tab
                second tab
                     third
                         fourth
0  1            2    3   4
```

```
\begin{tabbing}
The \=example line \=can
  \=be \=``killed''\kill\\
\>first tab\\ \>\>second tab\\
\>\>\>third\\ \>\>\>\>fourth\\
0 \>1 \>2 \>3 \>4
\end{tabbing}
```

Current tab positions can be saved and reloaded with the `\pushtabs` and `\poptabs` commands. They work like a LIFO-system: last in, first out.

```
1 2  3   4
1   2  3 4
1   2    3
1   2  3 4
1 2  3   4
```

```
\begin{tabbing}
00\=000\=0000\=\kill
\pushtabs          % save tabbing positions
1\>2\>3\>4\\
0000\=000\=00\=\kill % new tab positions
\pushtabs          % save also this ones
1\>2\>3\>4\\
0000\=00000\=\kill% new tab positions
1\>2\>3\\
\poptabs           % get last saved tabs
1\>2\>3\>4\\
\poptabs           % get previous saved tabs
1\>2\>3\>4\\
\end{tabbing}
```

01-02-3

accents Problems can arise when using some short commands if they are defined as accents at the same time. In these cases the accents within a `tabbing` environment have to be introduced by `\a`; an alternative is to use the `Tabbing` package (cf. Section 2.29 on page 109).

```
first café
              second café
                  maître
crème                 brûlée
```

```
\begin{tabbing}
The \=example line \=can \=be \=``killed''\kill\\
\>first caf\a'e\\ \>\>second caf\a'e\\
\>\>\>m\a^aitre\\
\>cr\a`eme\>\>\>br\a^ul\a'ee
\end{tabbing}
```

01-02-4

If the following lines need to be inset, the `\+` command can be used to set the left margin for the next (and future) lines one tab position further in. This saves you coding a `\>` at the start of the next (and future) lines as the current left margin of the text now corresponds to the position of that tab. This effect can be reversed through `\-`; the current left margin is moved to the left by exactly one tab. These two commands are especially useful when typesetting algorithms if you are unable to use the usual `listings` package.

As with a normal table, the individual elements between the tabs are typeset as a group, so if you want to change the font for a whole `tabbing` environment you must do it before the environment. Extra tab stops can be added after the example line by inserting `\=` at the appropriate place; however these new tabs are always added to the available list, existing ones are not deleted.

A normal line ...

```
function fact(n: integer): integer;
         begin
               if n > 1 then
               fact:= n * fact(n-1)
         else
               fact:= 1;
end;
```

A normal line ...

```
A normal line \ldots \ttfamily\small
\begin{tabbing}
function \=\textbf{fact(n: integer)}: integer;\\
\> begin \=\+ \\% left margin to tab
\> if \=n $>$ 1 then \+  \\
fact:= n * fact(n-1) \- \\
else \+ \\
fact:= 1; \-\-\\% back 2 tabs
end;
\end{tabbing}\normalfont\normalsize
A normal line \ldots
```

01-02-5

You don't need to use example text to specify tabs; you can also use \hspace, as in this example:

```
A normal line \ldots
\begingroup\small\ttfamily % keep change of font local
\begin{tabbing}
\=\hspace{0.25in} \=\hspace{0.25in} \=\hspace{0.25in} \=\hspace{0.25in}\kill
\> <category> \+ \\
    \> <pattern>WHAT IS A *</pattern> \+ \\
    \> <template><srai>DEFINE <star index ="1"></srai> \\
    \> </template> \-\-  \\
\> </category>   \\[0.5\normalbaselineskip]
\> <category> \+ \\
    \> <pattern>DO YOU KNOW WHAT A * IS</pattern> \+ \\
\> <template><srai>DEFINE <star index ="1"></srai></template> \-\- \\
\> </category>
\end{tabbing}
\endgroup
A normal line \ldots
```

01-02-6

A normal line ...

```
<category>
    <pattern>WHAT IS A *</pattern>
        <template><srai>DEFINE <star index ="1"></srai>
        </template>
</category>

<category>
    <pattern>DO YOU KNOW WHAT A * IS</pattern>
        <template><srai>DEFINE <star index ="1"></srai></template>
</category>
```

A normal line ...

You can use the \' and \` tab commands to left- or right-align words. The right-alignment of text after the \` command always refers to the line as a whole; further tabs after \` are ignored. The \' command, however, refers to the current tab, right-aligning the sequence of characters before the command and left-aligning the sequence that follows it; the difference can be seen clearly in the following examples. When using the \' command, the space between the right- and left-aligned sequences of characters is specified through \tabbingsep=5.0ptThis spacing can be changed arbitrarily, but this must be done globally within the tabbing environment, as the material between two tabs is held locally internally and a change of the length here would have no visible effect.

```
0    1              2   3  4
                 2  left-aligned
             2      left-aligned
      1 left-aligned
   0 left-aligned
```

01-02-7

```
\begin{tabbing}
The \=example line \=can
  \=be \=``killed''\kill\\
0 \>1 \>2 \>3 \>4\\
  \>  \>2 \'left-aligned\\
\global\setlength\tabbingsep{20pt}
  \>  \>2 \'left-aligned\\
\global\setlength\tabbingsep{0pt}
  \>1     \'left-aligned\\
0         \'left-aligned\\
\end{tabbing}
```

```
0    1              2   3  4
                    2      right-aligned on the line
     1                                  right-aligned
0                                               right
```

01-02-8

```
\begin{tabbing}
The \=example line \=can
  \=be \=``killed''\kill\\
0 \>1 \>2 \>3 \>4\\
  \>  \>2 \`right-aligned on the line\\
  \>1 \`right-aligned\\
0 \`right \\
\end{tabbing}
```

Horizontal centring of `tabbing` environments is surpriginly easy – just insert the environment into a `minipage` of maximal width; this "clips" it to the required width after the creation of the `tabbing` environment.

This is a normal text in a text line of normal width.

```
0    1              2   3  4
  right-aligned  left-aligned
```

This is a normal text in a text line of normal width.

01-02-9

```
This is a normal text in a text
line of normal width.
\begin{center}\begin{minipage}{\linewidth}
\begin{tabbing}
The \=example line \=can
  \=be \=``killed''\kill\\
0 \>1 \>2 \>3 \>4\\
  \>  \> right-aligned\'left-aligned\\
\end{tabbing}
\end{minipage}\end{center}
This is a normal text in a text
line of normal width.
```

footnote Footnotes in the `tabbing` environment behave similarly to footnotes in the `tabular` environment (cf. Section 1.1.4 on page 12); in theory they are not possible but can be achieved through the combination `\footnotemark` – `\footnotetext` or with special packages.

Remember when you use this combination of commands that `\footnotemark` increments the footnote counter, so it has to be reset before the text of the footnote is written with `\footnotetext`. This is shown in the following example:

01-02-10

f	fb	fbb
f[1]	fb	fbb
f	fb	fbb
f	fb[2]	fbb
f	fb	fbb
f	fb	fbb[3]

Normal line of text after the tabbing environment with normal footnote[4].

[1]foo
[2]foobar
[3]foobarbaz
[4]normal footnote

```
\begin{tabbing}
foo \= foobar \= foobarbaz\kill
f \> fb \> fbb\\
f\footnotemark \> fb \> fbb\\
f \> fb \> fbb\\
f \> fb\footnotemark \> fbb\\
f \> fb \> fbb\\
f \> fb \> fbb\footnotemark
\end{tabbing}     \addtocounter{footnote}{-2}
\footnotetext{foo}\stepcounter{footnote}
\footnotetext{foobar}\stepcounter{footnote}
\footnotetext{foobarbaz}

Normal line of text after the
\texttt{tabbing} environment with normal
footnote\footnote{normal footnote}.
```

Special packages for tabs are covered in Section 2.28 on page 108. They allow for easier setting of tabs and simplify the handling of accents.

1.3 Notes

This section summarizes some important facts and frequently made mistakes when using the `tabular` or `tabbing` environments:

- ▷ All definitions within a table *cell* are local to the cell; internally the contents of a table cell is enclosed in a `\begingroup` ... `\endgroup` sequence.
- ▷ Vertical line segments may be missing if rows are terminated prematurely by `\\` or `\tabularnewline` when using the `array` package. Empty cells should be marked as `& &` .
- ▷ A common mistake is caused by too few defined designators for column types. The following error message was caused by using three columns where only two were defined:

```
! Extra alignment tab has been changed to \cr.
<recently read> \endtemplate

l.7   text & text &
                    \\
?
```

- ▷ The space between two columns is `2\tabcolsep` by default; the space to the left and right of each column is `\tabcolsep`.
- ▷ `\multicolumn` overwrites the existing specification for the right hand side of the column or columns by default. This should be kept in mind especially for vertical lines. In the case of the first column, the left margin is affected as well.
- ▷ The `tabbing` environment has the advantage that it can be used in two-column mode (`\twocolumn`) and additionally allows for page breaks.

Chapter 2

Packages

This chapter describes all packages related to tables that are currently available on CTAN except for packages that support tables across several pages, which are covered in Chapter 4 on page 125. It's always worth checking before you use a package whether it has been updated in the meantime. To help you, the following table lists all packages with their respective version and date. Some packages are certainly more important than others, though as this is fairly subjective we've listed them mostly alphabetically, just distinguishing between certain thematic areas: "general – decimal numbers – colour – tabs – page break", and left it up to you to decide which packages are important and necessary.

Table 2.1: Summary of all LaTeX packages related to tables.

name	*date*	*version*	*description*
array	2008/09/09	2.4c	Extension of the array and tabular environments.
arydshln	2004/08/31	1.71	Horizontal and vertical dashed lines.
bigstrut	1994/05/31	1.0	Vertical lengths for better line spacing.
blkarray	1999/03/24	0.05	Extension of the array and tabular environments.
booktabs	2005/04/14	1.6183	Better table layout.
cellspace	2009/07/31	1.6	Simple arrangement of cell contents within a table.
ctable	2009/09/17	1.15	Centred, left-, or right-aligned tables.
datatool	2009/11/15	2.03	Comprehensive package to read and process external data (CSV) and display as a table.
delarray	1994/03/14	1.01	Several delimiters for the array and tabular environments.
easytable	2001/06/13	1.0	Tables with equal column width or row height and various vertical and horizontal lines.
hhline	1994/05/23	v2.03	Extended horizontal "lines" in tables.
makecell	2009/08/03	0.1e	Support for special headers and multi-line cells.
mdwtab	1998/04/28	1.9	A reimplementation of the tabular and array environments.
multirow	2004/05/05	1.6	Multi-line cells within a table.
slashbox	1993/05/31		Split cells within a table.
spreadtab	2009/11/01	0.1	Tables with a functionality like Excel.
tabls	2006/01/13	3.5	Improved vertical spacing in a table (tabular lineskip).
tabularht	2007/04/11	2.5	tabular environment with fixed height.
tabularkv	2006/02/20	1.1	tabular environment with a "key–value" interface.
tabularx	1999/01/07	2.07	Tables with variable column widths.
tabulary	2008/12/01	0.9	Tables with equal height and different widths.
threeparttable	2003/06/13	3.0	Supports tables with headers, footers, and footnotes of the same width.
threeparttablex	2009/12/28	0.06	Better support of notes.
warpcol	2007/11/21	1.0c	Relative alignment of cells with numerical contents.
widetable	2009/10/26	1.1	Extension of the longtable* environment.
dcolumn	2001/05/28	1.06	Align decimal numbers at the decimal separator.
rccol	2005/11/12	1.2c	Align decimal numbers at the decimal separator; places after the separator can be rounded.
siunitx	2010/10/08	2.0x	Typesetting of columns of numbers with or without a unit.
colortbl	2001/02/13	0.1j	Coloured table columns, rows, and cells.
xcolor	2007/01/21	v2.11	Extensions for coloured table columns, rows, and cells.
polytable	2005/04/26	0.8.2	tabular-like environment with symbolic column names.
tabto	2006/09/12	1.0	"Tab" to defined places on a line.
Tabbing	1997/12/18	1.0	tabbing environment that allows accents in the usual notation.
longtable	2004/02/01	4.11	Support for page breaks within tables. More flexible than the supertabular package.

continued...

... continued

name	*date*	*version*	*description*
ltablex	1995/11/06	1.0	Extension of the tabularx environment to support page breaks within the table similar to the longtable package.
ltxtable	1995/12/11	0.2	Combination of the longtable and tabularx packages.
stabular	1998/03/19		Tables that allow page breaks.
supertabular	2004/02/20	4.1e	Multi-page tables, similar to the longtable package.
xtab	2008/07/26	2.3c	Extended version of the supertabular package.

2.1 array

The array package by Frank Mittelbach and David Carlisle offers several better ways to typeset tables. The use of booktabs is recommended as well. The following table is laid out firstly with "normal" column definitions, and then each new method is shown for comparison. Again please note that we are only using horizontal and vertical lines in these tables to highlight the differences between the layouts; lines do not improve the readability of a table and, in principle, we recommend that you never use vertical lines and only use horizontal lines sparingly (cf. guidelines on page 3).

02-01-1

left	right	centred	box
l	r	c	p{2cm}

```
\begin{tabular}{|l|r|c|p{2cm}|}\hline
left & right & centred & box\\\hline
l      & r      & c      & p\{2cm\}\\\hline
\end{tabular}
```

\extrarowheight increases the **height** of the line without affecting the depth; therefore this space should not be set too large. Its main use is to avoid capital letters "hitting" an upper line.

02-01-2

left	right	centred	box
l	r	c	p{1.75cm}

```
\usepackage{array}

\setlength\extrarowheight{8pt}
\begin{tabular}{|l|r|c|p{1.75cm}|}\hline
left & right & centred & box\\\hline
l & r & c & p\{1.75cm\}\\\hline
\end{tabular}
```

\arraybackslash redefines the standard double backslash command for a table line break (\\). Without this redefinition it would not retain its meaning when using one of the formatting commands, \raggedright, \raggedleft or \centering, in a p (\parbox) column. Now for a new *row within a column* use the \newline command and for a new *table row* use \\ or the \tabularnewline command:

L	R	C	box
l	r	c	p{2.5cm} new line with \newline
l	r	c	new table row with \\
what now			

```
\usepackage{array}

\begin{tabular}{|l|r|c|>{\raggedright%
    \arraybackslash}p{2.5cm}|}\hline
L & R & C & box\\\hline
l & r & c & p\{2.5cm\}\newline
  new line with \verb+\newline+\\
l & r & c & new table row with \verb+\\+\\
  what now &&& \\\hline
\end{tabular}
```

02-01-3

When using the ragged2e package, however, you don't have to insert the \arraybackslash command explicitly:

L	R	C	box
l	r	c	p{2.5cm} new line with \newline
l	r	c	new table row with \tabularnewline
what now			

```
\usepackage{array,ragged2e}

\begin{tabular}{|l|r|c|
    >{\RaggedRight}p{2.5cm}|}\hline
L & R & C & box\tabularnewline\hline
l & r & c & p\{2.5cm\}
  \newline new line with \verb+\newline+\\
l & r & c & new table row
  with {\small\verb=\tabularnewline=}\\
what now&&&\tabularnewline\hline
\end{tabular}
```

02-01-4

>{...}, where "..." is any arbitrary code sequence, executes this code *before the start* of the respective column in each row. In the following example, bold font is selected for the first column:

left	right	centred	box
l	r	c	p{1.5cm}

```
\usepackage{array}

\begin{tabular}{|>{\bfseries}l|r|c|p{1.5cm}|}
left & right & centred & box\\
    l &      r &      c     & p\{1.5cm\}
\end{tabular}
```

02-01-5

<{...}, where "..." again is any arbitrary code sequence, executes this code *before the end* of the respective column in each row this time. In the following example, math mode was selected by switching on inline mode through >{$} and off again through the following <{$}:

left	*right*	centred	box
l	*r*	c	p{1.5cm}

```
\usepackage{array}

\begin{tabular}{l>{$}r<{$}c|p{1.5cm}|}
left & right & centred & box\\\hline
l & r & c & p\{1.5cm\}
\end{tabular}
```

02-01-6

!{...}, where "..." is any arbitrary code sequence, inserts this code *instead of* a separator in each row. The space to the left and right of the two columns remains the same. In this example, a colon and an arrow are inserted instead of the separator:

02-01-7

left	right	: centred	→ box
l	r	: c	→ p{1.5cm}

```
\usepackage{array}

\begin{tabular}{l ! {\vline}r !{:} c
    !{$\rightarrow$} p{1.5cm}}
left & right & centred & box\\\hline
l & r & c & p\{1.5cm\}
\end{tabular}
```

m{...}, where "..." is an arbitrary length (e.g. m{3cm}), centres (middle) a box aligned with the base line of the current row vertically.

02-01-8

left	right	a m-parbox
l	right	m{2cm} this cell is vertically centered

```
\usepackage{array}

\begin{tabular}{|l | r | m{2cm}|}\hline
left & right & a m-parbox \\\hline
l & right & m\{2cm\} this cell is
    vertically centered\\\hline
\end{tabular}
```

b{...}, where "..." is an arbitrary length (e.g. b{3cm}), aligns a box with the bottom of the current row.

02-01-9

left	r	a b-parbox
l	right	b{2cm} this cell is vertically alligned at the bottom

```
\usepackage{array}

\begin{tabular}{|l | r | b{2cm}|}\hline
left & r & a b-parbox \\\hline
l & right & b\{2cm\} this cell is vertically
        alligned at the bottom\\\hline
\end{tabular}
```

2.1.1 \newcolumntype

\newcolumntype{*character*} [n] {*column definition*}

The \newcolumntype command lets you define arbitrary new column types that can then be used in their abbreviated form as column definitions in the table head. You can only use a single case sensitive letter as the *character*, and it must be different from ones already defined unless you don't mind the earlier definition being overwritten. *n* specifies the number of parameters; it has no effect if the definition uses no parameters. The *column definition* must refer to a column type that exists already. The following example shows how to use the command:

```
\usepackage{array} \newcolumntype{L}{>{$}l<{$}} \newcolumntype{T}{>{\ttfamily\small}l}

\begin{tabular}{@{}lLT@{\qquad}lLT@{}}\hline
sine  & \sin(\alpha) &<value> sin &cosine & \cos(\alpha) & <value> cos \\
tangent&\tan(\alpha)&<value> tan &arcus tangent&\arctan(x)&<value1> <value2> atan\\\hline
\end{tabular}
```

sine	$\sin(\alpha)$	<value> sin	cosine	$\cos(\alpha)$	<value> cos
tangent	$\tan(\alpha)$	<value> tan	arcus tangent	$\arctan(x)$	<value1> <value2> atan

02-01-10

In the next example, the headers are rotated so as not to widen the columns needlessly, which would decrease the readability of the table. If a column has a header of multiple rows, it's better to use the varwidth package by Donald Arseneau and the environment of the same name. Its advantage over the minipage environment is that you don't need to specify the required width explicitly.

```
\usepackage{array,rotating}
\newcolumntype{B}{>{\bfseries}c}
\newcolumntype{T}{>{\ttfamily}l}
\newcolumntype{R}[1]{>{\begin{turn}{#1}}l<{\end{turn}}}

\begin{tabular}[b]{BTl}
\multicolumn{1}{R{45}}{abbreviation} & \multicolumn{1}{R{45}}{reference column} &
\multicolumn{1}{R{45}}{parameter}\\\hline B & c & - \\ T & l & - \\ R & l & 1\\\hline
\end{tabular} \qquad
\begin{tabular}[b]{@{}BTl@{}}
\multicolumn{1}{R{90}}{abbreviated} & \multicolumn{1}{R{90}}{reference column} &
\multicolumn{1}{R{90}}{parameter}\\ B & c & - \\ T & l & - \\ R & l & 1
\end{tabular}
```

02-01-11

abbreviation	reference column	parameter
B	c	-
T	l	-
R	l	1

abbreviated	reference column	parameter
B	c	-
T	l	-
R	l	1

hyphenation

TeX is set not to hyphenate the first word of a paragraph. However, sometimes hyphenation is desirable in a narrow column, and the workaround is to define a column type that starts the column by writing a \hspace{0pt}; this is recognised as a word of length zero by TeX, which then will be able to hyphenate the following regular word. This is clearly visible in the following example; the first table has an error in the last column, the second one is correct.

```
\usepackage{array} \newcolumntype{P}[1]{>{\hspace{0pt}}p{#1}}

\begin{tabular}[t]{|l r c | p{1cm}|}
left & right & centred & box          \\\hline
l    & r     & c       & correctilific
\end{tabular} \qquad
\begin{tabular}[t]{|l r c | P{1cm}|}
```

```
left & right & centred & box\\\hline
l    & r     & c       & correctilific
\end{tabular}
```

02-01-12

left	right	centred	box
l	r	c	correctilific

left	right	centred	box
l	r	c	cor- rec- tilific

Horizontal alignment can be adjusted with the three commands mentioned earlier: \raggedleft, \centering, and \raggedright. Alternatively you can use the modified commands \RaggedLeft, \Centering, and \RaggedRight from the ragged2e package by Martin Schröder, which allow hyphenation.

```
\usepackage{array,ragged2e}
\newcolumntype{L}[1]{>{\hspace{0pt}\RaggedRight}p{#1}}
\newcolumntype{C}[1]{>{\hspace{0pt}\Centering}p{#1}}
\newcolumntype{R}[1]{>{\hspace{0pt}\RaggedLeft}p{#1}}

\begin{tabular}{@{}L{3cm}C{3cm}R{3cm}@{}}\hline
A left aligned column with ragged right margin
  & A centred column with ragged left and ragged right margin
  & A right aligned column with ragged left margin\\
L & C & R\\\hline
\end{tabular}
```

02-01-13

A left aligned col- umn with ragged right margin	A centred column with ragged left and ragged right margin	A right aligned column with ragged left margin
L	C	R

\newcolumntype may define more than one column type as well; for example the definition \newcolumntype{x}{llcll} defines five columns. Here it is in use:

02-01-14

R	L	L	C	L	L
RR	LL	LL	CC	LL	LL

```
\usepackage{array} \newcolumntype{x}{llcll}

\begin{tabular}{ r x }
R & L & L & C & L & L\\
RR& LL& LL& CC& LL& LL
\end{tabular}
```

Especially when using larger packages, it can sometimes be helpful to set the defined column types to be output into the log file through \showcols.

```
\showcols
```

The log file for Example 02-01-13 contains the following lines:

```
Column L#1 -> >{\hspace {0pt}\RaggedRight }p{#1}
Column C#1 -> >{\hspace {0pt}\Centering }p{#1}
Column R#1 -> >{\hspace {0pt}\RaggedLeft }p{#1}
```

Vertical lines

When using the \multicolumn command, you need to be careful about the definition of vertical lines, especially if this definition is done in the parent column definition as well as in the argument of \multicolumn. In the following example, we have made the affected vertical line very wide to illustrate the potential problem:

L	L	C	L	L
LL	CCC			L

02-01-15

```
\usepackage{array}

\begin{tabular}{|l!{\vrule width 3pt}l|c|l|l|}\hline
L & L & C & L & L\\
LL&\multicolumn{3}{!{\vrule width 3pt}c|}{CCC} & L\\\hline
\end{tabular}
```

This shows that the vertical line was drawn by both the normal column definition as well as by the \multicolumn one. This only occurs when using the array package, because this considers vertical lines with their real width. In the normal tabular environment of standard LaTeX, the lines are not considered when determining the horizontal spacing – the lines are drawn on top of each other. The exception is a \multicolumn environment that starts in the first column though; in this case both left and right vertical lines have to be drawn if requried. Otherwise a line only has to be placed on the right hand side of the column definition. Remember, lines are always assigned to the previous column except for the first column.

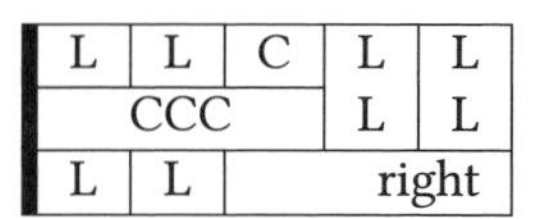

L	L	C	L	L
CCC			L	L
L	L	right		

02-01-16

```
\usepackage{array}

\begin{tabular}{!{\vrule width 3pt}l|l|c|l|l|}\hline
L & L & C & L & L                        \\\cline{1-3}
\multicolumn{3}{!{\vrule width 3pt}c|}{CCC} & L & L\\\hline
L & L & \multicolumn{3}{r|}{right} \\\hline
\end{tabular}
```

Horizontal lines

As long as a framed table is in its own paragraph or centred vertically on a line, for example like this one two table, there are no problems with the display – apart from the typographically adverse line spacing. If, however, you align the upper edge of a table with the base line of the current line through the optional argument [t], for example like this one two table, then there is a problem with the first horizontal line of the table, which is a long way below the current text line. The fact that the bottom line is too close to the following line of text is only a small problem in comparison. The array package has two special commands to help you align both the first and last horizontal lines more appropriately:

```
\firsthline
\lasthline
```

In the following example the first table has the usual alignment, the second is shifted up using the `\firsthline` command to align the first text line with the existing text, and the third one has a small amount of additional space inserted before the following line using the `\lasthline` command.

02-01-17

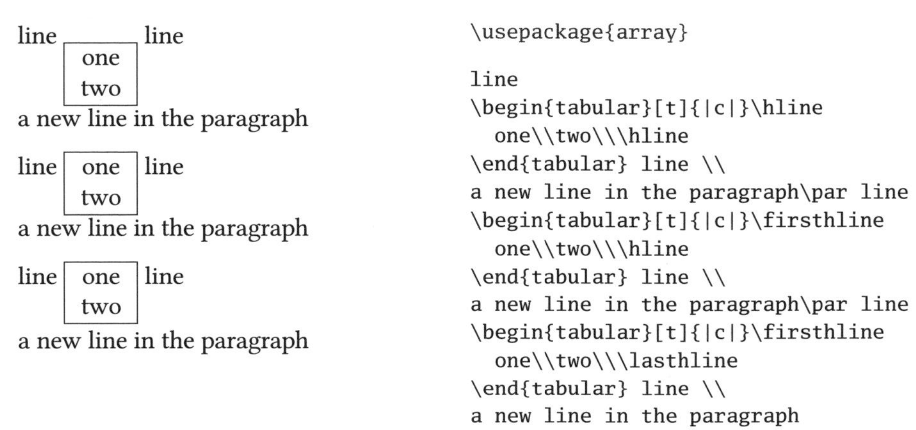

```
\usepackage{array}

line
\begin{tabular}[t]{|c|}\hline
  one\\two\\\hline
\end{tabular} line \\
a new line in the paragraph\par line
\begin{tabular}[t]{|c|}\firsthline
  one\\two\\\hline
\end{tabular} line \\
a new line in the paragraph\par line
\begin{tabular}[t]{|c|}\firsthline
  one\\two\\\lasthline
\end{tabular} line \\
a new line in the paragraph
```

You can change the spacing above and below the table using the `\extratabsurround` length. The default value of this length is 2.0pt.

02-01-18

A line in the paragraph before the table.
line | one / two | line
A line in a paragraph after the table.
A line in a paragraph before the table and
`\addtolength\extratabsurround{10pt}`.

line | one / two | line

A line in a paragraph after the table.

```
\usepackage{array}

A line in the paragraph before the table.
\par line
\begin{tabular}[t]{|c|}\firsthline
  one\\two\\\lasthline
\end{tabular} line \\
A line in a paragraph after the table.\par
A line in a paragraph before the table and\\
\verb+\addtolength\extratabsurround{10pt}+.
\par line
\addtolength\extratabsurround{10pt}
\begin{tabular}[t]{|c|}\firsthline
  one\\two\\\lasthline
\end{tabular} line \\
A line in a paragraph after the table.
```

2.2 arydshln

The arydshln package by Hiroshi Nakashima lets you use dashed vertical or horizontal lines; it works in conjunction with the normal line commands. If you are loading several table-specific packages, make sure to always load arydshln last, in order to avoid interferences with other packages.

load arydshln last

left	right	centred	box
l	r	c	p{1.5cm}
l	r	c	p{1.5cm}

```
\usepackage{arydshln}

\begin{tabular}{|l:r:|:c:p{1.5cm}|}\hline
left & right & centred & box\\\hdashline
l & r & c & p\{1.5cm\}\\\hline
l & r & c & p\{1.5cm\}\\\hdashline\hdashline
\end{tabular}
```

02-02-1

The example above shows that a colon defines a vertical dashed line and `\hdashline` a horizontal dashed line; they are used in the usual way. Instead of the colon, you can also use a semicolon, which has an argument that lets you modify the the lengths of the dashes and the gaps. And similarly to the standard lines, you can use `\cdashline` to draw a partial horizontal line across a subset of columns. Both `\hdashline` and `\cdashline` also have optional arguments, allowing you to define the appearance of the dashed line. This box shows the syntax for each:

vertical	*horizontal*
:	\hdashline [dash/gap]
;{*dash/gap*}	\cdashline{*from–to*} [dash/gap]

This example shows all four lines in use:

left	right	centred	box
l	r	c	p{1.5cm}
l	r	c	p{1.5cm}
l	r	c	p{1.5cm}
l	r	c	p{1.5cm}

```
\usepackage{arydshln}

\begin{tabular}
  {|l:r:|:c;{2pt/2pt}p{1.5cm};{2pt/4pt}}
  \hdashline[3pt/1.5pt]
left & right & centred & box\\
  \cdashline{2-3}[1pt/3pt]
l & r & c & p\{1.5cm\}\\\hdashline[5pt/3pt]
l & r & c & p\{1.5cm\}\\\hline
l & r & c & p\{1.5cm\}\\\hdashline[3pt/5pt]
l & r & c & p\{1.5cm\}\\\hline
\end{tabular}
```

02-02-2

When using the `array` package (N.B. you *must* load it before loading `arydshln`), there are also corresponding versions of `\firsthline` and `\lasthline` available (cf. Section 2.1.1 on page 26). They have an optional argument to specify the lengths of the gaps and dashes as well. Here is the syntax followed by an example:

```
\firsthdashline [dash/gap]
\lasthdashline [dash/gap]
```

02-02-3

a new line on the paragraph

line | one | line
two
a new line on the paragraph

line | one | line
two
a new line on the paragraph

```
\usepackage{array,arydshln}

a new line on the paragraph\par line
\begin{tabular}[t]{:c:}\firsthdashline
  one\\two\\\hdashline
\end{tabular} line \\
a new line on the paragraph\par line
\begin{tabular}[t]{:c:}\firsthdashline[3pt/1pt]
  one\\two\\\lasthdashline[1pt/3pt]
\end{tabular} line \\
a new line on the paragraph
```

You can change the line style globally through the \dashlinedash and \dashlinegap lengths. Both are set internally to a length of 4 pt.

02-02-4

left	right	centred	box
l	r	c	p{1.5cm}
l	r	c	p{1.5cm}

```
\usepackage{arydshln}
\setlength\dashlinedash{2pt}
\setlength\dashlinegap{2pt}

\begin{tabular}{|l:r:|:c:p{1.5cm}:}
    \hdashline
left & right & centred & box\\
    \cdashline{2-3}
l & r & c & p\{1.5cm\}\\\hdashline
l & r & c & p\{1.5cm\}\\\hdashline
\end{tabular}
```

The different behaviour of standard LaTeX and the array package when creating vertical lines has already been mentioned in sections 1.1.1 on page 6 and 2.1.1 on page 26. The arydshln package provides two commands that let you switch between the different behaviours:

```
\ADLnullwide    \ADLsomewide
```

\ADLnullwide enables the behaviour of standard LaTeX: the width of the row has no effect on the width of the table. \ADLsomewide has the opposite effect. In general you won't need to worry about the distinction as the line width will usually be less than 1 pt. However, in the following example we have set the line width to be excessively large to illustrate the difference between the two commands:

02-02-5

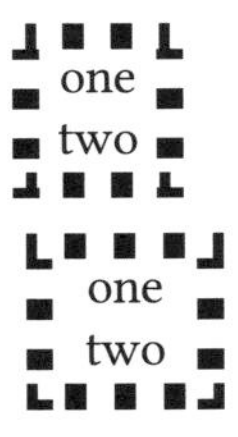


```
\usepackage{arydshln}

\setlength\arrayrulewidth{5pt}
\begin{tabular}{:c:}\hdashline
  one\\two\\\hdashline
\end{tabular}\par\medskip
\ADLsomewide% switch to array style
\begin{tabular}{:c:}\hdashline
  one\\two\\\hdashline
\end{tabular}
```

In some circumstances the dashed lines may not end properly at the right or lower margin. If this happens, you can change the character mode to improve the joins using `\ADLdrawingmode`:

```
\ADLdrawingmode{mode}
```

There are three different modes available (numbered 1, 2, and 3); in many cases the results of the first (default) one will be perfectly satisfactory. The following example uses each mode in turn for the same table; you have to look closely at the intersections of the dashed lines to see the difference.

```
\usepackage{arydshln}

\setlength\dashlinedash{3.01pt}\setlength\dashlinegap{3.01pt}
 \newcommand\Tabelle[1]{\begin{tabular}[b]{|c:c;{2pt/2pt}c|}\hline
    \noalign{\vskip-\arrayrulewidth}
  \mb{A}&\mb{A}&\mb{A}\\[-\arrayrulewidth]\hdashline
  \mb{B}&\mb{B}&\mb{B}\\[-\arrayrulewidth]\hdashline[2pt/2pt]
  \mb{C}&\mb{C}&\mb{C}\\[-\arrayrulewidth]\hline
  \multicolumn3c{(#1)}
\end{tabular}}
\begin{center}
\Tabelle1\qquad\ADLdrawingmode{2}\Tabelle2\qquad\ADLdrawingmode{3}\Tabelle3
\end{center}
```

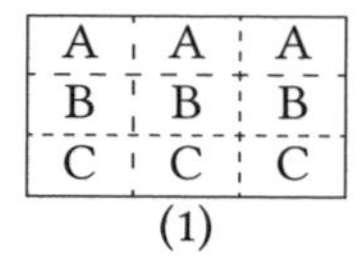

A	A	A
B	B	B
C	C	C

(1)

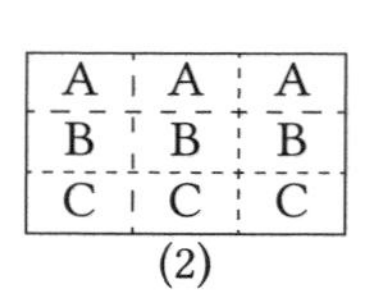

A	A	A
B	B	B
C	C	C

(2)

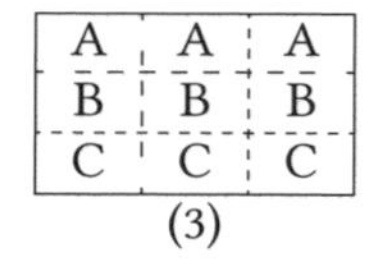

A	A	A
B	B	B
C	C	C

(3)

02-02-6

2.3 bigdelim, bigstrut, and multirow

These three packages by Jerry Leichter and Piet van Oostrum are actually one unit and mainly offer support for creating table cells across several rows.

In general, every `\multirow` arrangement can be replaced by a nested table, as shown in Example 1.1.3 on page 9. This is often even the better way. The other two packages provide functionality to create delimiters around tables or parts of tables.

2.3.1 multirow

The `\multirow` package provides just one command, with the following alternatives as its syntax:

```
\multirow{rows} [sum \bigstrut] {width} [shift] {text}
\multirow{rows} [sum \bigstrut] * [shift] {text}
```

The meaning of the individual mandatory and optional parameters is explained below:

rows	Number of table rows that are combined to a `multirow` cell.
sum `\bigstrut`	This optional parameter can be helpful especially in the `array` environment to achieve better spacing of the rows.
width	The column type of the superior table is ignored and changed locally to a p column of the specified width.
*	Assumes the column type of the superior table.
shift	The optional specification of a length makes fine-tuning of the vertical position of the text possible.
text	The contents of the `\multirow` cell; may be another table or other complex objects, for example a parbox.

02-03-1

col1 row0	col2 row0	col3 row0
col1 row1	col2 row1	
col1 row2	col2 row2	col 3
col1 row3	col 2	
col1 row4	and	col3 row4
	more	
	text	

```
\usepackage{multirow}

\begin{tabular}{|l|l|l|}\hline
  col1 row0 & col2 row0 & col3 row0\\
  col1 row1 & col2 row1
    & \multirow{3}{2cm}{col 3}\\\cline{1-1}
  col1 row2 & col2 row2 & \\\cline{1-2}
  col1 row3
    & \multirow{2}{1cm}{col 2 and more text} &\\
    \cline{1-1}\cline{3-3}
  col1 row4 &          & col3 row4\\\hline
\end{tabular}
```

The principle is easily understood – you place the `\multirow` command in the cell of the table that marks the start of the multi-row cell. *After that*, i.e. in the next rows of the table, you leave cells empty according to the definition of the `\multirow`. By default, the text is inserted left-aligned horizontally and centred vertically if a column width has been given for `\multirow`; the cell then corresponds to the `p` column type. There is no check to see whether the given text fits into the specified number of rows, as is shown in the example above; the required number of rows must be provided manually, as below:

02-03-2

col1 row0	col2 row0	col3 row0
col1 row1	col2 row1	
col1 row2	col2 row2	col 3
col1 row3	col 2	
col1 row4	and	col3 row4
	more	
	text	

```
\usepackage{multirow,bigstrut}

\begin{tabular}{|l|l|l|}\hline
  col1 row0 & col2 row0 & col3 row0\\
  col1 row1 & col2 row1 &
      \multirow{3}{2cm}{col 3}\\\cline{1-1}
  col1 row2 & col2 row2 & \\\cline{1-2}
  col1 row3
    & \multirow{4}{1cm}{col 2 and more text} &\\
    \cline{1-1}\cline{3-3}
  col1 row4 &          & col3 row4\\
         &          &          \\
         &          &          \\\hline
\end{tabular}
```

Using the star in the `\multirow` command instead of specifying a width simply means that the type of the current column as declared in the header of the table is used, as in the following example:

col1 row0	col2 row0	col3 row0
col1 row1	col2 row1	
col1 row2	col2 row2	col 3
col1 row3	col 2	
col1 row4		col3 row4

```
\usepackage{multirow}

\begin{tabular}{|l|r|c|}\hline
  col1 row0 & col2 row0 & col3 row0\\
  col1 row1 & col2 row1
    & \multirow{3}*{col 3}\\\cline{1-1}
  col1 row2 & col2 row2 & \\\cline{1-2}
  col1 row3 & \multirow{2}*{col 2} &  \\
    \cline{1-1}\cline{3-3}
  col1 row4 &           & col3 row4\\\hline
\end{tabular}
```

02-03-3

The horizontal lines look bad as they appear very close to the text, especially in the left column. You can increase the space by specifying an additional line feed, `\\[`*Dim*`]`. To do this, you should use the `\bigstrut` command from the `bigstrut` package to make `multirow` aware of the change. `\bigstrut` corresponds to a box of a specific height and depth in relation to the base line, but zero width (height above base line 2.0pt, depth below base line 2.0ptand width 0.0pt.). Then if you also use the optional sum `\bigstrut` argument to tell the `\multirow` command how many such `\bigstrut` commands there are, you will still be able to centre the text vertically.

The following example shows what happens when the optional argument is not used. This leads to a result where the `\multirow` entries are not centred vertically anymore.

col1 row0	col2 row0	col3 row0
col1 row1	col2 row1	
col1 row2	col2 row2	col 3
col1 row3	col 2	
col1 row4		col3 row4

```
\usepackage{multirow,bigstrut}

\begin{tabular}{|l|r|c|}\hline
  col1 row0 & col2 row0 & col3 row0\\
  col1 row1 & col2 row1 &
   \multirow{3}{1.25cm}{col 3}\bigstrut\\\cline{1-1}
  col1 row2 & col2 row2 & \bigstrut\\\cline{1-2}
  col1 row3 & \multirow{2}{1.25cm}{col 2} & \bigstrut\\
    \cline{1-1}\cline{3-3}
  col1 row4 &           & col3 row4\bigstrut\\\hline
\end{tabular}
```

02-03-4

If you do use the optional argument to tell `\multirow` the number of additional active `\bigstruts`, then the appopriate adjustment will be made for them. The number of "active" `\bigstrut` commands results from the way the command is used. With `\bigstrut` `[`*position*`]` , where position may take the values `t` for top and `b` for bottom, additional space is only inserted above, or below, so this command is only counted once. Without an optional argument, however, space is inserted above and below, so the command counts twice.

In the following example, the first `\multirow` command extends across three rows and the second one across two rows. This determines the values of the optional arguments; `\bigstrut` was used in each respective row.

02-03-5

c1 r0	c2 r0	c3 r0
c1 r1	c2 r1	
c1 r2	c2 r2	c 3
c1 r3	c 2	
c1 r4		c3 r4

```
\usepackage{multirow,bigstrut}

\begin{tabular}{|l|r|c|}\hline
  c1 r0 & c2 r0 & c3 r0\\
  c1 r1 & c2 r1 &
   \multirow{3}[6]{1.25cm}{c 3}\bigstrut\\\cline{1-1}
  c1 r2 & c2 r2 & \bigstrut\\\cline{1-2}
  c1 r3 & \multirow{2}[4]{1.25cm}{c 2} & \bigstrut\\
    \cline{1-1}\cline{3-3}
  c1 r4 &       & c3 r4\bigstrut\\\hline
\end{tabular}
```

Fine-tuning is usually necessary when using displayed mathematical environments because they insert vertical space themselves, which leads to incorrect vertical centring.

02-03-6

c1 r0	c2 r0	c3 r0
c1 r1	c2 r1	
c1 r2	c2 r2	c 3
c1 r3		
c1 r4	$f(x,y) = x \cdot y$	c3 r4

```
\usepackage{multirow,bigstrut}

\begin{tabular}{|l|r|c|}\hline
  c1 r0 & c2 r0 & c3 r0\\
  c1 r1 & c2 r1 & \multirow{3}[6]{1.25cm}{c 3}
        \bigstrut\\\cline{1-1}
  c1 r2 & c2 r2 & \bigstrut\\\cline{1-2}
  c1 r3 & \multirow{2}[4]{2cm}{\[f(x,y)=x\cdot y\]}
                & \bigstrut\\\cline{1-1}\cline{3-3}
  c1 r4 &       & c3 r4\bigstrut\\\hline
\end{tabular}
```

We can correct this using the \abovedisplayskip space, which is already defined in LaTeX and the factor 0.8, which has been determined through trial and error here.

02-03-7

c1 r0	c2 r0	c3 r0
c1 r1	c2 r1	
c1 r2	c2 r2	c 3
c1 r3	$f(x,y) = x \cdot y$	
c1 r4		c3 r4

```
\usepackage{multirow,bigstrut}

\begin{tabular}{|l|r|c|}\hline
 c1 r0 & c2 r0 & c3 r0\\ c1 r1 & c2 r1 &
  \multirow{3}[6]{1.25cm}{c 3}\bigstrut\\\cline{1-1}
 c1 r2 & c2 r2 & \bigstrut\\\cline{1-2}
 c1 r3 &
 \multirow{2}[4]{2cm}[0.8\abovedisplayskip]{%
  \[f(x,y)=x\cdot y\]} &
  \bigstrut\\\cline{1-1}\cline{3-3}
 c1 r4 &       & c3 r4\bigstrut\\\hline
\end{tabular}
```

We mentioned earlier that \multirow assumes a p column type by default unless you use the star, in which case \multirow assumes the superior column definition. A p column is by definition always typeset left-aligned and justified. You can change this behaviour by redefining the \multirowsetup command. This makes horizontal centring within a r column possible, as can be seen in column 3 in the following example.

c1 r0	c2 r0	c3 r0
c1 r1	c2 r1	
c1 r2	c2 r2	c3
c1 r3	$f(x,y) = x \cdot y$	
c1 r4		c3 r4

02-03-8

```
\usepackage{multirow,bigstrut}
\renewcommand\multirowsetup{\centering}

\begin{tabular}{| l | r | r |}\hline
 c1 r0 & c2 r0 & c3 r0\\  c1 r1 & c2 r1
& \multirow{3}[6]{1.5cm}{c3}\bigstrut\\\cline{1-1}
 c1 r2 & c2 r2 & \bigstrut\\\cline{1-2}
 c1 r3 &
 \multirow{2}[4]{2cm}[0.8\abovedisplayskip]{%
  \[f(x,y)=x\cdot y\]} &
  \bigstrut\\\cline{1-1}\cline{3-3}
 c1 r4 &        & c3 r4\bigstrut\\\hline
\end{tabular}
```

The column definition has no impact on the display of the equation as displayed formulae are always centred horizontally.

2.3.2 bigstrut

The `bigstrut` package just defines the `\bigstrut` command, and can be used on its own without the `\multirow` package. As mentioned before (see on page 32), it defines a box of a specific height and depth above and below the base line, but with width zero.

`\bigstrut` [position]

The optional argument lets you restrict the invisible box to height or depth only, by specifying `t` or `b`. In these cases, the counting for the optional argument per row has to be adjusted as well – single instead of double counting. In the following example, the left table with `\bigstrut` was typeset without optional argument ( ), the middle one with `t` ( ), and the right one with `b` ( ).[1]

```
\usepackage{multirow,bigstrut}

\begin{tabular}{|l|r|c|}\hline
  11 & 21 & \multirow{3}[6]{1cm}{3}\bigstrut\\\cline{1-1}
  12 & 22 &                        \bigstrut\\\cline{1-2}
  13 & \multirow{2}[4]{1cm}{2} &   \bigstrut\\\cline{1-1}\cline{3-3}
  14 &     & 34                    \bigstrut\\\hline
\end{tabular}\quad
\begin{tabular}{@{}|l|r|c|@{}}\hline
  11 & 21 & \multirow{3}[3]{1cm}{3}\bigstrut[t]\\\cline{1-1}
  12 & 22 &                        \bigstrut[t]\\\cline{1-2}
  13 & \multirow{2}[2]{1cm}{2} &   \bigstrut[t]\\\cline{1-1}\cline{3-3}
  14 &     & 34                    \bigstrut[t]\\\hline
\end{tabular}\quad
```

[1] The "frames" inside the brackets here were created with `\fbox` and a `\fboxsep` of 0 pt to make the boxes visible and show their position relative to the base line.

```
\begin{tabular}{@{}|l|r|c|@{}}\hline
  11 & 21 & \multirow{3}[3]{1cm}{3}\bigstrut[b]\\\cline{1-1}
  12 & 22 &                          \bigstrut[b]\\\cline{1-2}
  13 & \multirow{2}[2]{1cm}{2} &    \bigstrut[b]\\\cline{1-1}\cline{3-3}
  14 &    & 34                       \bigstrut[b]\\\hline
\end{tabular}
```

02-03-9

11	21	3
12	22	
13	2	
14		34

11	21	3
12	22	
13	2	
14		34

11	21	3
12	22	
13	2	
14		34

You can change the spacing by redefining `\bigstrut` or by changing the `\bigstrutjot` length, which is used to determine the box. The default for this length is 0.0pt. By increasing it by 2 pt, the tables would look like this:

02-03-10

11	21	3
12	22	
13	2	
14		34

11	21	3
12	22	
13	2	
14		34

11	21	3
12	22	
13	2	
14		34

In theory you can also use `\multirow` and `\bigstrut` within the eqnarray environment. However, its not straightforward as LaTeX already inserts a space of size `\jot`=3.0pt before and after each line, which may lead to small vertical shifts as `\multirow` can't use this length for vertical centring. In fact it's best to avoid using eqnarray anyway as there can be other problems with the vertical spacing. Use the corresponding commands from the amsmath package in preference. [56]

amsmath

02-03-11

1	1	1	1
2	2	2	2
3	3	3	3
8	4		4
	5		5
	6	8	6
	7		7
	8		8
9	9	9	9
10	10	10	10

```
\usepackage{bigstrut,multirow}

\begin{minipage}{2cm}
\begin{eqnarray*}
  1&1\\2&2\\3&3\\
  \multirow{5}*{8} &4\\ &5\\ &6\\ &7\\ &8\\
  9&9\\10&10
\end{eqnarray*}
\end{minipage}\setlength\bigstrutjot{\jot}
\begin{minipage}{2cm}
\begin{eqnarray*}
  1&1\\2&2\\3&3\\
  \multirow{5}[20]*{8} &4\\ &5\\ &6\\ &7\\ &8\\
  9&9\\10&10
\end{eqnarray*}
\end{minipage}
```

2.3.3 bigdelim

The \bigdelim package is a special application of the \multirow command and lets you typeset brackets across multiple rows, for tables and matrices. Its syntax is:

\ldelim{*bracket symbol*}{*rows*}{*space*} [text]	\ldelim{*bracket symbol*}{*rows*}* [text]
\rdelim{*bracket symbol*}{*rows*}{*space*} [text]	\rdelim{*bracket symbol*}{*rows*}* [text]

bracket symbol Any delimiter can be used as the bracket symbol. They are also allowed for \left and \right in math mode; in principle curly, round, angled, and square brackets.

rows Number of rows enclosed by the left or right bracket.

space Determines the space between the bracket and the table or matrix; the column width of the bracket is set to *space*.

* The star assumes the column type of the enclosing tabular or array environment. The number of lines is not taken into account; the height of the symbol is only one line.

text Optional text, inserted outside the bracket.

	0	...
if $f(n)$ = {	1	then do...
	2	then do...
	3	then do...
	4	then do...
	5	then do...
	6	...
	7	...

02-03-12

```
\usepackage{multirow,bigdelim}

\begin{tabular}{lll}
 & 0 &\ldots\\
\ldelim\{{6}{1.9cm}[if $f(n)=$]
 & 1 & then do\ldots\\
 & 2 & then do\ldots\\
 & 3 & then do\ldots\\
 & 4 & then do\ldots\\
 & 5 & then do\ldots\\
 & 6 &\ldots\\
 & 7 &\ldots
\end{tabular}
```

	0	...	
if $f(n)$ = {	1	then do...	] foo
	2	then do...	
	3	then do...	
	4	then do...	
	5	then do...	
	6	...	]bar

02-03-13

```
\usepackage{multirow,bigdelim}

\begin{tabular}{lllr}
 & 0 & \ldots            &\\
\ldelim{\{}{6}{1.9cm}[if $f(n)=$]
 & 1 & then do\ldots & \rdelim{]}{3}{1cm}[foo]\\
 & 2 & then do\ldots &\\
 & 3 & then do\ldots & \\
 & 4 & then do\ldots &\\
 & 5 & then do\ldots & \rdelim{]}{3}{*}[bar]\\
 & 6 &\ldots          &\\
\end{tabular}
```

These two examples show how \bigdelim works; the brackets including the optional text are simply part of a \multirow command and as such part of a normal table column.

Therefore the cells before and after the `\ldelim` and `\rdelim` commands must remain empty. This is especially important for the first column, otherwise the corresponding content would appear in those cells. You must bear in mind whether you need special columns for `\ldelim` and `\rdelim` when defining the columns of a table; if there are going to be three normal columns and a right bracket, you need to define four columns in the header of `tabular` or `array`.

2.3.4 Coloured table rows

When using either the `colortbl` or `xcolor` packages, you need to adapt the way you use `\multirow`, `\bigdelim`, or `\rdelim`. This is because the colouring packages colour individual cells one by one, rather than colouring whole columns or rows. So the current cell is first coloured and then the text is inserted. With `\multirow`, this text is inserted across several cells, but only the first one has been coloured so far. When the colouring process reaches the respective column's cell in the next row, the colouring of the cell hides the text. This can be seen in the left hand table in the following example.

Using colour

```
\usepackage{multirow,bigstrut} \usepackage[table]{xcolor}
\renewcommand\multirowsetup{\centering}

\begin{tabular}{|l|>{\columncolor{black!30}}r|>{\columncolor{black!20}}r|}\hline
  col1 row1 & col2 row1 & \multirow{3}[6]{1.5cm}{col3} \bigstrut\\\cline{1-1}
  col1 row2 & col2 row2 & \bigstrut                     \\\cline{1-2}
  col1 row3 & \multirow{2}[4]{2cm}[0.8\abovedisplayskip]{\[f(x,y)=x\cdot y\]} &
                                         \bigstrut\\\cline{1-1}\cline{3-3}
  col1 row4 &        & col3 row4\bigstrut\\\hline
\end{tabular} \quad
\begin{tabular}{|l|>{\columncolor{black!30}}r|>{\columncolor{black!20}}r|}\hline
  col1 row1 & col2 row1 & \bigstrut                    \\\cline{1-1}
  col1 row2 & col2 row2 & \bigstrut                    \\\cline{1-2}
  col1 row3 &  & \multirow{-3}[6]{1.5cm}{col3} \bigstrut  \\\cline{1-1}\cline{3-3}
  col1 row4 &  \multirow{-2}[4]{2cm}[0.8\abovedisplayskip]{\[f(x,y)=x\cdot y\]}
     & col3 row4                         \bigstrut\\\hline
\end{tabular}
```

02-03-14

col1 row1	col2 row1	
col1 row2	col2 row2	
col1 row3	$f(x,y)=x\cdot y$	
col1 row4		col3 row4

col1 row1	col2 row1	col3
col1 row2	col2 row2	
col1 row3	$f(x,y)=x\cdot y$	
col1 row4		col3 row4

The second part of the example illustrates the way round this problem is to specify a negative value for the number of rows in the `\multirow` command. This means that they are counted from bottom to top, rather than from top to bottom. By reversing the order, all cells that are affected by the `\multirow` command are already coloured before `\multirow` inserts the text. In principle, negative numbers could always be used, but it can be confusing, so it only makes sense to do this if you are colouring the table cells.

2.4 blkarray

The blkarray package by David Carlisle lets you form custom blocks (blockarray) within a tabular or array environment and provides commands to define cells that span more than one column. The package never went past the experimental stage, but has some very interesting features that are not provided by any other package.

math mode The package requires the size of the math font to be specified; this means that before using the blockarray environment for the first time, math mode must have been active at least once. In cases where this was not taken care of by other commands already – for example the default tabular environment – it has to be done manually by the user. You can do this in the document preamble by just inserting the following code:

```
\usepackage{blkarray}
\AtBeginDocument{\setbox0\hbox{$ $}}
```

Of course, if the blockarray environment is embedded in a math environment anyway, you won't need to do this. The syntax for the blockarray environment is:

```
\begin{blockarray} [position] {column definition}
...
\end{blockarray}
```

We discussed the problems that can occur when using the \multicolumn command and vertical lines in Section 2.1.1 on page 26. blkarray offers a special way of defining columns that avoids problems. You simply prefix a line definition with & in the column definition, and then use the \BAmulticolumn command, which cannot overwrite vertical lines. The syntax of \BAmulticolumn is identical to the usual \multicolumn command in standard LaTeX. The following example shows you the difference between using the \multicolumn command in a tabular environment and using the \BAmulticolumn command in a blockarray environment:

11	21	31
12	22	32
13	23	33

11	21	31
12	22	32
13	23	33

02-04-1

```
\usepackage{blkarray}

\begin{tabular}{c|c|c}
11 & 21 & 31\\
12 & \multicolumn{1}{r}{22} & 32\\
13 & 23 & 33
\end{tabular}

\begin{blockarray}{c|c&|c}
11 & 21 & 31\\
12 & \BAmulticolumn{1}{r}{22} & 32\\
13 & 23 & 33
\end{blockarray}
```

blkarray supports nested tables through a special block environment, though this has to refer to an entire row of the superordinate table. The syntax is:

```
\begin{blockarray} [position] {column definition}
...
  \begin{block*}{column definition}
  ...
  \end{block*}
...
\end{blockarray}
```

02-04-2

11	21	31
12		*23–32*
13		*23–33*
14	24	34

```
\usepackage{blkarray}

\begin{blockarray}{c|c|c}
11 & 21 & 31\\
\begin{block}{>{\itshape}c\BAmulticolumn{2}{>{\itshape}r}}
12 & 23--32\\ 13 & 23--33\\
\end{block}
14 & 24 & 34
\end{blockarray}
```

The above example showed how to use the block environment, but its advantage only becomes apparent when using the extended column types that let you insert delimiters at arbitrary positions, as in the following example. This can only be done in math mode though; you have to use \text from the amsmath package or \mbox from standard LaTeX to enter text.

math mode

02-04-3

$$\begin{array}{c|cc}c 11 & 21 & 31 & 41\\ 12 & 22 & 32\rbrace & 42\\ 13 & 23 & 33 & 43\\ 14 & 24 & 34 & 44\end{array}$$

```
\usepackage{blkarray}

\begin{blockarray}{cccc}
11 & 21 & 31 & 41\\
\begin{block}{c | cc \} c}
12 & 22 & 32 & 42\\ 13 & 23 & 33  & 43\\
\end{block}
14 & 24 & 34 & 44
\end{blockarray}
```

The starred version of the block environment adopts the superordinate delimiter definition, which is then not interrupted by the block environment anymore.

02-04-4

$$\begin{matrix} 11 \\ 12 \\ 13 \\ 14 \end{matrix} \left\{ \begin{matrix} 21 \quad 31 \\ 23\text{–}32 \\ 23\text{–}33 \\ 24 \quad 34 \end{matrix} \right\} \begin{matrix} 41 \\ 42 \\ 43 \\ 44 \end{matrix}$$

```
\usepackage{blkarray}

\begin{blockarray}{c \{ c c \} c}
11 & 21 & 31 & 41\\
\begin{block*}{c \BAmulticolumn{2}{c} c}
12 & 23\mbox{--}32 & 42\\13 & 23\mbox{--}33 & 43\\
\end{block*}
14 & 24 & 34 & 44
\end{blockarray}
```

The blockarray and block environment are particularly useful for numbering individual rows or columns of a matrix. In contrast to the normal \bordermatrix (see [56]), you can apply simple font changes for the numbers.

$$\begin{array}{cccc} \scriptstyle 1 & \scriptstyle 2 & \scriptstyle 3 & \scriptstyle 4 \end{array}$$
$$\begin{array}{c} \scriptstyle 2 \\ \scriptstyle 3 \\ \scriptstyle 4 \end{array}\begin{pmatrix} 22 & 32 & 42 \\ 23 & 33 & 43 \\ 24 & 34 & 44 \end{pmatrix}$$

02-04-5

```
\usepackage{blkarray}

\begin{blockarray}{>{\scriptsize}cccc}
\begin{block}{*{4}{>{\scriptsize}c}}
1 & 2 & 3 & 4\\
\end{block} \begin{block}{>{\scriptsize}c(ccc)}
2 & 22 & 32 & 42\\ 3 & 23 & 33  & 43\\
4 & 24 & 34 & 44\\
\end{block}
\end{blockarray}
```

The following additional commands make marking blocks with text easier:

`\Right{`*delimiter*`}{`*text*`}`	`\Left{`*text*`}{`*delimiter*`}`
`\BAmultirow{`*width*`}{`*text*`}`	`\BAnoalign*`
`\BAenum`	`\BAtablenotes`

`\Right`	Text right of the delimiter.
`\Left`	Text left of the delimiter.
`\BAmultirow`	Similar to `\multirow` (cf. Section 2.3 on page 30) but with specified width; the height is specified by the block.
`\BAnoalign`	Block of text that spans the whole width of the block.
`\BAnoalign*`	Ditto, but superordinate delimiters are not interrupted.
`\BAenum`	Increments the internal line counter `BAenumi` and outputs the result formatted with `\theBAenumi`. A subsequent `!` operator can be used to get right-aligned space.
`\BAtablenotes`	By setting `\BAtablenotestrue`, the footnotes appear underneath the table and within its width. `\BAtablenotesfalse` achieves the standard footnote behaviour of appearing at the bottom of the page. This command is discussed in Section 2.4.1 on page 42.

`\Right` and `\Left` need to be placed in the respective column definition for the `block` environment.

$$\begin{array}{ccccc} & \scriptstyle 1 & \scriptstyle 2 & \scriptstyle 3 & \scriptstyle 4 \quad \scriptstyle \text{columns} \end{array}$$
$$\text{demo}\left\{\begin{array}{cccc} \scriptstyle 2 & 22 & 32 & 42 \\ \scriptstyle 3 & 23 & 33 & 43 \\ \scriptstyle 4 & 24 & 34 & 44 \end{array}\right\} 3\times 3 \text{ matrix}$$
$\scriptstyle \text{rows}$

02-04-6

```
\usepackage{blkarray}

\begin{blockarray}{>{\scriptsize}ccccl}
\begin{block}{*{5}{>{\scriptsize}c}}
1 & 2 & 3 & 4 & columns\\
\end{block}
\begin{block}{\Left{demo} \{ >{\scriptsize}cccc
    \Right\}{3$\times$3 matrix} l}
2 & 22 & 32 & 42\\ 3 & 23 & 33  & 43\\
4 & 24 & 34 & 44\\
\end{block}
\makebox[0pt][l]{\scriptsize rows}
\end{blockarray}
```

\BAnoalign* can be used to insert arbitrary text that spans all columns. It corresponds to a \multicolumn command defining a \parbox that spans the whole width of the specified table. Delimiters are only not interrupted with the starred version, similar to block*.

In the following example, the ! operator in the definition of the table is used for formatting as well as making space. \BAenum!{.\quad} means that the value of the counter BAenumi is printed and the dot with space \quad is used as the next "column separator". Within a table, all cells are local; any changes that should affect subsequent rows must be done globally. In the example, \gdef\theBAenumi{\Roman{BAenumi}} sets the counter output to Roman numerals.

```
\usepackage{blkarray,ragged2e}

\begin{blockarray}{\BAenum!{.\quad}cc\Right{\}}{\texttt{block 1}}}
   ccc & cc        \\
   c   & ccccccccc \\
  \BAnoalign*{\texttt{\textbackslash BAnoalign*} typesets the text exactly in the
                                                    width of the table.}
  \begin{block}{\BAenum!{.\quad}(rr\Right{\}}
              {\parbox{3cm}{block 2, with a nested \texttt{block*}}}}
    \phantom{XX}rrr & rr \\
               rrr & r  \\  % next row empty "field" for BAenum
    \begin{block*}{!{\quad}ll}
      & ll & ll\phantom{XX}\\
      & l  & l\\
    \end{block*}
    r & r \\ \end{block}
  ccc \\
  \begin{block}{\BAenum!{.\quad}>{\bfseries}l \{c\Right{\}}{\texttt{block 3}}}
    \gdef\theBAenumi{\Roman{BAenumi}}
    LLL & \BAmultirow{50pt}{\Centering All columns in one block.} \\
    LL  & \\
    L   & \\
  \end{block}
  \begin{block}{\BAenum \{l\}l\Right{\}}{\texttt{block 4}}}
    ll & l\\ \BAnoalign{In contrast to \texttt{\textbackslash BAnoalign*},
      \texttt{\textbackslash BAnoalign} interrupts all delimiters in the current block.}
    l  & lll \\
  \end{block}
  c & c
\end{blockarray}
```

02-04-7

1.	ccc	cc	block 1
2.	c	ccccccccc	
\BAnoalign* typesets the text exactly in the width of the table.			
3.	rrr	rr	block 2, with a nested block*
4.	rr	r	
	ll	ll	
	l	l	
7.	r	r	
8.	ccc		block 1
9.	**LLL**	All columns in one block.	block 3
X.	**LL**		
XI.	**L**		
XII	ll { l }		block 4
In contrast to \BAnoalign*, \BAnoalign interrupts all delimiters in the current block.			
XIII	l { lll}		block 4
XIV.	c	c	block 1

2.4.1 Footnotes

In standard LaTeX you can't typeset footnotes in a table, but this is possible with `blkarray`. There are two variants: specifying `\BAtablenotestrue` lets you insert footnotes within the respective current block; specifying `\BAtablenotestrue` puts the footnotes at the bottom of the page as usual. The following two examples illustrate the two options:

```
\usepackage{blkarray}
\BAtablenotestrue

\begin{blockarray}{|c||c|}
   I\footnotetext[\textsc{sourceA:}]{Chicago Manual of Style.}
 & II\footnote{Note on II. This is a particularly long footnote to demonstrate a line break
    in the footnote.}\\
   \begin{blockarray}{(ll)}
     \footnotetext[\textsc{sourceB:}]{Chicago Manual of Style.}
     \footnotetext[\textsc{noteA:}]{The statement above is incorrect.}
     left column--1 & left--2 \\
     left--3\footnote{Footnote on left-3.} & left--4\\
   \end{blockarray} & \begin{blockarray}{(ll)}
     \footnotetext[\textsc{sourceC:}]{Chicago Manual of Style.}
     \footnotetext[\textsc{noteB:}]{The statement above is incorrect.}
     right column--1 & right--2 \\
     right--3\footnote{Footnote on right-3.} & right--4\\
   \end{blockarray}\\
```

```
 III\footnote{Note on THREE.} & IV \\
\end{blockarray}
```

02-04-8

I	II*
(left column−1 left−2 / left−3* left−4)	(right column−1 right−2 / right−3* right−4)
SOURCEB: Chicago Manual of Style. NOTEA: The statement above is incorrect. * Footnote on left-3.	SOURCEC: Chicago Manual of Style. NOTEB: The statement above is incorrect. * Footnote on right-3.
III†	IV

SOURCEA: Chicago Manual of Style.
* Note on II. This is a particularly long footnote to demonstrate a line break in the footnote.
† Note on THREE.

02-04-9

$$\begin{bmatrix} \text{I}^1 & \text{II}^2 \\ \begin{pmatrix} \text{l-1}^3 & \text{l-2} \\ \text{l-3}^4 & \text{l-4} \end{pmatrix} & \begin{pmatrix} \text{r-1}^5 & \text{r-2} \\ \text{r-3}^6 & \text{r-4} \end{pmatrix} \\ \text{III}^7 & \text{IV} \end{bmatrix}$$

[1]Chicago Manual of Style (CMoS).
[2]This is a long footnote to demonstrate the line break.
[3]Chicago Manual of Style.
[4]Footnote on l-3.
[5]CMoS
[6]...
[7]Note on III.

```
\usepackage{blkarray} \BAtablenotesfalse

\begin{blockarray}{[c c]}
  I\footnote{Chicago Manual of Style (CMoS).} &
 II\footnote{This is a long footnote to demonstrate
             the line break.}\\
 \begin{blockarray}{(ll)}
   l-1\footnote{Chicago Manual of Style.} & l-2 \\
   l-3\footnote{Footnote on l-3.} & l-4 \\
   \end{blockarray}
 & \begin{blockarray}{(ll)}
   r-1\footnote{CMoS}
 & r-2\\r-3\footnote{\ldots} & r-4\\
 \end{blockarray}\\
 III\footnote{Note on III.} & IV \\
\end{blockarray}
```

2.4.2 Lines

Vertical lines are created similarly to standard LaTeX; you can also use the extensions known from the hhline package (cf. Section 2.10 on page 64). However, you can't use \hline for horizontal lines, but blkarray provides its own commands instead. There are also two further commands for improving vertical spacing as well.

\BAhline	\BAhhline{*line notation*}
\BAextrarowheight	\BAextraheightafterhline

The following notation applies to vertical and horizontal lines; it is an extension of the notation from the hhline package.

- `-` A single line of column width.
- `=` A double line of column width.
- `.` A single dashed line of column width.
- `"` A double dashed line of column width.
- `~` A column without line.
- `|` A vertical line which intersects double horizontal lines.
- `:` Ditto, but not intersecting double horizontal lines.
- `#` A single line between two vertical ones.
- `t` The upper half of a double horizontal line.
- `b` The lower half of a double horizontal line.
- `*` Repetition operator. `*{3}{==#}` expands to `==#==#==#`; similar to the definition of several equal column types.

You can only use the `t` and `b` notation between two types of vertical lines.

0	1	2	3	4	5
0	1	2	3	4	5
0	1	2	3	4	5
0	1	2	3	4	5
0	1	2	3	4	5

```
\usepackage{blkarray}

\begin{blockarray}{||c||c|cc||cc||}
   \BAhhline{|t:=:t:=|==#==:t|}
 0 & 1 & 2 & 3 & 4 & 5\\\BAhline
 0 & 1 & 2 & 3 & 4 & 5\\\BAhline\BAhline
 0 & 1 & 2 & 3 & 4 & 5\\\BAhhline{||-||-..||.-}
 0 & 1 & 2 & 3 & 4 & 5\\\BAhhline{=::="":":"=}
 0 & 1 & 2 & 3 & 4 & 5\\\BAhhline{|b:=:b:="":":"=:b|}
\end{blockarray}
```

02-04-10

The individual lines of this example are explained in depth below; it can be difficult to understand especially the corners and intersections.

`||c||c|cc||cc||` ▷ The default vertical Lines.

`\BAhhline{|t:=:t:=|==#==:t|}`

`|t:` ▷ A vertical line (`|`), the upper half of a double horizontal (`t`), and a vertical line (`:`) which does not intersect horizontal lines: In conjunction with the column definition this produces:

`=` ▷ A default double horizontal line: , together with the previous lines this produces:

`:t:` ▷ A vertical (`:`), upper half of a horizontal one (`t`), and again a vertical line (`:`), where these do not intersect the horizontal ones: Together with the previous lines this produces:

`==#==` ▷ Two columns with double lines (`==`), a double line between two vertical ones (`#`), and again two columns with double horizontal lines: Together with the previous lines this produces:

`:t|` ▷ A vertical line (`:`), the upper half of a double horizontal one (`t`), and a vertical line (`t`) which intersects horizontal lines. The whole is the mirrored start of the table: Together with the previous lines this produces:

`\BAhline` ▷ Creates a line across the whole width of the table:

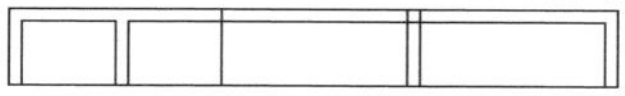

`\BAhline\BAhline` ▷ Creates a double line across the whole width of the table:

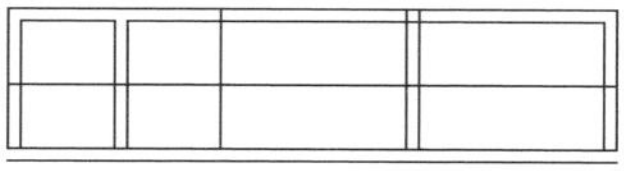

`\BAhhline{||-||-..||.-}` ▷ The middle line of the table.

`||-||-]` ▷ Two vertical lines each (`||`), followed by a simple line of column width: 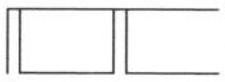 Together with the previous lines this produces:

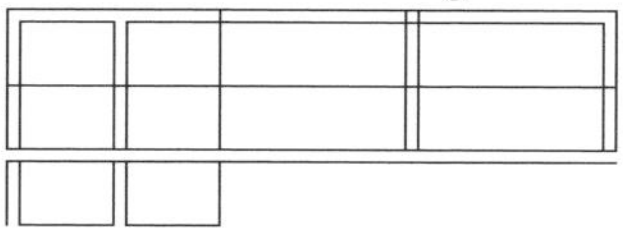

`..||.-` ▷ Two dashed lines across the width of the column each (`..`), followed by two vertical lines (`||`), a dashed line (`.`), and a single solid line (-), of column width each:  Together with the previous lines this produces:

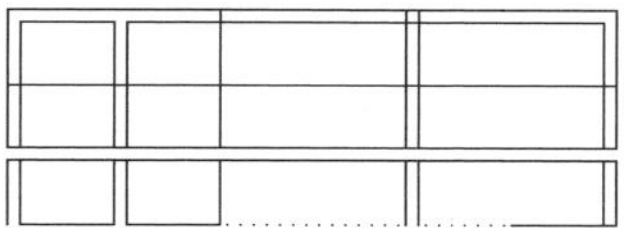

`=::=""::"=` ▷ A double horizontal line (=), followed by two vertical ones (`::`), another horizontal line (=), a double dashed line ("), and finally a normal double line (=): 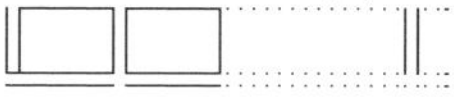 Together with the previous lines this produces:

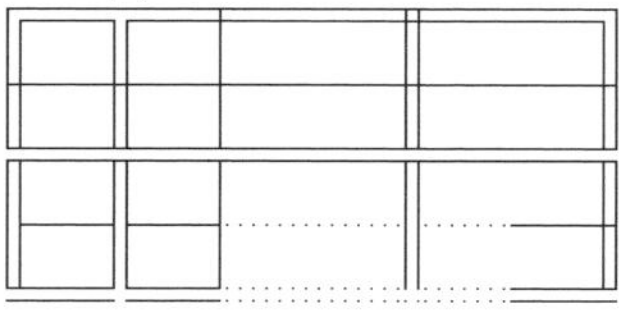

`|b:=:b:=""::"=:b|` ▷ A vertical line (`|`), the lower half of a double one (b), a vertical one (`:`), a double horizontal one (=), a vertical line (`:`), the lower half of a double one (b), a vertical one (`:`), a double horizontal line (=), two double dashed ones (`""`), two vertical ones (`::`), a double dashed line ("), a double horizontal one (=), a vertical one (`:`), the lower half of a double one (b), and finally a vertical line (`|`):  . Everything together yields Example 02-04-10 on the preceding page, given before.

2.4.3 Vertical alignment

The *position* optional argument of the `blockarray` environment can have the same values `tcb` as the standard `tabular` environment. However, the next example shows that the result of applying one of these values for this optional argument is not what you might expect:

```
\usepackage{blkarray}

Text \begin{blockarray}[t]{|c|} 1\\2\\3 \end{blockarray} text
     \begin{blockarray}[c]{|c|} 1\\2\\3 \end{blockarray} text
     \begin{blockarray}[b]{|c|} 1\\2\\3 \end{blockarray} text
```

02-04-11

Text 1 2 3 text 1 2 3 text 1 2 3 text

2.5 booktabs

The booktabs package by Simon Fear certainly belongs to the "highly recommended" category and should always be used. It primarily refers to typographical conventions to be kept in mind when creating tables, which are valid in general and have already been mentioned in Chapter 1 on page 3. These specifications are applied by booktabs, especially for vertical lines; they are not supported by the package in any special way. An example from [34, page 73] is given as starting point for a typographically *bad* table.

gnome	pound	€13.65
	piece	.01
gnu	filled	92.50
emu		33.33
duckbill	frozen	8.99

```
\begin{tabular}{||l|lr||} \hline
gnome        & pound     & \euro13.65\\
                                \cline{2-3}
             & piece     & .01    \\\hline
gnu          & filled  & 92.50 \\
                  \cline{1-1}\cline{3-3}
emu          &           & 33.33 \\\hline
duckbill & frozen & 8.99   \\\hline
\end{tabular}
```

02-05-1

Of course the original point of this example was to discuss applications of commands and not typographical questions. Nevertheless this table is suitable as a starting point for a discussion of good and less good options for a table layout. For comparison, let us take a look at the same table without vertical lines.

gnome	pound	€13.65
	piece	.01
gnu	filled	92.50
emu		33.33
duckbill	frozen	8.99

```
\usepackage{eurosym}

\begin{tabular}{@{}llr@{}} \hline
gnome & pound   & \euro13.65\\\cline{2-3}
      & piece   & .01   \\\hline
gnu   & filled & 92.50\\\cline{1-1}\cline{3-3}
emu   &           & 33.33\\\hline
duckbill & frozen & 8.99 \\\hline
\end{tabular}
```

02-05-2

The text becomes easier to see, which is always a worthwhile aim. We can also omit some of the horizontal lines, and use the \multirow or \raisebox command to shift the one common entry "filled" and centre it vertically.

02-05-3

gnome	pound	€13.65
	piece	.01
gnu	filled	92.50
emu		33.33
duckbill	frozen	8.99

```
\usepackage{eurosym,multirow}

\begin{tabular}{@{}llr@{}} \hline
gnome & pound & \euro13.65    \\
      & piece    & .01        \\
gnu   & \multirow{2}*{filled} & 92.50\\
emu   &          & 33.33      \\
duckbill & frozen & 8.99\\\hline
\end{tabular}
```

The booktabs package offers further ways to improve this table. In particular, it lets you employ different line widths more easily, with several commands defined:

```
\toprule [width]
\midrule [width]
\cmidrule [width] (horizontal trim) {from–to}
\morecmidrules
\bottomrule [width]
\addlinespace [space]
\specialrule{width}{space above}{space below}
```

The default values for the widths of the individual lines, with their associated lengths and space above/below and for \cmidrule with the optional horizontal trim are summarized in Table 2.2.

Table 2.2: Summary of the relevant lengths and their assignment to commands; the column *current* gives the values for the class used here.

length	*default*	*current*	*line type*
\heavyrulewidth	0.08 em	0.79982pt	\toprule, \bottomrule
\lightrulewidth	0.05 em	0.4999pt	\midrule
\cmidrulewidth	0.03 em	0.29991pt	\cmidrule
\belowrulesep	0.65 ex	2.7979pt	\toprule, \midrule, \cmidrule
\belowbottomsep	0 pt	0.0pt	\bottomrule
\aboverulesep	0.4ex	1.72177pt	\midrule, \cmidrule, \bottomrule
\abovetopsep	0 pt	0.0pt	\toprule
\cmidrulesep	2\p@	2.0pt	\cmidrule, \morecmidrules
\cmidrulekern	0.5 em	4.99878pt	\cmidrule
\defaultaddspace	0.5 em	4.99878pt	\addlinespace

We can improve our example table further by using the booktabs line types and adding a caption. In many fonts, the digits all have the same width; so right-aligning is sufficient to format the column of numbers.

meats		
animal	unit	price in €
gnome	pound	13.65
	piece	0.01
gnu	filled	92.50
emu		33.33
duckbill	frozen	8.99

```
\usepackage{eurosym,array,multirow,booktabs}

\begin{tabular}{@{}ll>{$}r<{$}@{}} \toprule
\multicolumn{2}{c}{meats}\\\cmidrule(r){1-2}
animal& unit  &\textrm{price in \euro}\\\midrule
gnome & pound & 13.65      \\
      & piece &  0.01      \\
gnu   & \multirow{2}*{filled} & 92.50\\
emu   &       & 33.33      \\
duckbill & frozen & 8.99\\\bottomrule
\end{tabular}
```

02-05-4

Using booktabs, you can also create simple bar charts with tables as well, without the need for other packages or external programs:

```
\usepackage{xcolor,booktabs}
\newlength{\basis}\setlength{\basis}{10cm} \newlength{\barlength}
\newcommand*{\Bar}[1]{%
  \setlength{\barlength}{0.01\basis}\setlength{\barlength}{#1\barlength}%
  \textcolor{black!40}{\rule{\barlength}{1.5ex}} #1\,\%}

\begin{tabular}{@{}ll@{}}\toprule
\multicolumn{2}{c}{General opinion on social differences in Germany (n=509)}
    \\\midrule
\Bar{57}  & very large   \\ \Bar{23}  & large\\
\Bar{12}  & less large\\ \Bar{8}    & small\\\bottomrule
\end{tabular}
```

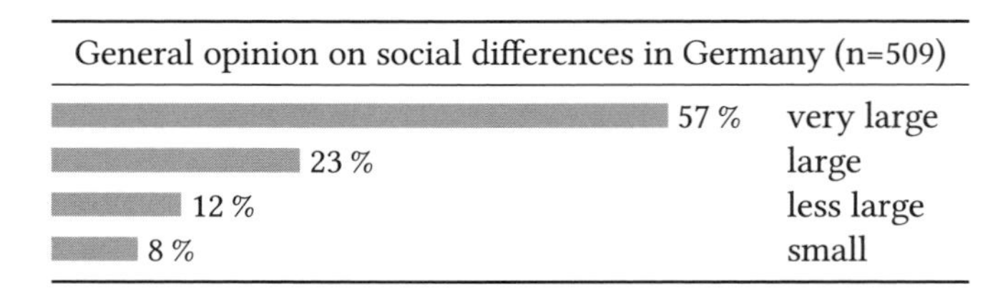

02-05-5

The \cmidrule command gives you more control over alignment than the default \cline command, as the values l and r create horizontal adjustment. The following two simple examples illustrate using the command: the first differs from the second only by the table header in the code – in the second case the table is left-/right-aligned.

02-05-6

one	two	three	four
one	two	three	four
one	two	three	four
one	two	three	four
one	two	three	four
one	two	three	four

```
\usepackage{booktabs}

\begin{tabular}{cccc}
one& two& three& four\\\cmidrule{1-2}\cmidrule{3-4}
one& two& three& four\\\cmidrule{1-1}\cmidrule{2-2}
                        \cmidrule{3-3}\cmidrule{4-4}
one& two& three& four\\\cmidrule(lr){1-2}\cmidrule(lr){3-4}
one& two& three& four\\\cmidrule(lr){1-1}\cmidrule(lr){2-2}
                        \cmidrule(lr){3-3}\cmidrule(lr){4-4}
one& two& three& four\\\cmidrule(r){1-2}\cmidrule(l){3-4}
one& two& three& four\\\cmidrule(r){1-1}\cmidrule(lr){2-2}
                        \cmidrule(lr){3-3}\cmidrule(l){4-4}
\end{tabular}
```

02-05-7

one	two	three	four
one	two	three	four
one	two	three	four
one	two	three	four
one	two	three	four
one	two	three	four

```
\usepackage{booktabs}

\begin{tabular}{@{}cccc@{}}
one& two& three& four\\\cmidrule{1-2}\cmidrule{3-4}
one& two& three& four\\\cmidrule{1-1}\cmidrule{2-2}
                        \cmidrule{3-3}\cmidrule{4-4}
one& two& three& four\\\cmidrule(lr){1-2}\cmidrule(lr){3-4}
one& two& three& four\\\cmidrule(lr){1-1}\cmidrule(lr){2-2}
                        \cmidrule(lr){3-3}\cmidrule(lr){4-4}
one& two& three& four\\\cmidrule(r){1-2}\cmidrule(l){3-4}
one& two& three& four\\\cmidrule(r){1-1}\cmidrule(lr){2-2}
                        \cmidrule(lr){3-3}\cmidrule(l){4-4}
\end{tabular}
```

You can see various differences in how the layout differs between the two tables. The first two rows show that neighbouring `\cmidrule` commands that don't use the horizontal alignment notation form a series of joined lines in the table. If on the other hand one or more of the optional trim parameters `l` or `r` are used, the partial line is shortened by the value `\cmidrulekern`. `\cmidrule` doesn't distinguish between cells in the centre of the table and at the edge, which is why the display in the second, left-/right-aligned table is different to the first table.

`\cmidrulekern` defaults to 0.5 em and can be changed at any time. Alternatively, a length can be specified explicitly as a parameter to `l` and `r`; for example `r{\`*`tabcolsep`*`}` shortens by `\tabcolsep`. Negative values extend the line to the left or right.

The following example is a rather complex application of the booktabs commands. By setting `@{\kern-30pt}` (negative column spacing) in the head of the table between the first and second column, we achieve an "attraction" of the following column. It is getting nearer to the first column.

```
\usepackage{eurosym,array,booktabs}

\begin{tabular}{@{}>{\raggedright}p{4.5cm}@{\kern-30pt}*{6}{>{\small}r}@{}}\toprule
\textit{alternative 1}  &  time of & year\\[-2pt]
                        &  investment    & 2006 & 2007 & 2008 & 2009 & 2010 \\
```

```
\cmidrule(lr){3-3}\cmidrule(lr){4-4}\cmidrule(lr){5-5}
                   \cmidrule(lr){6-6}\cmidrule(l){7-7}
introductory payments   & 0 &      0 &      0 &      0 &      0 &      0 \\
current personnel cost & 0 &  7.187 &  7.187 &  7.187 &  7.187 &  7.187 \\
current cost for\newline
system maintenance & 0 & 13.572 & 13.572 & 13.572 & 13.572 & 13.572\\
   \cmidrule[0.8pt](r){1-2}\cmidrule(lr){3-3}\cmidrule(lr){4-4}\cmidrule(lr){5-5}
   \cmidrule(lr){6-6}\cmidrule(l){7-7}
total payments for the investment
  & 0 & 20.759 & 20.759 & 20.759 & 20.759 & 20.759\\\bottomrule
%
\multicolumn{7}{c}{\rule{0pt}{3ex}\small(all amounts in \euro)}
\end{tabular}
```

02-05-8

alternative 1	time of investment	year 2006	2007	2008	2009	2010
introductory payments	0	0	0	0	0	0
current personnel cost	0	7.187	7.187	7.187	7.187	7.187
current cost for system maintenance	0	13.572	13.572	13.572	13.572	13.572
total payments for the investment	0	20.759	20.759	20.759	20.759	20.759

(all amounts in €)

As with the default LaTeX `\cline` command, calling `\cmidrule` several times consecutively does not draw multiple lines. However, inserting the `\morecmidrules` command between two identical `\cmidrule` commands gets round this; repeating the sequence creates more lines. The line spacing is specified by `\doublerulesep`=2.0pt and can be changed as usual through a length command.

one	two	three	four
one	two	three	four
one	two	three	four

02-05-9

```
\usepackage{booktabs}

\begin{tabular}{cccc}
one & two & three & four\\\cmidrule{2-3}\cmidrule{2-3}
one & two & three & four\\
             \cmidrule{2-3}\morecmidrules\cmidrule{2-3}
one & two & three & four\\\cmidrule{2-3}\morecmidrules
             \cmidrule{2-3}\morecmidrules\cmidrule{2-3}
\end{tabular}
```

The `\specialrule` command is helpful for colour tables, as it lets you create lines that don't have any vertical space before or after them and therefore can be placed immediately after coloured blocks. This also makes using vertical lines possible, which would otherwise be interrupted before and after horizontal lines because of the additional vertical spacing associated with `booktabs` line types.

colour tables

```
\usepackage{array,booktabs}
\usepackage[table]{xcolor}                    \definecolor{cLightRed}{rgb}{1,.70,.70}
\definecolor{cLightYellow}{rgb}{.90,.85,.55}\definecolor{cLightGray}{rgb}{.90,.90,.90}
\definecolor{cMediumGray}{rgb}{.70,.70,.70} \definecolor{cDarkGray}{rgb}{.50,.60,.70}
\newcommand\thickc[1][0.5pt]{\vrule width #1}
\newcommand\myMidrule{\specialrule{0.6pt}{0pt}{0pt}}

\renewcommand{\arraystretch}{1.35}
\begin{tabular}{|l|c|c|m{4cm}|} \specialrule{2pt}{5pt}{0pt}
  \multicolumn{4}{!{\thickc[2pt]}c!{\thickc[2pt]}}{%
     \large \textbf{Boot Loader Header Table}}\\\specialrule{2pt}{0pt}{0pt}
  \multicolumn{4}{!{\thickc[1pt]}>{\columncolor{cLightYellow}}r!{\thickc[1pt]}}{%
     \large Version Independent }\\\specialrule{1pt}{0pt}{0pt}
  \multicolumn{1}{!{\thickc[1pt]}>{\columncolor{cDarkGray}}c|}{Entry}
  & \multicolumn{1}{|>{\columncolor{cDarkGray}}c|}{Location}
  & \multicolumn{1}{|>{\columncolor{cDarkGray}}c|}{Size}
  & \multicolumn{1}{|>{\columncolor{cDarkGray}}c!{\thickc[1pt]}}{Comments} \\
        \specialrule{1pt}{0pt}{0pt}
  \rowcolor{cLightGray} JmpTrap & 0 & Word & 0EBFEh (JMP \$)\\\myMidrule
  \rowcolor{cMediumGray} MagicNumber & 2 & Word & 0AA55h \\\myMidrule
  \rowcolor{cLightGray} Name & 4 & 4 Bytes & 'EBLH' \\\myMidrule
  \rowcolor{cMediumGray} Version & 8 & Word & Version of BLH table\\\myMidrule
  \rowcolor{cLightGray} Size & 10 & Byte & Size of BLH table \\\myMidrule
  \rowcolor{cMediumGray}SizeVDT & 11 & Byte & Size of following version
    dependent table\\\myMidrule
  \multicolumn{4}{!{\thickc[1pt]}>{\columncolor{cLightYellow}}r!{\thickc[1pt]}}{%
    \large Version 1.x }\\\myMidrule
  \rowcolor{cLightGray} Empty & 0 & 0 & No Data for 1.x\\\myMidrule
  \multicolumn{4}{!{\thickc[2pt]}c!{\thickc[2pt]}}{%
    \large \textbf{End of Boot Loader Header Table}}\\[-2pt]\bottomrule[2pt]
\end{tabular}
```

02-05-10

Boot Loader Header Table			
			Version Independent
Entry	Location	Size	Comments
JmpTrap	0	Word	0EBFEh (JMP $)
MagicNumber	2	Word	0AA55h
Name	4	4 Bytes	'EBLH'
Version	8	Word	Version of BLH table
Size	10	Byte	Size of BLH table
SizeVDT	11	Byte	Size of following version dependent table
			Version 1.x
Empty	0	0	No Data for 1.x
End of Boot Loader Header Table			

In the above example, additional vertical spacing was not desired because of using coloured cells. In the next example, however, the exact opposite is wanted: we can insert additional vertical space arbitrarily at any place in the table using \addlinespace. When using a longtable environment (Section 4.1 on page 125), \specialrule also helps to control the space after a table caption. However, remember that when using longtable and booktabs together, the syntax of the commands is slightly different:

longtable

```
\toprule (horizontal trim) [width]
\midrule (horizontal trim) [width]
\bottomrule (horizontal trim) [width]
\specialrule (horizontal trim) {width}{space above}{space below}
```

The optional argument for the horizontal trim is now possible for all commands. This is important to know because for example in the following code, the \relax after the last \midrule is required. Otherwise the parenthesis in the following line would cause an error message – \midrule would regard it as the start of an optional argument.

```
\usepackage{longtable}  \usepackage{booktabs}

\begin{longtable}{@{}lrccccr@{}}
\caption{Summary.}\\          \specialrule{1pt}{5pt}{5pt}
\multicolumn{1}{l}{compound} & \multicolumn{1}{c}{Lit.}
   & \multicolumn{1}{c}{X-Ray} & \multicolumn{1}{c}{Lsm.}
   & \multicolumn{1}{c}{$^{125}$Te-shift}
   & \multicolumn{1}{c}{$^{19}$F-shift} \\\midrule
\addlinespace[0.3em]
\endhead
%
\addlinespace[0.5em]
\endfoot
%
\bottomrule
\endlastfoot
%
(CF$_3$C$_6$F$_4$)$_2$Te$_2$ &---&---&---&---&--- \\\midrule
Ph$_2$Te                     &---&---&---&729&--- \\\midrule\relax
(C$_6$F$_4$)$_2$Te$_2$       &---& ja&---&762& $-108,0$; $-152,0$
\end{longtable}
```

Table 1: Summary.

02-05-11

compound	Lit.	X-Ray	Lsm.	^{125}Te-shift	^{19}F-shift
$(CF_3C_6F_4)_2Te_2$	—	—	—	—	—
Ph_2Te	—	—	—	729	—
$(C_6F_4)_2Te_2$	—	ja	—	762	$-108,0$; $-152,0$

2.6 cellspace

The cellspace package by Josselin Noirel automatically loads the ifthen, array, and calc packages and provides better line spacing for displayed equations in tables and matrices. Otherwise, especially when using fractions, roots, or exponents in tabular environments, problems can occur such as the one in the following example:

02-06-1

$f(x) = \frac{\sqrt{x^2-1}}{x^2+1}$
$f(x) = \frac{\sqrt{x^2-1}}{x^2+\frac{1}{x^2}}$

```
\begin{tabular}{c}\hline
$ f(x)=\frac{\sqrt{x^2-1}}{x^2+1}$                    \\\hline
$ f(x)=\frac{\sqrt{x^2-1}}{x^2+\frac{1}{x^2}}$\\\hline
\end{tabular}
```

In general, you could just use the \arraystretch command to stretch the table. But this doesn't always lead to equal spacing across different tables, because the value for \arraystretch has to be adjusted. Furthermore a lot of experience is required to come up with sensible values, which nevertheless still do not always yield the expected solution.

02-06-2

$f(x) = \frac{\sqrt{x^2-1}}{x^2+1}$
$f(x) = \frac{\sqrt{x^2-1}}{x^2+\frac{1}{x^2}}$

```
\renewcommand\arraystretch{2.5}
\begin{tabular}{c}\hline
$ f(x)=\frac{\sqrt{x^2-1}}{x^2+1}$ \\\hline
$ f(x)=\frac{\sqrt{x^2-1}}{x^2+\frac{1}{x^2}}$\\\hline
\end{tabular}
```

The cellspace package tries to determine sensible spacings above and below by calculating the required height of the cell. To achieve this, a new S column type was defined through the \newcolumntype command. It takes the actual type as a parameter; possible values are l, c, r, p, m, and b. For the simple types, no parentheses are necessary and the following character is automatically assumed to be the argument, i.e. Sl and S{l} are identical.

02-06-3

$f(x) = \frac{\sqrt{x^2-1}}{x^2+1}$
$f(x) = \frac{\sqrt{x^2-1}}{x^2+\frac{1}{x^2}}$

```
\usepackage{cellspace}

\begin{tabular}{Sc}\hline
$ f(x)=\frac{\sqrt{x^2-1}}{x^2+1}$ \\\hline
$ f(x)=\frac{\sqrt{x^2-1}}{x^2+\frac{1}{x^2}}$\\\hline
\end{tabular}
```

The space above and below a tabular cell is controlled by the package-defined lengths \cellspacetoplimit=1 pt and \cellspacebottomlimit=1 pt. These default values are quite small, so we recommende you change them. You can do this by using either \setlength or \addtolength.

02-06-4

$f(x) = \frac{\sqrt{x^2-1}}{x^2+1}$
$f(x) = \frac{\sqrt{x^2-1}}{x^2+\frac{1}{x^2}}$

```
\usepackage{cellspace}\addtolength\cellspacetoplimit{3pt}
\addtolength\cellspacebottomlimit{3pt}

\begin{tabular}{Sc}\hline
$ f(x)=\frac{\sqrt{x^2-1}}{x^2+1}$ \\\hline
$ f(x)=\frac{\sqrt{x^2-1}}{x^2+\frac{1}{x^2}}$\\\hline
\end{tabular}
```

cellspace lets you add further column types with the \addparagraphcolumntypes command. This mostly refers to custom types defined by the user, which are not known to cellspace otherwise. A typical case is the addition of a X column type when using the package tabularx (cf. Section 2.18 on page 87).

x	the independent variable which can be assigned arbitrarily
y	the dependent variable
$f(x)$	the function $y = f(x)\dfrac{1}{\sqrt{x}}$

```
\usepackage{amsmath,cellspace,tabularx}
\addparagraphcolumntypes{X}
\addtolength\cellspacetoplimit{3pt}
\addtolength\cellspacebottomlimit{3pt}

\begin{tabularx}{\linewidth}{S{p{3em}}SX}\hline
$x$ & the independent variable which can be
      assigned arbitrarily\\\hline
$y$ & the dependent variable\\\hline
$f(x)$ & the function
      $y=f(x)\dfrac{1}{\sqrt{x}}$\\\hline
\end{tabularx}
```

02-06-5

2.7 ctable

The ctable package by Wybo Dekker combines the functionality of the array, tabularx, and booktabs packages. Additionally, the rotating, xspace, color, and xkeyval packages are loaded. ctable defines the command of the same name, which is used to change the layout of a table, controlled by keywords. It also provides additional commands for footnotes and lines.

\ctable [options] {*column declarations*}{*footnotes*}{*table rows*}
\tmark [symbol]
\tnote [symbol] {*text*}
\NN [spacing]   \FL [spacing]   \ML [spacing]   \LL [spacing]

In the simplest case, the ctable command is used without options and with an empty argument for the footnotes:

left	*centre*	*right*
l	c	r
left	center	right

```
\usepackage{ctable}

\ctable{lcr}{}{% <-- empty footnote argument!
  \emph{left} & \emph{centre} & \emph{right}\\\hline
  l    & c      & r     \\
  left & center & right }
```

02-07-1

Table 2.3 summarizes all possible optional parameters and also gives the corresponding default values. Several of the options refer to the table as the floating environment; this is not important here though and will not be explained further. [42]

Table 2.3: Summary of the options for the \ctable command.

name	*description*
caption	Table caption (above or below); *must* be enclosed in parentheses if the text contains a comma or an equals sign.
cap	Alternative short form for the list of tables (\listoftables).
captionskip	Space between caption and table, default is 2 ex.
mincapwidth	Minimum width of the table caption. Useful for very narrow tables; footnotes are always typeset with the "caption" width.
pos	Float position, default is tbp.
label	Requires a table caption. Corresponds to the \label command.
width	If a width is specified, the tabularx environment is used to typeset the table; therefore the X column type is used for at least one column.
maxwidth	If the table does not extend to the maximum width, each X column is converted to a normal l column.
center	Centres the table on the current line (default).
left	Left-aligns the table on the current line.
right	Right-aligns the table on the current line.
figure	A figure floating environment is used for the table instead of the table environment.
botcap	Places the caption at the bottom.
sideways	Rotates the table counter-clockwise (oneside) or clockwise (twoside) by 90 degrees and places it on its own page. The pos option must not be used in this case.
nosuper	Typesets the footnote symbols *not* in "superscript" mode.
notespar	Typesets all footnote texts consecutively in *one* paragraph.
star	Uses the starred versions of the floating environments; this only makes sense in \twocolumn mode to have the table span both columns.
framerule	The table is *always* fitted with a frame; the line width is 0 pt by default though – it is invisible unless another value is specified.
framesep	Corresponds to \fboxsep and determines the spacing between frame and table; default is 0 pt.
framefg	Expects three values separated by spaces (RGB), each from the range [0...1] for the frame colour; default is 0 0 0 for black.
framebg	Expects three values separated by spaces (RGB), each from the range [0...1] for the background colour of the frame; default is 1 1 1 for white.

Footnotes are always placed underneath the table and their width (mark and text) depends on the table caption. If there is no caption, the width of the table itself is taken. A separating line is drawn when using the standard \footnotetext command. The counting is done in the usual minipage form; i.e. \tmark is to be replaced by the "real" letter and \footnotetext the corresponding number (f→6). If \tmark and \tnote are used without optional argument, the label *a* is assumed automatically. The footnote counter is not incremented automatically.

I[SOURCE:]	II[a]
left col–1	right col–1
left–2	right–2
left–3[b]	right–3[*]
left–4	right–4
III[c]	IV[f]

SOURCE: Chicago Manual of Style. [a] Note on II. This is a very long footnote to demonstrate the line break in a footnote. [b] Footnote on left-3. [*] Footnote on right-3 [c] Footnote on III.

[f] Another "real" footnote on III.

02-07-2

```
\usepackage{ctable}

\ctable[notespar=true]{|c||c|}{%
 \tnote[\textsc{source:}]{Chicago Manual of Style.}%
 \tnote{Note on II. This is a very long footnote to
        demonstrate the line break in a footnote.}%
 \tnote[b]{Footnote on left-3.}%
 \tnote[*]{Footnote on right-3}%
 \tnote[c]{Footnote on III.}%
 \footnotetext[6]{Another ‘‘real’’ footnote on III.}%
}{%
  I\tmark[\textsc{source:}] & II\tmark\\
  left col--1      & right col--1      \\
  left--2          & right--2          \\
  left--3\tmark[b]& right--3\tmark[*] \\
  left--4          & right--4          \\
  III\tmark[c]     & IV\tmark[f] }
```

Frames are only drawn around the table; the footnotes appear outside it. When specifying the line width you need to take into account that very thin lines are sometimes not visible on the screen. In this case the document can be magnified or printed. Colour specifications in one of the extended xcolor notations like red!70!blue!30 are not possible.

xcolor

I[SOURCE:]	II[a]
left column–1	right column–1
left–2	right–2
left–3[b]	right–3[*]
left–4	right–4
III[c]	IV[f]

SOURCE: Chicago Manual of Style.
[a] Note on II. This is a very long footnote to demonstrate the line break in the footnote.
[b] Footnote on left-3.
[*] Footnote on right-3
[c] Footnote on III.

[f] Another "real" footnote on III.

02-07-3

```
\usepackage{ctable}

\ctable[framerule=0.5pt,framesep=5pt,
    framebg=0.8 0.5 0.6]{@{}c||c@{}}{%
 \tnote[\textsc{source:}]{Chicago Manual of Style.}%
 \tnote{Note on II. This is a very long footnote
        to demonstrate the line break
        in the footnote.}%
 \tnote[b]{Footnote on left-3.}%
 \tnote[*]{Footnote on right-3}%
 \tnote[c]{Footnote on III.}%
 \footnotetext[6]{Another ‘‘real’’ footnote on III.}%
}{%
  I\tmark[\textsc{source:}] & II\tmark\\
  left column--1  & right column--1   \\
  left--2         & right--2          \\
  left--3\tmark[b]& right--3\tmark[*] \\
  left--4         & right--4          \\
  III\tmark[c]     & IV\tmark[f]
}
```

The sideways parameters always put the table on its own page so using them only makes sense for large tables. If the table is very wide but not very high, its better to use a simple rotation with \rotatebox.

Instead of the standard line break commands like \\ or \tabularnewline, ctable provides alternative variants like \NN (normal newline); they are listed on page 54. *All* line commands must be within the table block. For lines, the \FL (first line), \ML (middle line), and \LL (last line) commands refer to the booktabs versions, \toprule, \midrule, and \bottomrule, with the option of specifying the width of the line.

\FL

```
\usepackage{ctable}

Here is some pretty useless text before the following table, which will appear
on its own page because of the \texttt{sideways} option.

\ctable[sideways,maxwidth=\textheight,
  caption=A table with \texttt{\textbackslash ctable}.]{@{}>{\ttfamily}l X@{}
}{\tnote[*]{A demonstration with \texttt{\textbackslash ctable}.}}%
 {\FL% FirstLine with default width
sideways\tmark[*] & Rotates the table counter-clockwise (oneside) or clockwise
    (twoside) by 90 degrees and places it on its own table. The \texttt{pos}
    option must not be used in this case.\ML[0.1pt]% MidLine
star & Uses the starred version as floating environment; this only makes
    sense in \texttt{\textbackslash twocolumn} mode to have the table span both
    columns.\LL[0.5pt]% LastLine
}% end of the table argument
```

02-07-4

Here is some pretty useless text before the following table, which will appear on its own page because of the sideways option.

Table 1: A table with \ctable.

sideways*	Rotates the table counter-clockwise (oneside) or clockwise (twoside) by 90 degrees and places it on its own table. The pos option must not be used in this case.
star	Uses the starred version as floating environment; this only makes sense in \twocolumn mode to have the table span both columns.

* A demonstration with \ctable.

The maxwidth option is helpful when tables are generated by external scripts or programs where the content of the table is not necessarily known before. The general use of a X column in conjunction with the tabularx package can be irritating if the specified width of the table (mandatory) is larger than necessary. By specifying a maximum width through maxwidth, a X column can be converted automatically to a l column if the table as a whole is narrower than the maximum width.

The horizontal alignment of the table, which is centred on the current line by default, can be changed through the options `left`, `center`, and `right`.

left	*centred*	*right*
l	c	r
left	center	right

left	*centred*	*right*
l	c	r
left	center	right

left	*centred*	*right*
l	c	r
left	center	right

```
\usepackage{ctable}

\ctable{@{}lcr@{}}{}{%
  \emph{left} & \emph{centred}
    & \emph{right}\\\hline
  l    & c       & r\\
  left & center & right }
\ctable[left]{@{}lcr@{}}{}{%
  \emph{left} & \emph{centred}
    & \emph{right}\\\hline
  l    & c       & r\\
  left & center & right }
\ctable[right]{@{}lcr@{}}{}{%
  \emph{left} & \emph{centred}
    & \emph{right}\\\hline
  l    & c       & r\\
  left & center & right }
```

02-07-5

2.8 datatool

The `datatool` package by Nicola Talbot supersedes the old `csvtools` package by the same author. `datatool` is actually a collection of several packages, all of which read external files and display them in some form or another – as table, pie chart, or function graph. All data sets are read line by line and must have a consistent separator, which can be specified by the user.

In the standard case, the external file contains a comma-separated list. Additionally, individual entries can be enclosed in quotes if they contain a comma themselves, as can be seen in the second line of the following data set. The first line of a data set *must* contain identifiers for the individual columns, which may then be referenced with `\DTLforeach`.

```
givenName,surname,passportNo,age
Hannes,"Wader, sen.",102689,68
Jane,Austen,102647,75
James,Brown,103569,42
Jana,Voss,105488,26
Roger,Daltry,106872,58
Claire,Waldoff,104356,45
Felix,Voss,513110,29
```

`\DTLloaddb`{*list of data*}{*file name*}
`\DTLforeach` * [condition] {*list of data*}{*identifier list*}{*table row*}

02-08-1

given name	**surname**	**age**
Hannes	Wader, sen.	68
Jane	Austen	75
James	Brown	42
Jana	Voss	26
Roger	Daltry	58
Claire	Waldoff	45
Felix	Voss	29

```
\usepackage{datatool}

\DTLloaddb{list}{data0.csv}
\begin{tabular}{llc}
\bfseries given name & \bfseries surname
  & \bfseries age
\DTLforeach{list}{\givenName=givenName,
  \surname=surname,\age=age}{%
  \\ \givenName & \surname & \age}
\end{tabular}
```

The starred version works faster, so is better for larger data sets, but it provides the data read only, allowing no changes to the individual entries. The first required argument of `\DTLforeach` expects the logical file name, the second one specifies the assignment of individual columns to macro names, and the last argument specifies the formatting of an individual row in the table. The double backslash can be inserted before or after the new row. We can number the individual rows easily with the internal counter `DTLrowi`; it can be queried in the usual way and also used for labels. This allows it to reference the individual rows of the table.

02-08-2

no	*given name*	*surname*	*age*
1.	Hannes	Wader, sen.	68
2.	Jane	Austen	75
3.	James	Brown	42
4.	Jana	Voss	26
5.	Roger	Daltry	58
6.	Claire	Waldoff	45
7.	Felix	Voss	29

The entry for James Brown can be found in row 3 of the table and the one for Claire in row 6.

```
\usepackage{datatool}
\DTLloaddb{list}{data0.csv}

\begin{tabular}{cllc}
\emph{no} & \emph{given name} &
  \emph{surname} & \emph{age}
\DTLforeach{list}{\givenName=givenName,
  \surname=surname,\age=age}{%
\label{tab:\surname}\\ \theDTLrowi.
  & \givenName & \surname  & \age}
\end{tabular}\par
The entry for James Brown can be found in
row~\ref{tab:Brown} of the table and the
one for Claire in row~\ref{tab:Waldoff}.
```

You can then reference items in the usual way with the `\ref` command. You *must* add the label before the line break `\\` to keep the reference to the internal command `\refstepcounterDTLrowi`; all counters are set at the beginning of the argument *table row* (cf. syntax of the command). The counters are assigned to the elements of *identifier list* and similar to the normal list denoted with consecutive lowercase Roman numerals. The first one is `DTLrowi`, the second one `DTLrowii`, etc.

> `\DTLisopenbetween{`*list*`}{`*start symbol*`}{`*end symbol*`}`
> `\DTLifoddrow{`*true*`}{`*false*`}`
> `\DTLiffirstrow{`*true*`}{`*false*`}`

The optional argument of `\DTLforeach` can be used to specify a condition for filtering entries; for example each person whose surname starts with "W". The `\DTLisopenbetween` command defines the region for which the list of data is "open"; the start is inclusive and the end is exclusive.

no	*given name*	*surname*	*age*
1.	Hannes	Wader, sen.	68
2.	Claire	Waldoff	45

```
\usepackage{datatool}\DTLloaddb{list}{data0.csv}

\begin{tabular}{cllc}
\emph{no} & \emph{given name} &
  \emph{surname} & \emph{age}
\DTLforeach[\DTLisopenbetween{\surname}{W}{X}]%
    {list}{\givenName=givenName,
  \surname=surname,\age=age}{\\
  \theDTLrowi.&\givenName&\surname&\age}
\end{tabular}
```

02-08-3

no	*given name*	*surname*	*age*
1.	Hannes	Wader, sen.	68
2.	Jane	Austen	75
3.	James	Brown	42
4.	Jana	Voss	26
5.	Roger	Daltry	58
6.	Claire	Waldoff	45
7.	Felix	Voss	29

```
\usepackage{datatool}
\usepackage[table]{xcolor}

\DTLloaddb{list}{data0.csv}
\begin{tabular}{cllc}
\emph{no} & \emph{given name} &
  \emph{surname} & \emph{age}
\DTLforeach{list}{\givenName=givenName,
 \surname=surname,\age=age}{\\
 \DTLifoddrow%
   {\rowcolor{black!20}}{\rowcolor{black!40}}
 \theDTLrowi.&\givenName&\surname&\age}
\end{tabular}
```

02-08-4

The `\DTLifoddrow` command helps you create a "double" table, by inserting a line break `\\` or a column separator `&` depending on the row. The order is important here; first, the missing line break for the header must be created. The counting of rows is done the same way as the data list; the first line contains the column identifiers (cf. the data set on page 58).

```
\usepackage{datatool} \DTLloaddb{list}{data0.csv}

\begin{tabular}{cllc@{\qquad}cllc}
\emph{no} & \emph{given name} & \emph{surname} & \emph{age} &
\emph{no} & \emph{given name} & \emph{surname} & \emph{age}
\DTLforeach{list}{\givenName=givenName,\surname=surname,\age=age}%
  {\DTLifoddrow{\\}{&} \theDTLrowi. & \givenName & \surname   & \age}
\end{tabular}
```

no	*given name*	*surname*	*age*	*no*	*given name*	*surname*	*age*
1.	Hannes	Wader, sen.	68	2.	Jane	Austen	75
3.	James	Brown	42	4.	Jana	Voss	26
5.	Roger	Daltry	58	6.	Claire	Waldoff	45
7.	Felix	Voss	29				

02-08-5

Use `\DTLiffirstrow` for example to insert a horizontal line after the first row.

02-08-6

no	*given name*	*surname*	*age*
1.	Hannes	Wader, sen.	68
2.	Jane	Austen	75
3.	James	Brown	42
4.	Jana	Voss	26
5.	Roger	Daltry	58
6.	Claire	Waldoff	45
7.	Felix	Voss	29

```
\usepackage{datatool}
\DTLloaddb{list}{data0.csv}

\begin{tabular}{cllc}
\emph{no} & \emph{given name} &
   \emph{surname} & \emph{age}
\DTLforeach{list}{\givenName=givenName,
  \surname=surname,\age=age}{%
  \DTLiffirstrow{\\\hline}{\\}
  \theDTLrowi.&\givenName&\surname&\age}
\end{tabular}
```

Another interesting feature of the datatool package is its ability to sort the data rows.

\DTLsort * [sorting order] {*sorting criteria*}{*list of data*}

The optional specification of the sorting order is only interesting in the case where the actual sorting criteria fails because there is no corresponding entry in the column of the list of data, similar to a null entry in a SQL database. In the following example, we are sorting primarily on *age* in descending order; the optional specification of *descending* sorts in descending order while *ascending* sorts in the default ascending order. *surname* is given as an alternative sorting order to the *age* sorting criteria.

02-08-7

no	*given name*	*surname*	*age*
1.	Jane	Austen	75
2.	Hannes	Wader, sen.	68
3.	Roger	Daltry	45
4.	Claire	Waldoff	45
5.	James	Brown	42
6.	Felix	Voss	29
7.	Jana	Voss	26

```
\usepackage{datatool}\DTLloaddb{list}{data0.csv}

\DTLsort[surname]{age=descending}{list}
\begin{tabular}{@{}cllc@{}}
\emph{no} & \emph{given name} &
  \emph{surname} & \emph{age}
\DTLforeach{list}{\givenName=givenName,
  \surname=surname,\age=age}{%
  \DTLiffirstrow{\\\hline}{\\}
  \theDTLrowi.&\givenName&\surname&\age}
\end{tabular}
```

When using \DTLsort to sort, whether text is upper- or lowercase does matter. However, in the starred version all strings are converted to lowercase before sorting, so then case doesn't matter.

02-08-8

no	*given name*	*surname*	*age*
1.	Jane	Austen	75
2.	James	Brown	42
3.	Roger	Daltry	58
4.	Jana	Voss	26
5.	Felix	Voss	29
6.	Hannes	Wader, sen.	68
7.	Claire	Waldoff	45

```
\usepackage{datatool}\DTLloaddb{list}{data0.csv}

\DTLsort*{surname}{list}
\begin{tabular}{@{}cllc@{}}
\emph{no} & \emph{given name} &
  \emph{surname} & \emph{age}
\DTLforeach{list}{\givenName=givenName,
  \surname=surname,\age=age}{%
  \DTLiffirstrow{\\\hline}{\\}
  \theDTLrowi.&\givenName&\surname&\age}
\end{tabular}
```

The functionality of the `datatool` package is much larger than what we can present here. You can find many further examples in the documentation of the package. [53]

2.9 easytable

The `easytable` package by Enrico Bertolazzi provides a simplified method for drawing tables. The package is part of the `easy` package series and automatically loads the main `easy` package. The general line width is set when loading the package, but there are two package options – `thinlines` and `thicklines`. The default values for these options are shown in Figure 2.4 on the next page. If you get the LaTeX error message "no room for a new dimen" when loading additional packages, you need to load the `etex` package, which allows for more than the usual dimension registers.

etex

Figure 2.1: Specification of the line width through the package option.

Option	\@tab@size@rule	\@tab@size@dash
thinlines	0.7 pt	0.5 pt
thicklines	1.5 pt	1.2 pt

The `easytable` package provides a simplified version of the `tabular` environment with its `TAB` environment, though it also offers some additional functionality. The syntax takes some getting used to:

```
\begin{TAB}(type ,xMin,yMin ) [margin,xMin,yMin] {columns}{rows}
```

type ,xMin,yMin
: Must be one of the following values:
  @ No effect.
  r Equal row heights.
  c Equal column widths.
  b Equal row heights and column widths.
  e Equal row heights and column widths (identical values).
  The optional values `xMin,yMin` enforce a minimum size of the box and have to be specified as a length with a TeX unit, for example 10pt,30pt.

margin ,xMin,yMin
: Optionally specifies the outer margin of the individual cells, similar to `\fboxsep`, and defaults to 2 pt. The additional optional arguments `xMin,yMin` specify the minimum size of the whole table, for example 10cm,5cm.

columns
: These are the default column definitions of LaTeX; they may only take the three standard values `l`, `c`, and `r`, however.

rows
: The alignment of the rows must be specified here; possible values are `c`, `t`, and `b`. The number of rows *must* be fixed at the beginning of the environment, or changed afterwards if the number of rows increases. Internally the maximum number of columns and rows is fixed to 30.

`easytable` uses different syntax for horizontal lines, so it can't be used together with the `booktabs` package.

no `\hline` and no `\cline`

When you want to format columns and rows uniformly, `easytable` offers clear advantages. The following example creates a table with quadratic cells, achieved by assigning column type with value `e`. Within these cells, the cells and rows are aligned according to the specifications `lrc` and `ctb`. Not having the `\hline` and `\cline` commands available is no restriction; you can set up the horizontal lines in the row formattin definition with the same notation as for vertical lines in column definitions.

02-09-1

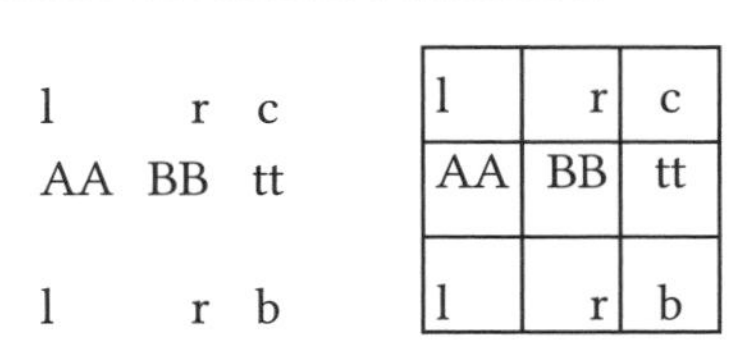

```
\usepackage[thinlines]{easytable}

\begin{TAB}(e){lrc}{ctb}
l  & r  & c \\
AA & BB & tt\\
l  & r  & b
\end{TAB}\qquad
\begin{TAB}(e){|l|r|c|}{|c|t|b|}
l  & r  & c\\AA & BB & tt\\l  & r  & b
\end{TAB}
```

The example above shows that the format specification for the row always applies to all columns of a table. In the first row only the `l` can be vertically centred correctly; `r` and `c` do not have an upper length like the l, so are not centred vertically.

02-09-2

l	r	c
AA	BB	tt
l	r	b

```
\usepackage[thinlines]{easytable}

\fbox{%
\begin{TAB}(e,12pt,12pt)[5pt,2.5cm,2.5cm]{l:r:c}{c:t:b}
l  & r  & c  \\
AA & BB & tt \\
l  & r  & b
\end{TAB}}
```

Horizontal and vertical lines don't need different commands or symbols for their own syntax anymore. The syntax provided by the TAB environment treats columns and rows the same; all lines can, and must, be specified with the same symbols. The symbols listed in Table 2.4 are valid for lines.

symbol	*description*	*symbol*	*description*
|	solid line	:	dashed line
;	dash-dot line	.	dotted line
0	like |, 1/5 of the width	1	like |, 1/4 of the width
2	like |, 1/3 of the width	3	like |, 1/4 of the width
4	like |	5	like |, double width
6	like |, triple width	7	like |, quadruple width
8	like |, quintuple width	9	like |, sextuple width

Table 2.4: Summary of the symbols for horizontal and vertical lines.

You can't insert partial lines in the TAB environment, but environments can be nested arbitrarily, which can be used to achieve the same effect:

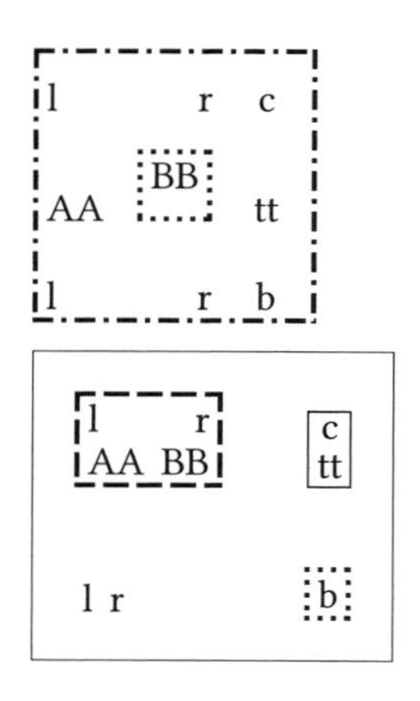

02-09-3

```
\usepackage[thicklines]{easytable}

\begin{TAB}(e){;lrc;}{;ctb;}
l  & r  & c \\
AA & \begin{TAB}(e){.r.}{.t.}BB\end{TAB} & tt\\
l  & r  & b
\end{TAB}\\[\medskipamount]
\begin{TAB}(@)[10pt]{0lr0}{0tt0}
  \begin{TAB}(@){:lr:}{:ct:}
    l  & r  \\ AA & BB
  \end{TAB} &
  \begin{TAB}(@){1c1}{2bb2}
    c\\tt
  \end{TAB}\\
  \begin{TAB}(@){lr}{c}
    l  & r
  \end{TAB} & \begin{TAB}(@){.c.}{.c.} b \end{TAB}
\end{TAB}
```

2.10 hhline

The `hhline` package by David Carlisle extends the standard line commands. The `blkarray` package by the same author was presented earlier in Section 2.4 on page 38; it also provides line extensions, partly with the same syntax. `hhline` defines the command of the same name, which expects only one parameter:

`\hhline{`*line definition*`}`

The symbols listed in Table 2.5 are valid for lines.

Table 2.5: Symbols for creating the line styles for rows, columns, and cells.

<table>
<tr><th>symbol</th><th>meaning</th></tr>
<tr><td>-</td><td>A single line of column width.</td></tr>
<tr><td>=</td><td>A double line of column width.</td></tr>
<tr><td>~</td><td>A column without line.</td></tr>
<tr><td>|</td><td>A vertical line that intersects double horizontal lines.</td></tr>
<tr><td>:</td><td>Ditto, but not intersecting double horizontal lines.</td></tr>
<tr><td>#</td><td>A single line between two vertical ones.</td></tr>
<tr><td>t</td><td>The upper half of a double horizontal line.</td></tr>
<tr><td>b</td><td>The lower half of a double horizontal line.</td></tr>
<tr><td>*</td><td>Repetition operator; *{3}{==#} expands to ==#==#==#, similar to the definition of multiple equal column types.</td></tr>
</table>

The following example can be understood with the help of the very elaborate explanations for Example 02-04-10 on page 44; no further explanations will be provided here.

02-10-1

0	1	2	3	4	5
0	1	2	3	4	5
0	1	2	3	4	5
0	1	2	3	4	5
0	1	2	3	4	5

```
\usepackage{hhline}

\begin{tabular}{||c||c|cc||cc||}
   \hhline{|t:=:t:=|==#==:t|}
 0 & 1 & 2 & 3 & 4 & 5\\\hline
 0 & 1 & 2 & 3 & 4 & 5\\\hhline{======}
 0 & 1 & 2 & 3 & 4 & 5\\\hhline{||-||-..||.-}
 0 & 1 & 2 & 3 & 4 & 5\\\hhline{=::=~~::~=}
 0 & 1 & 2 & 3 & 4 & 5\\\hhline{|b:=:b:=--::-=:b|}
\end{tabular}
```

2.11 makecell

The `makecell` package by Olga Lapko is particularly suitable for formatting individual table cells separately. In principle, the functionality of all the special commands that this package provides can be achieved with commands from other packages as well.

`\makecell` * [column/row type] {*cell contents*}

The name of the command already indicates that it is designed for the formatting of an individual cell. The parameter for the horizontal alignment may take any value allowed by the `array` package: `l`, `c`, `r`, `p`, `m`, and `b`. The last three expect a separate parameter for the column width, so they must be enclosed in parentheses again, for example `{p{4cm}}` or `{>{\ttfamily}m{4em}}`. The mandatory parameter for the horizontal alignment maybe empty (`{}`) but must be specified. For the vertical alignment, the usual three values `b`, `c`, and `t` are allowed. `\makecell` creates a cell which consists of a single-column table. If the optional values are missing, the contents are centred horizontally and vertically. The starred version of `\makecell` adds the vertical space `1\jot`=3.0pt before and after the current cell. The order of the parameter values doesn't matter.

02-11-1

1st	without parameter
2nd	without parameter but on two lines
3rd	horizontal left
4th	horizontal left
5th	horizontal right
6th	horizontal right

7th	fixed width
8th	fixed width

```
\usepackage{makecell}

\begin{tabular}{|c|c|}\hline
1st & \makecell{without parameter} \\\hline
2nd & \makecell{without parameter\\
                 but on two lines}\\\hline
3rd & \makecell[l]{horizontal left}   \\\hline
4th & \makecell[l]{horizontal\\ left} \\\hline
5th & \makecell[r]{horizontal right}  \\\hline
6th & \makecell[r]{horizontal\\ right}\\\hline
\end{tabular}\\[5pt]
\begin{tabular}{|c|c|}\hline
7th & \makecell[{}{p{3cm}}]{fixed width} \\\hline
8th & \makecell[{}{p{3cm}}]{fixed\\width}\\\hline
\end{tabular}
```

1st	without parameter
2nd	vertical top
3rd	vertical top
4th	vertical bottom
5th	vertical bottom

```
\usepackage{makecell}

\begin{tabular}{|c|c|}\hline
1st & \makecell{without parameter}    \\\hline
2nd & \makecell[t]{vertical top}      \\\hline
3rd & \makecell[t]{vertical\\ top}    \\\hline
4th & \makecell[b]{vertical bottom}   \\\hline
5th & \makecell[b]{vertical\\ bottom}\\\hline
\end{tabular}
```

02-11-2

1st	without parameter
2nd	vertical top horizontal left
3rd	vertical top horizontal right
4th	vertical bottom horizontal left
5th	vertical bottom horizontal right

```
\usepackage{makecell}

\begin{tabular}{|c|c|}\hline
1st & \makecell{without parameter}\\\hline
2nd & \makecell*[tl]{vertical top\\
                   horizontal left}\\\hline
3rd & \makecell[tr]{vertical top\\
                  horizontal right}\\\hline
4th & \makecell*[bl]{vertical bottom\\
                   horizontal left}\\\hline
5th & \makecell[br]{vertical bottom\\
                  horizontal right}\\\hline
\end{tabular}
```

02-11-3

In contrast to \makecell, the \thead command uses predefined values to format headers of a table.

\thead [column type] {*text*}	\rothead{*text*}	\theadfont*text*

Title for column 1	column 2	column 3
A	vertical top horizontal left	B
C	vertical top horizontal right	RIGHT

```
\usepackage{makecell}

\begin{tabular}{ccc}
\thead{Title for\\column 1}
    & \thead[l]{column 2}
    & \thead[r]{column 3} \\\hline
A & \makecell*[tl]{vertical top\\
    horizontal left} & B\\
C & \makecell[tr]{vertical top\\
    horizontal right} & RIGHT \\\hline
\end{tabular}
```

02-11-4

The optional parameter only affects the horizontal alignment; everything else is determined by the following commands:

\cellset{*definition*}	\cellalign{*horizontal/vertical column type*}
\cellrotangle{*angle*}	\theadalign{*horizontal/vertical column type*}
\theadfont{*font size macro*}	\theadset{*definition*}

The package defines the following default values for the individual commands, but you can of course use \renewcommand to modify them:

```
\newcommand\cellset{\def\arraystretch{1}\extrarowheight\z@\nomakegapedcells}
\newcommand\cellgape{}
\newcommand\cellalign{cc}
\newcommand\cellrotangle{90}
\newcommand\theadfont{\footnotesize}
\newcommand\theadset{}
\newcommand\theadgape{\gape}
\newcommand\rotheadgape{}
\newcommand\theadalign{cc}
\newcommand\bottopstrut{\gape{\strut}}
\newcommand\topstrut{\gape[t]{\strut}}
\newcommand\botstrut{\gape[b]{\strut}}
```

The individual commands execute the respective commands listed below:

```
\makecell  \cellalign\cellset
\thead     \theadalign\cellset\theadfont\theadset
\rothead   \cellset\theadfont\theadset
```

The following example specifies new values for \cellalign, \theadalign, and \theadfont. The changes were made globally, which is recommended for the title row. All cells are formatted with lt (left/top) and the captions with lb (left/bottom).

02-11-5

Title for column 1	*column 2*	*column 3*
A	vertical top LEFT	B
C	vertical top LEFT	RIGHT

```
\usepackage{makecell}

\renewcommand\cellalign{lt}
\renewcommand\theadalign{lb}
\renewcommand\theadfont{\itshape\small}
\begin{tabular}{@{}ccc@{}}
\thead{Title for\\column 1}
  & \thead{column 2}
    & \thead{column 3} \\\hline
A & \makecell*{vertical top\\LEFT} & B\\
C & \makecell{vertical top\\ LEFT}
  & RIGHT \\\hline
\end{tabular}
```

For rotated captions, you *must* specify the height of the text beforehand by assigning a length to \rotheadsize. This is easy to do with the \settowidth command, by passing it the longest line in the desired font. If \rotheadsize is not assigned a length, 0 pt is assumed automatically, which leads to output that makes no sense. The rotation angle is specified by \cellrotangle, which can be changed with \renewcommand. If the rotating package were not loaded for the rotation, a warning would be written to the log file.

load rotating *package*

Title for column 1	*column 2*	*column 3*
A	vertical top LEFT	B
C	vertical top LEFT	RIGHT

```
\usepackage{makecell,rotating}

\renewcommand\cellalign{lt}
\renewcommand\theadalign{lb}
\renewcommand\theadfont{\itshape\normalsize}
\settowidth\rotheadsize{\theadfont Title for}
\begin{tabular}{@{}ccc@{}}\hline
\rothead{Title for\\column 1}
  & \thead{column 2}
    & \renewcommand\cellrotangle{45}
      \rothead{column 3} \\\hline
A & \rotcell{vertical top\\LEFT} & B\\
C & \makecell*{vertical top\\ LEFT}
  & RIGHT \\\hline
\end{tabular}
```

02-11-6

2.11.1 Cell size

You can move the contents of individual table cells up and down with respect to the base line with the standard `\raisebox` command. However, the `makecell` package simplifies the task by defining two special commands for vertical translations.

```
\gape [position] {text}
\Gape [height] [depth] {text}
```

The `\gape` command is the same as `\smash` from the `amsmath` package and changes the vertical size of the box of *text*. Without arguments, the depth as well as the height of the box are increased by `\jot`=3.0pt. The optional argument can take the values `b` and `t`; `b` adds size only to the depth of the box and likewise `t` adds size only to the height of the box. The respective other length is minimized so that *text* just fits the box.

```
\usepackage{makecell}

\rule{1em}{0.5pt}\fbox{good text}\rule{1em}{0.5pt}\fbox{\gape{good text}}%
\rule{1em}{0.5pt}\fbox{\gape[b]{good text}}\rule{1em}{0.5pt}
\fbox{\gape[t]{good text}}\rule{1em}{0.5pt}
```

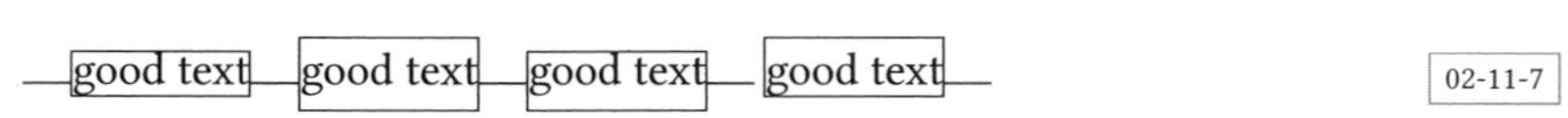

02-11-7

While `\gape` translates the box taking its current size into account, you can make individiual adjustments with `\Gape`:

```
\usepackage{makecell}

\rule{1em}{0.5pt}\fbox{good text}\rule{1em}{0.5pt}\fbox{\Gape{good text}}%
\rule{1em}{0.5pt}\fbox{\Gape[5pt]{good text}}\rule{1em}{0.5pt}
\fbox{\Gape[5pt][-5pt]{good text}}\rule{1em}{0.5pt}
```

02-11-8

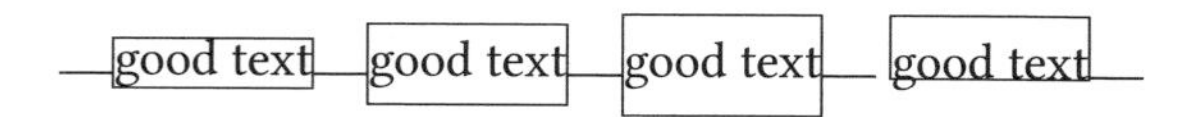

So using \gape and \Gape lets you change the depth and height of *one* cell, but the following commands let you do this for one or all of the cells of a row or the whole of a table.

```
\bottopstrut
\topstrut
\botstrut
\setcellgapes [position] {length}
\makegapedcells
\nomakegapedcells
```

The first three commands increase the default value for \strut by \jot=3.0pt respectively, either for depth and height (\bottopstrut), only the depth (\botstrut), or only the height (\topstrut).

02-11-9

normal row
top and bottom
only bottom
only top

```
\usepackage{makecell}

\begin{tabular}{@{}c@{}}\hline
normal row\\\hline
\bottopstrut top and bottom\\\hline
\botstrut only bottom\\\hline
\topstrut only top\\\hline
\end{tabular}
```

\setcellgapes lets you adjust the height and/or depth of all cells of a table by a manually chosen length. If you don't use an optional parameter (b or t), both the height and depth are increased by the specified length. The two switches \makegapedcells and \nomakegapedcells activate and deactivate the additional insertion of vertical space.

02-11-10

normal row
top and bottom
top and bottom

normal row
top and bottom
top and bottom

```
\usepackage{makecell}

\setcellgapes{5pt}\makegapedcells
\begin{tabular}{@{}c@{}}\hline
normal row\\\hline
top and bottom\\\hline
top and bottom\\\hline
\end{tabular}\\[10pt]
\nomakegapedcells
\begin{tabular}{@{}c@{}}\hline
normal row\\\hline
top and bottom\\\hline
top and bottom\\\hline
\end{tabular}
```

2.11.2 Multi-line cells

The `\multirow` command, already described in Section 2.3 on page 30, is reimplemented by the `makecell` package through two of its own commands. It does however use other internal commands of the `multirow` package, which therefore has to be loaded as well.

load `multir` *package*

`\multirowcell{`*rows*`}` [vertical shift] [pos] {*text*}
`\multirowhead{`*rows*`}` [vertical shift] [pos] {*text*}

The behaviour of these two commands is similar to `\makecell` and `\thead`, as shown in Example 02-11-6 on page 68.

```
\usepackage{multirow,makecell}

\begin{tabular}{ l c c }\hline
\multirowthead{4}{First column head}
  & \multicolumn{2}{c}{\thead{Multi-column head}}\\\cline{2-3}
  & \thead{Second and\\multi-line\\column head} & \thead{Third\\column head}\\\hline
cell text & A &\multirowcell{4}{28--31}\\ \cline{1-2}
\makecell{multi-line      \\ cell text}  & B & \\ \hline
\makecell[l]{left-aligned  \\ cell text} & C
  & \multirowcell{4}[.5\normalbaselineskip][l]{37--43}\\\cline{1-2}
\makecell[r]{right-aligned \\ cell text} & D & \\\hline
\makecell[b]{bottom-aligned    \\ cell text} & E
  & \multirowcell{6}[\normalbaselineskip][r]{37--43\\52--58}\\\cline{1-2}
\makecell[{{p{5cm}}}]{long long long cell text with fixed width} & F & \\\cline{1-2}
\makecell[{{>{\setlength\parindent{1em}}p{5cm}}}]{long long long
            cell text with fixed width} & G & \\\hline
\end{tabular}
```

02-11-11

First column head	Multi-column head	
	Second and multi-line column head	Third column head
cell text	A	28–31
multi-line cell text	B	
left-aligned cell text	C	37–43
right-aligned cell text	D	
bottom-aligned cell text	E	37–43 52–58
long long long cell text with fixed width	F	
long long long cell text with fixed width	G	

```
\usepackage{booktabs,multirow,makecell}
\renewcommand\theadfont{\itshape\footnotesize}

\begin{tabular}{@{}llr@{--}rrlr@{--}rrl@{}}\toprule
  & \multicolumn{8}{l}{\thead{to convert}} & \\\cmidrule(lr){2-9}
  & \multicolumn{4}{l}{\thead{from frequencies in the}}
  & \multicolumn{4}{l}{\thead{to frequencies in the}}\\
                                          \cmidrule(lr){2-5}\cmidrule(lr){6-9}
 \thead[b]{type} & \thead[t]{television\\range} & \multicolumn{2}{l}{\thead{channel}}
  & \thead{MHz} & \thead[t]{television\\range} & \multicolumn{2}{l}{\thead{channel}}
  & \thead{MHz} & \thead[t]{configuration}\\\cmidrule(r){1-1}\cmidrule(lr){2-2}
     \cmidrule(lr){3-4}\cmidrule(lr){5-5}\cmidrule(lr){6-6}\cmidrule(lr){7-8}
     \cmidrule(lr){9-9}\cmidrule(l){10-10}
  SAFE 381 WK & F I   &  2 &  4 & 174 & F III & 5 & 12 & 174 & DO \\
  SAFE 382 WK & F II  &  5 & 12 &  68 & F I   & 2 &  4 &  47 & DO \\
  SAFE 383 WK & F III & 21 & 38 & 174 & F III & 5 & 12 & 174 & ES \\
  SAFE 384 WK & F IV  & 42 & 48 &  47 & F III & 5 & 12 & 174 & ET \\\bottomrule
\end{tabular}
```

02-11-12

	to convert							
	from frequencies in the			*to frequencies in the*				
type	*television range*	*channel*	*MHz*	*television range*	*channel*	*MHz*	*configuration*
SAFE 381 WK	F I	2– 4	174	F III	5– 12	174	DO
SAFE 382 WK	F II	5– 12	68	F I	2– 4	47	DO
SAFE 383 WK	F III	21– 38	174	F III	5– 12	174	ES
SAFE 384 WK	F IV	42– 48	47	F III	5– 12	174	ET

2.11.3 Column numbering

You can also use the makecell package to automatically number columns, using the \nline command; \eline lets you skip a specified number of columns. You can choose the numbering format through the optional argument *type*, which can make use of the common LaTeX formats: arabic (6), alph (f), Alph (F), roman (vi), and Roman (VI).

```
\eline{columns}
\nline [type] [start] {columns}
\rnline [type] [start] {columns}
```

\rnline is similar to \nline, except that the counting is done with Cyrillic symbols.

1	2	3	4	5	6	7	8	9	10
2	A								Z
3	1	2						1	2
4	S4	S5	S6	S7	S8	S9	S10	S11	S12
5	(2)	(3)	(4)	(5)	(6)	(7)			
6					4	5	6		

```
\usepackage{makecell}

\begin{tabular}{@{}c|*{9}{c}@{}}
1 & \nline[1][2]{9}\\\hline
2 & A & \eline{7} & Z\\
3 & \nline{2} & \eline{5} & \nline{2}\\
4 & \nline[S1][4]{9} \\
5 & \nline[(a)][2]{6}\\
6 & \eline{4} & \nline[1][4]{3}
\end{tabular}
```

02-11-13

2.12 mdwtab

The mdwtab package by Mark Wooding is part of a whole series of mdwtools. The package is not an extension of the standard tabular and array environments as such, but reimplements them from scratch. Therefore you might encounter problems when using mdwtab in conjunction with other packages that extend these two environments, but assume the standard definition.

Here are the main differences in how the environments work:

- A major innovation is the way the column definitions are read and interpreted. You can use an expression like {|@{}|} in standard LaTeX, but not when using mdwtab. The "abuse" of @{} to avoid \doublerulesep between two vertical lines is explicitly forbidden. If you tried to use it, you would get this error message:

```
! Package mdwtab Error: Missing column type.
See the mdwtab package documentation for explanation.
```

  On the other hand, constructs like {c@*{4}{{:}@}{-}c} are allowed when using mdwtab. This particular example expands to the expression {c@{:}@{:}@{:}@{:}@{-}c}.
- If a @ expression follows a vertical line, it refers to the *next* column and not the current one.
- mdwtab defines some new column types in addition to the usual ones:

Ml, Mc, Mr	M stands for *Math* and denotes columns with mathematical expressions; l, c, and r have the usual meaning.
Tl, Tc, Tr	The same for pure text.
#{*pre*}{*post*}	User-defined column type that can be specified additionally through *pre* (code before cell) and *post* (code after cell).

Several new commands are available in mdwtab:

\tabpause{*text*}   \vline [length]   \vgap [length]   \hlx{*arguments*}

\tabpause provides an easy way to break a table in order to draw lines or insert text across all columns, without having to use the \multicolumn command. The *text* is typeset in paragraph mode, so line breaks are possible. You can use \vline with an optional argument to insert a vertical line of specified width. \vgap inserts vertical space at any arbitrary position on a table row, though using \hlx is more effective; this command is discussed in more detail below. In the following example, the column type is set to Mc, which means that the mathematical expressions don't have to be enclosed in $...$. However, this has no effect on the argument of \tabpause, which is always typeset in text mode.

02-12-1

	equations
1st	$f(x) = \frac{\sqrt{x^2-1}}{x^2+1}$
2nd	$f(x) = \frac{\sqrt{x^2-1}}{x^2+\frac{1}{x^2}}$

Now the same equations again!

3rd	$f(x) = \frac{\sqrt{x^2-1}}{x^2+1}$
4th	$f(x) = \frac{\sqrt{x^2-1}}{x^2+\frac{1}{x^2}}$

```
\usepackage{mdwtab}

\begin{tabular}{!{\vline[3pt]}l@{\quad}|Mc|}\hlx{shv[1,2]}
   & equations\\\hlx{v[1][10pt]hv[][5pt]}
1st& f(x)=\frac{\sqrt{x^2-1}}{x^2+1} \\\hlx{vhv}
2nd& f(x)=\frac{\sqrt{x^2-1}}{x^2+\frac{1}{x^2}}\\\hlx{vh}
\tabpause{Now the same equations\\
          again!}\hlx{hv}
3rd& f(x)=\frac{\sqrt{x^2-1}}{x^2+1} \\\hlx{vhv}
4th& f(x)=\frac{\sqrt{x^2-1}}{x^2+\frac{1}{x^2}}\\\hlx{vh}
\end{tabular}
```

The special line command \hlx (**hl**ine**ex**tended) lets you manipulate the row spacing without any additional commands. The following arguments are available for \hlx:

h — Effect like \hline; several h correspond to as many \hline commands.

v [line] [H] — Inserts a vertical space of *H*; all vertical lines, apart from the ones specified, are extended accordingly. If the optional specification of the height is missing, \doublerulesep=2.0pt is assumed. In the example above, the command \hlx{v[1][10pt]hv[][5pt]} means that a vertical space of 10 pt is inserted on top of the tabular row and the vertical line no 1 is not stretched. The the horizontal line is drawn with a following vertical space of 5 pt and all verticval lines are stretched. The vertical lines are counted from 0 to n (number of columns). Several lines can be excluded by giving a comma-separated list, a from–to specification, or both.

s [H] — Like the option v, but without extension of the vertical lines.

c [from–to] — Similar to \cline.

b — Adds a negative horizontal feed (backspace) of the line width; usually only required for the longtable environment.

/ [number] — Similar to the normal \pagebreak[*number*] command, where *number* specifies the priority of the page break.

. — Starts a new table row immediately afterwards and is only required in special cases. You can't place a table-specific command like \hline immediately after the dot.

In Example 02-12-1, the individual arguments, which always must be interpreted one after the other, have the following meaning:

shv[1,2]	vertical space without extending the lines, \hline, vertical space, do not extend line number 1 and 2
v[1][10pt]hv[][5pt]	vertical space of 10pt without extending line 1, \hline, vertical space of 5pt
vhv	vertical space, \hline, vertical space
vh	vertical space, \hline
hv	\hline, vertical space
vhv	vertical space, \hline, vertical space
vh	vertical space, \hline

When using mdwtab, the \newcolumntype command also has a different syntax. In contrast to array, mdwtab allows an optional argument.

\newcolumntype{*character*} [number of parameters] [default]
{*number of columns*}{*column type*}{*contents*}

arbitrary text	arbitrary text again

```
\usepackage{mdwtab}
\newcolumntype{P}[1][2cm]{%
  >{\raggedright\hspace{0pt}}p{#1}}

\begin{tabular}{| P[1cm] | P | }\hlx{hv}
arbitrary text & arbitrary text again\\\hlx{vh}
\end{tabular}
```

02-12-2

2.13 slashbox

The slashbox package by Koichi Yasuoka provides support for divided cells. A common use is to specify both a column label and a row label in the upper left cell of a table:

```
\usepackage{slashbox}
\usepackage{pict2e}

\begin{tabular}{l|*{5}{c}}
\backslashbox{holiday}{year} & 2007 & 2008 & 2009 & 2010 & 2011\\\hline
Easter    & 08.04. & 23.03. & 12.04. & 04.04. & 24.04.\\
Pentecost & 27.05. & 11.05. & 31.05. & 23.05. & 12.06.
\end{tabular}
```

holiday \ year	2007	2008	2009	2010	2011
Easter	08.04.	23.03.	12.04.	04.04.	24.04.
Pentecost	27.05.	11.05.	31.05.	23.05.	12.06.

02-13-1

It's a good idea to load slashbox package together with the pict2e package by Hubert Gäßlein and Rolf Niepraschk to produce better lines. slashbox has two commands:

```
\slashbox [width] [position] {L text}{R text}
\backslashbox [width] [position] {L text}{R text}
```

The only difference between the commands is where the line is drawn: `\slashbox` draws it from the lower left corner to the upper right corner and `\backslashbox` from the upper left to the lower right.

```
\usepackage{slashbox,pict2e}

\begin{tabular}{r|*{5}{c}|l}
\backslashbox{holiday}{year}& 2007& 2008& 2009& 2010& 2011&
    \slashbox{year}{holiday}\\\hline
Easter    & 08.04. & 23.03. & 12.04. & 04.04. & 24.04. & Easter\\
Pentecost & 27.05. & 11.05. & 31.05. & 23.05. & 12.06. & Pentecost
\end{tabular}
```

02-13-2

year / holiday	2007	2008	2009	2010	2011	year / holiday
Easter	08.04.	23.03.	12.04.	04.04.	24.04.	Easter
Pentecost	27.05.	11.05.	31.05.	23.05.	12.06.	Pentecost

The arguments of *L text* and *R text* are typeset in paragraph mode; therefore `\\` can be used. This automatically makes the column wider however. Using the optional argument for the width can make sense; it only has an effect if it is larger than the width calculated internally. In the following example the specification of 20 mm is not taken into account because it is smaller than the calculated width.

```
\usepackage{slashbox,pict2e}

\begin{tabular}{l|*{5}{c}}
\backslashbox[20mm]{two\\ holidays}{year} & 2007 & 2008 & 2009 & 2010 & 2011\\\hline
Easter    & 08.04. & 23.03. & 12.04. & 04.04. & 24.04.\\
Pentecost & 27.05. & 11.05. & 31.05. & 23.05. & 12.06.
\end{tabular}
```

02-13-3

year / two holidays	2007	2008	2009	2010	2011
Easter	08.04.	23.03.	12.04.	04.04.	24.04.
Pentecost	27.05.	11.05.	31.05.	23.05.	12.06.

`\slashbox` and `\backslashbox` assume by default that the space `\tabcolsep` is present to the left and right of the table. If the `@{}` operator is used when defining columns, the resulting line is exactly `\tabcolsep` too far to the left or right. However, you can use the two optional arguments to correct this; they tell the command how much space is available. The argument for the *position* may be `l` for left (i. e. there is no `\tabcolsep` to the left), `r` for right, or `lr` for both.

```
\usepackage{slashbox,pict2e}

\begin{tabular}{|@{}r|*{5}{c}|l@{}|}\hline
\backslashbox[0pt][l]{holiday}{year} & 2007 & 2008 & 2009 & 2010 & 2011
   & \slashbox[0pt][r]{year}{holiday}\\\hline
Easter    & 08.04. & 23.03. & 12.04. & 04.04. & 24.04. & Easter\\
Pentecost & 27.05. & 11.05. & 31.05. & 23.05. & 12.06. & Pentecost\\\hline
\end{tabular}
```

year / holiday	2007	2008	2009	2010	2011	year / holiday
Easter	08.04.	23.03.	12.04.	04.04.	24.04.	Easter
Pentecost	27.05.	11.05.	31.05.	23.05.	12.06.	Pentecost

02-13-4

2.14 spreadtab

The `spreadtab` package by Christian Tellechea provides a simple spreadsheet and makes it possible to sum numerical values in columns. The `spreadtab` environment replaces the `tabular` environment.

```
\begin{spreadtab} [settings] {{name of the table}{column definition}}
... table rows and columns...
\end{spreadtab}

\STautoroundnumber of digits
```

A table cell is uniquely identified by its row and column. The columns are designated by [*a..z*] and the rows by [*1..*]. The case is not significant for the column; more than 26 columns are not possible. If a `\multicolumn` command is used, the combined cells are identified by the identifier of the leftmost cell. The following diagram illustrates the structure:

a1	b1	c1	d1	e1	f1	g1
a2	b2		d2	e2	f2	g2
a3			d3	e3		g3

```
\begin{tabular}{|*7{c|}}\hline
a1&b1&c1&d1&e1&f1&g1\\\hline
a2&\multicolumn{2}{l|}{b2}
  &d2&e2&f2&g2\\\hline
\multicolumn{3}{|l|}{a3}&d3&
\multicolumn{2}{l|}{e3}&g3\\\hline
\end{tabular}
```

02-14-1

You can apply the usual arithmetic operators to perform operations on the contents of cells, as shown in the following example. Internally, the `fp` package is used; divisions can be done with precision of up to 18 digits after the decimal point.

02-14-2

27	54	81
58	45	13
50	25	1250
60	47	1.276595744680851063
135	146	0.924657534246575342

```
\usepackage{spreadtab}

\begin{spreadtab}{{tabular}{rr |r}}
        27 &         54 & a1+b1 \\
        58 &         45 & a2-b2 \\
        50 &         25 & a3*b3 \\
        60 &         47 & a4/b4 \\\hline
a1+a2+a3 & b1+b2+b4 & a5/b5
\end{spreadtab}
```

However, visually it's a good idea to use the \STautoround command to limit the number of digits after the decimal point, especially for divisions.

02-14-3

27	54	81
58	45	13
50	25	1250
60	47	1.277
135	146	281

```
\usepackage{spreadtab}  \STautoround{3}

\begin{spreadtab}{{tabular}{rr |r}}
        27 &         54 & a1+b1 \\
        58 &         45 & a2-b2 \\
        50 &         25 & a3*b3 \\
        60 &         47 & a4/b4 \\\hline
a1+a2+a3 & b1+b2+b4 & a5+b5
\end{spreadtab}
```

2.14.1 Relative references to table cells

Starting from the current cell, relative cell addresses can be given through two numerical values in square brackets. The specification [-1,3] denotes the cell that is one column to the left and three rows down. Using this functionality means we can produce Pascal's triangle by specifying just one number; the matrix math environment then determines the number of columns automatically. In this case no column definitions are needed.

```
\usepackage{spreadtab,amsmath}

$\begin{spreadtab}{{matrix}{}}
1\\
[0,-1] & [-1,-1]\\
[0,-1] & [-1,-1]+[0,-1] & [-1,-1]\\
[0,-1] & [-1,-1]+[0,-1] & [-1,-1]+[0,-1] & [-1,-1]\\
[0,-1] & [-1,-1]+[0,-1] & [-1,-1]+[0,-1] & [-1,-1]+[0,-1] & [-1,-1]\\
[0,-1] & [-1,-1]+[0,-1] & [-1,-1]+[0,-1] & [-1,-1]+[0,-1] & [-1,-1]+[0,-1] & [-1,-1]
\end{spreadtab}$
```

02-14-4

$$\begin{matrix} 1 \\ 1 & 1 \\ 1 & 2 & 1 \\ 1 & 3 & 3 & 1 \\ 1 & 4 & 6 & 4 & 1 \\ 1 & 5 & 10 & 10 & 5 & 1 \end{matrix}$$

2.14.2 Text columns

By default, the spreadtab package assumes that a table cell contains either purely numerical contents, a command, or a relative reference. If you want a cell to contain text, you must insert a @ symbol at the beginning of the cell.

month	income	tax
1	5409	1622.7
2	4523	1356.9
3	4711	1413.3
	14643	4392.9

```
\usepackage{spreadtab}

\begin{spreadtab}{{tabular}{rr |r}}
@ month & @ income & @ tax \\\hline
      1 &   5409     & b2*0.3 \\
      2 &   4523     & b3*0.3 \\
      3 &   4711     & b4*0.3 \\\hline
        & b2+b3+b4 & B5*0.3
\end{spreadtab}
```

02-14-5

If the @ symbol can't be used for TEXnical reasons, you can use \STtextcell instead; it is identical to the @ symbol.

2.14.3 Mixed cells

If a cell contains text as well as code specific to spreadtab, you must separate the numerical contents from the text part by the assignment operator :=. The general syntax for mixed cells is

<*text*>:={*numerical field*}<*end text*>

The numerical content has to be enclosed in curly braces. The \STnumericfieldmarker command is an alternative to the assignment operator, if the := symbol can't be used for TEXnical reasons (for example when activating French, where the colon is an active symbol).

month	income	tax
1	5409	1622.7
2	4523	1356.9
3	4711	1413.3
	sum: 14643 €	$\sum$: 4392.9

```
\usepackage{spreadtab,eurosym}

\begin{spreadtab}{{tabular}{rr |r}}
@ month & @ income & @ tax \\\hline
      1 &   5409     & b2*0.3 \\
      2 &   4523     & b3*0.3 \\
      3 &   4711     & b4*0.3 \\\hline
        & \llap{sum: :={b2+b3+b4} \euro}
          & $\sum$: :={B5*0.3}
\end{spreadtab}
```

02-14-6

2.14.4 Omitting rows or columns

You can omit individual rows or columns from the output using the corresponding command in the row or column:

`\SThiderow` `\SThidecol`

An omitted column also does *not* appear in the column definition of the table. In the following example there are five columns internally, but with the spreadtab environment, only the four "active" columns r|ccc are defined. Hiding a row may be useful if the values need to be taken into account but shouldn't be visible to the user.

```
\usepackage{spreadtab}

\begin{spreadtab}{{tabular}{r | ccc}}\hline
@ $x$ \emph{values}    & -1          & 0 \SThidecol & 2            & 3            \\\hline
@ $f(x)=2\cdot x-1$    & 2*[0,-1]-1& 2*[0,-1]-1   & 2*[0,-1]-1 & 2*[0,-1]-1\\
@ $g(x)=x-10$\SThiderow& [0,-2]-10 & [0,-2]-10    & [0,-2]-10  & [0,-2]-10 \\
@ $h(x)=1-x$           & 1-[0,-3]  & 1-[0,-3]     & 1-[0,-3]   & 1-[0,-3]  \\\hline
@ $j(x)=x^2$           & [0,-4]*[0,-4] & [0,-4]*[0,-4] & [0,-4]*[0,-4]
                           & [0,-4]*[0,-4] \\\hline
\end{spreadtab}
```

02-14-7

x *values*	-1	2	3
$f(x) = 2 \cdot x - 1$	-3	3	5
$h(x) = 1 - x$	2	-1	-2
$j(x) = x^2$	1	4	9

2.14.5 Saving of cell contents

If you want to use the contents of a cell outside the current cell, you can use the \STsavecell command to save the contents of the cell in a macro name, which can be chosen arbitrarily. It has to be specified in the optional argument of spreadtab.

\STsavecell\\<*macro*>{*cell*}

The cell must be defined as an absolute reference, i. e. the unique combination of column and row, for example h3.

02-14-8

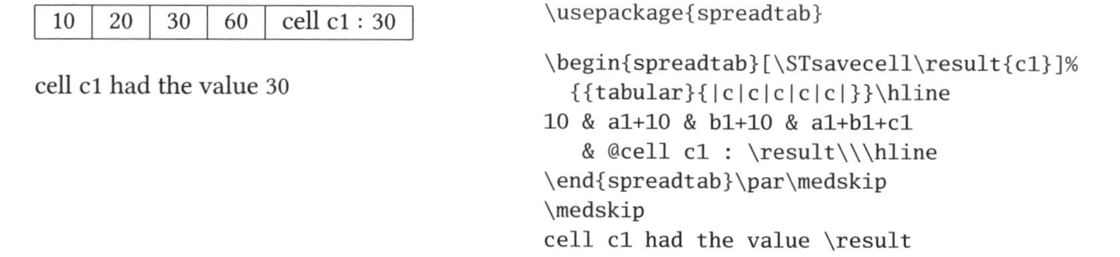

10	20	30	60	cell c1 : 30

cell c1 had the value 30

```
\usepackage{spreadtab}

\begin{spreadtab}[\STsavecell\result{c1}]%
  {{tabular}{|c|c|c|c|c|}}\hline
10 & a1+10 & b1+10 & a1+b1+c1
   & @cell c1 : \result\\\hline
\end{spreadtab}\par\medskip
\medskip
cell c1 had the value \result
```

There is no limit to the number of cells that can be saved in spreadtab; you just need to list them all one after the other in the optional argument.

month	income	tax
1	5409	1622.7
2	4523	1356.9
3	4711	1413.3
	sum: 14643 €	$\sum$: 4392.9

The income was 14643 € and the tax was 4392.9 €!

```
\usepackage{spreadtab,eurosym}
```

02-14-9

```
\begin{spreadtab}[\STsavecell\EK{b5}%
  \STsavecell\ST{c5}]{{tabular}{rr |r}}
@ month & @ income & @ tax \\\hline
      1 &   5409    & b2*0.3 \\
      2 &   4523    & b3*0.3 \\
      3 &   4711    & b4*0.3 \\\hline
        & \llap{sum: :={b2+b3+b4} \euro}
         & $\sum$: :={B5*0.3}
\end{spreadtab}\par\medskip
The income was \EK~\euro\ and the tax was \ST~\euro!
```

2.14.6 Math and date functions

spreadtab provides the following mathematical and date operations for manipulating cell contents:

sum(<*region1*>;<*region2*>;...) Sum the cells, starting with the first *region* and ending with the nth *region*. A *region* can be

- ▷ a single cell or
- ▷ a *from–to region* of the form <*from*>:<*to*>; a rectangular region that contains several rows and columns is possible as well.

month	income	tax
1	5409	1622.7
2	4523	1356.9
3	4711	1413.3
	sum: 14643 €	$\sum$: 4392.9

```
\usepackage{spreadtab,eurosym}
```

02-14-10

```
\begin{spreadtab}{{tabular}{rr |r}}
@ month & @ income & @ tax \\\hline
      1 &   5409    & b2*0.3 \\
      2 &   4523    & b3*0.3 \\
      3 &   4711    & b4*0.3 \\\hline
        & \llap{sum: :={sum(b2:b4)} \euro}
         & $\sum$: :={sum(C2:C4)}
\end{spreadtab}
```

fact(<*number*>) Outputs the factorial of *number*.

```
\usepackage{spreadtab} \setlength\tabcolsep{2pt}

\begin{spreadtab}{{tabular}{@{} *9{p{3em}} @{}}}
  0     &  1    &  2    &  3    &  4    &  5    &   6   &  7    &8\\\hline
fact(a1)&fact(b1)&fact(c1)&fact(d1)&fact(e1)&fact(f1)&fact(g1)&fact(h1)&fact(i1)
\end{spreadtab}
```

0	1	2	3	4	5	6	7	8
1	1	2	6	24	120	720	5040	40320

02-14-11

sumprod(<*region1*>;<*region2*>;...) The corresponding cells are first multiplied (first cell in region 1 by first cell in region 2, etc.) and then the products are added. All regions need to be the same length and correspond to the syntax given above. Cells that do not contain a numerical value or that don't exist because of a `\multicolumn` command are assigned the value zero.

```
\usepackage{spreadtab}

\begin{spreadtab}{{tabular}{ @{} r *6c @{}}}
@age      & 10 & 11 & 12 & 13 & 14 & 15\\
@number    &  5 &  8 & 20 & 55 &  9 &  3\\\hline
\multicolumn{7}{@{}l}{mean age: :={sumprod(b1:g1;b2:g2)/sum(b2:g2)}}
\end{spreadtab}
```

02-14-12

age	10	11	12	13	14	15
number	5	8	20	55	9	3
mean age: 12.64						

rand Outputs a random number between 0 and 1. If you need to output the same random series more than once, the internal `\ST@seed` command must be overwritten:

```
\makeatletter\renewcommand\ST@seed{}\makeatletter
```

Now the random number generator can be started individually with `\FPseed`=<*number*>. If you set the number to be the same, the same series will be output.

randint(min, max) Outputs a random integer between *min* and *max*. If *min* is not given, an integer between 0 and *max* is produced.

```
\usepackage{spreadtab} \STautoround{4}

\begin{spreadtab}{{tabular}{@{} l|cccc @{}}}
@random number $\in [0;1]$  &rand()          &rand()          &rand()          &rand()          \\
@random number $\in [-5;5]$ &randint(-5,5)&randint(-5,5)&randint(-5,5)&randint(-5,5)\\
@random number $\in [0;20]$ &randint(20)   &randint(20)   &randint(20)   &randint(20)   \\
\end{spreadtab}
```

02-14-13

random number $\in [0;1]$	0.6515	0.7522	0.1592	0.8468
random number $\in [-5;5]$	1	1	-1	-5
random number $\in [0;20]$	15	1	14	15

ifeq(number1,number2,number3,number4) If *number1*=*number2*, then *number3*, else *number4*.

ifgt(number1,number2,number3,number4) If *number1*>*number2*, then *number3*, else *number4*.

iflt(number1,number2,number3,number4) If *number1*<*number2*, then *number3*, else *number4*.

engshortdatetonum(cell) Converts a date in the short form *YYYY/MM/DD* to its corresponding number (the number of days that have passed since the first of March in the year zero) to allow you to compare dates and calculate timespans. *cell* can be an absolute or relative reference to a cell that must contain a date in short form. It may also be a command that yields a date in short form, for example `\today`.

englongdatetonum(cell) Converts a date of the long form *name of month DD, YYYY* to the number of the day in the year.

```
\usepackage{spreadtab}

\begin{spreadtab}{{tabular}{cc}}
@1789/7/14              & engshortdatetonum(a1)\\
2001/1/1 :={}           & engshortdatetonum([-1,0])\\
engshortdatetonum(0/3/1) & engshortdatetonum(\number\year/\number\month/\number\day)\\
englongdatetonum(February 13, 2005) & englongdatetonum(\today)\\
@July 1, 1970                     & englongdatetonum(a5)\\\hline
@2010/11/23             & engshortdatetonum([-1,0])\\
@2010/1/1               & engshortdatetonum([-1,0])\\
@difference              & :={[0,-2]-[0,-1]} days
\end{spreadtab}
```

02-14-14

1789/7/14	653554
2001/1/1	730791
0	734213
732295	734213
July 1, 1970	719649
2010/11/23	734404
2010/1/1	734078
difference	326 days

numtoengshortdate(number) Converts a number to a date in the short form *YYYY/MM/DD*.

numtoenglongdate(number) Converts a number to a date in the long form *name of month DD, YYYY*.

numtoengmonth(number) Converts a number to the name of the month that corresponds to the date.

numtoengday(number) Converts a number to the name of the day that corresponds to the date.

2010/3/17	
365	2011/3/17
365	March 17, 2011
365	March
365	thursday
-365	2009/3/17
-365	March 17, 2009
-365	March
-365	tuesday

```
\usepackage{spreadtab}

\begin{spreadtab}{{tabular}{cc}}\hline
\multicolumn{2}{|c|}{@2010/3/17}                        \\\hline
 365 & numtoengshortdate(engshortdatetonum(a1)+[-1,0])\\
 365 & numtoenglongdate(engshortdatetonum(a1)+[-1,0]) \\
 365 & numtoengmonth(engshortdatetonum(a1)+[-1,0])    \\
 365 & numtoengday(engshortdatetonum(a1)+[-1,0])      \\\hline
-365 & numtoengshortdate(engshortdatetonum(a1)+[-1,0])\\
-365 & numtoenglongdate(engshortdatetonum(a1)+[-1,0]) \\
-365 & numtoengmonth(engshortdatetonum(a1)+[-1,0])    \\
-365 & numtoengday(engshortdatetonum(a1)+[-1,0])
\end{spreadtab}
```

02-14-15

2.15 tabls

The tabls package by Donald Arseneau has the sole aim of optimizing the vertical row spacing, which is often not good with the standard LaTeX tables. tabls defines three additional lengths and modifies the \hline command to insert optional vertical space of a chosen length like the one for \\.

```
\tablinesep    \arraylinesep    \extrarulesep
\hline [length]
```

\tablinesep Minimal space between two adjacent cells in a tabular environment; negative values and 0 pt don't alter the standard behaviour. The default is 1 pt and text within @{...} is not taken into account when determining the spacing.

\arraylinesep The same for the array environment.

\extrarulesep Vertical space that is inserted before and after the line commands \hline and \cline. The minimum space between a line and text is then \extrarulesep + 0.5\tablinesep. Negative values are possible, but only as long as no line touches the text. The default for \extrarulesep is 3 pt.

The default LaTeX behaviour is achieved with the following settings:

```
\setlength\tablinesep{0pt}
\setlength\arraylinesep{0pt}
\setlength\extrarulesep{0pt}
```

The following example firstly uses the default lengths in tabls and then repeats the table using the standard LaTeX settings for comparison.

02-15-1

$$f(x) = \frac{\sqrt{x^2-1}}{x^2+1}$$
$$f(x) = \frac{\sqrt{x^2-1}}{x^2+\frac{1}{x^2}}$$

$$f(x) = \frac{\sqrt{x^2-1}}{x^2+1}$$
$$f(x) = \frac{\sqrt{x^2-1}}{x^2+\frac{1}{x^2}}$$

```
\usepackage{tabls}

\begin{tabular}{c}\hline[10pt]
$ f(x)=\frac{\sqrt{x^2-1}}{x^2+1}$\\\hline
$ f(x)=\frac{\sqrt{x^2-1}}{x^2+\frac{1}{x^2}}$\\\hline
\end{tabular}\\[10pt]
%
\setlength\tablinesep{0pt}%   Standard-LaTeX
\setlength\arraylinesep{0pt}% Standard-LaTeX
\setlength\extrarulesep{0pt}% Standard-LaTeX
\begin{tabular}{c}\hline
$ f(x)=\frac{\sqrt{x^2-1}}{x^2+1}$ \\\hline
$ f(x)=\frac{\sqrt{x^2-1}}{x^2+\frac{1}{x^2}}$\\\hline
\end{tabular}
```

The tabls package works in conjunction with many packages, but you don't necessarily get the results that you expect. For example, for the slashbox package it fails to take account of any changed spacings, so the diagonals don't end in the corners:

Using tabls a slashbox

```
\usepackage{tabls,slashbox,pict2e}

\begin{tabular}{|@{}r|*{5}{c}|l@{}|}\hline
\backslashbox[0pt][l]{holiday}{year} & 2007 & 2008 & 2009 & 2010 & 2011
    & \slashbox[0pt][r]{year}{holiday}\\\hline[3pt]
```

```
Easter    & 08.04. & 23.03. & 12.04. & 04.04. & 24.04. & Easter\\
Pentecost & 27.05. & 11.05. & 31.05. & 23.05. & 12.06. & Pentecost\\\hline
\end{tabular}
```

02-15-2

year / holiday	2007	2008	2009	2010	2011	year / holiday
Easter	08.04.	23.03.	12.04.	04.04.	24.04.	Easter
Pentecost	27.05.	11.05.	31.05.	23.05.	12.06.	Pentecost

The following table makes use of the extra space provided by the tabls package; without this space it would have been much harder to read.

```
\usepackage{tabls}
\newcommand{\T}{\textsf{T}}\newcommand{\Z}{\mathcal{Z}}\newcommand{\C}{\textsf{c}}

\begin{tabular}{@{}c|c|ccccc@{}}\hline
 BV \rule[-0.3cm]{0cm}{0.8cm}& R & $d$ & $u_\Z$
   & $u_{\Z^\C}$ & $v_\Z$ & $v_{\Z^\C}$\\\hline
 $u_\Z$ \rule[-0.3cm]{0cm}{0.8cm}& $y_\Z$&$A_\Z$ & $I$ & $0$ & $-I$ & $0$ \\
 $u_{\Z^\C}$ \rule[-0.3cm]{0cm}{0.8cm}& $y_{\Z^\C}$
   & $A_{\Z^\C}$&$0$ & $I$ & $0$ & $-I$\\\hline
 ZF/GK & $e_m^\T
   \left(\begin{array}{c} y_\Z \\ y_{\Z^\C}\end{array}\right)$
   & $e_m^\T\left(\begin{array}{c}A_\Z \\A_{\Z^\C}\end{array}\right) $
   & $0$ & $0$ & $-2e_n^\T$ & $-2e_{m-n}^\T$  \\\hline
\end{tabular}
```

02-15-3

BV	R	d	$u_\mathcal{Z}$	$u_{\mathcal{Z}^\mathsf{c}}$	$v_\mathcal{Z}$	$v_{\mathcal{Z}^\mathsf{c}}$
$u_\mathcal{Z}$	$y_\mathcal{Z}$	$A_\mathcal{Z}$	I	0	$-I$	0
$u_{\mathcal{Z}^\mathsf{c}}$	$y_{\mathcal{Z}^\mathsf{c}}$	$A_{\mathcal{Z}^\mathsf{c}}$	0	I	0	$-I$
ZF/GK	$e_m^\mathsf{T}\left(\begin{array}{c} y_\mathcal{Z} \\ y_{\mathcal{Z}^\mathsf{c}}\end{array}\right)$	$e_m^\mathsf{T}\left(\begin{array}{c} A_\mathcal{Z} \\ A_{\mathcal{Z}^\mathsf{c}}\end{array}\right)$	0	0	$-2e_n^\mathsf{T}$	$-2e_{m-n}^\mathsf{T}$

2.16 tabularht

The tabularht package by Heiko Oberdiek lets you specify the height of the table and therefore a variable row height to achieve the respective height.

The package can be loaded with the option vlines, which offers – albeit experimental – support for correct vertical lines if additional vertical space was inserted. This option requires ε-TEX, which is standard in current TEX distributions. Additional possible options concern the output driver, e.g. dvips, pdftex,.... It must only be specified however if there are problems with the automatic detection (for example for dvips).

specify ...s driver

The package supports the following environments:

\begin{tabularht}{*options*} [pos] {*column definition*}... \end{tabularht}
\begin{tabularht * }{*options*} [pos] {*width*}{*column definition*}... \end{tabularht * }
\begin{arrayht}{*options*} [pos] {*column definition*}... \end{arrayht}
\begin{tabularhtx}{*options*}{*width*}{*column definition*}... \end{tabularhtx}

The tabularht environment is similar to the tabular environment, while arrayht corresponds to the array environment. The tabularhtx environment is only defined if the tabularx package has been loaded as well.

If the calc package is loaded, the corresponding calc length definitions are also considered by tabularht. Possible options are \to and \spread; both can be assigned a length and \to defines the height of the table (standard) and \spread extends it by the specified length.

\begin{tabularht}{*1cm*} → height is 1cm
\begin{tabularht}{*to=1cm*} → height is 1cm
\begin{tabularht}{*spread=0cm*} → normal height, corresponds to \begin{tabular}
\begin{tabularht}{*spread=1cm*} → normal height, extended by 1cm

Within the table, you can use the following three commands: \interrowspace and \interrowfill insert additional fixed or dynamic vertical space, while an arbitrary command sequence can be inserted between \interrowstart and \interrowstop. The comma-separated list of lines specifies which of them are extended across the inserted space; all other lines are discontinued. If you want all lines to be discontinuous, set 0 as the argument.

\interrowspace [line1,line2,...] {*length*}
\interrowfill [line1,line2,...]
\interrowstart [line1,line2,...] ...\interrowstop

The \interrowspace command is identical to \noalign{*vspace*{*length*}}, and the \interrowfill command is identical to \interrowspace{*fill*}, which is also identical to \noalign{*vfill*}.

```
\usepackage{booktabs}
\usepackage{tabularht}

\fbox{%
\begin{tabularht*}{0.8in}{4in}{@{} l @{\extracolsep{\fill}} r @{}}
  top left& top right\\\interrowfill
  \multicolumn{2}{@{}c@{}}{bounding box}\\\interrowfill
  bottom left & bottom right
\end{tabularht*}}
```

top left		top right
	bounding box	
bottom left		bottom right

02-16-1

Vertical lines are counted starting at 1 on the left. In the following example, only the second and third line are set to be continuous.

column 1	column 2	column 3	column 4
column 1	column 2	column 3	column 4

```
\usepackage[vlines]{tabularht}

\begin{tabularht}{1.75cm}{*{4}{|c}|}\hline
column 1 & column 2 & column 3
  & column 4\\\hline
\interrowfill[2,3]\hline
column 1 & column 2 & column 3
  & column 4\\\hline
\end{tabularht}
```

02-16-2

The last example uses a fixed `\interrowspace` and a command called in an `\interrowstart`-`\interrowstop` sequence:

first	line
second	line
third	line
fourth	line

```
\usepackage{booktabs}
\usepackage[pdftex,vlines]{tabularht}% specify driver

\begin{tabularht}{spread=0pt}{|l|l|}\hline
  first & line\\\hline
\interrowstart \addlinespace[10mm]\interrowstop\hline
  second & line\\
\interrowstart \hline\hline \interrowstop
  third & line\\\hline
\interrowspace[1,3]{15mm}\hline
  fourth & line\\\hline
\end{tabularht}
```

02-16-3

2.17 tabularkv

The `tabularkv` package by Heiko Oberdiek is virtually identical to the `tabularht` package (which is loaded automatically, cf. Section 2.16 on page 84), but it uses the "key-value" interface and therefore also loads the `keyval` package. The optional parameters are:

name	*type*	*description*
`width`	length	Width of the table, automatically uses `tabularht*`.
`x`		Use `tabularhtx`; don't forget to load the `tabularx` package before using this.
`height`	length	Height of a table.
`valign`	`top/bottom/center`	Vertical position.

For all options, you use a tabularkv environment, and the package automatically selects the table environment that corresponds to the parameters that you have assigned. The second optional argument for the vertical position *pos* (t, b, c) isn't really necessary, as you can easily specify the vertical position through valign in the options.

```
\begin{tabularkv} [settings] [pos] {column definition}... \end{tabularkv}
```

02-17-1

top left	top right
bounding box	
bottom left	bottom right

```
\usepackage{booktabs, tabularkv}

\fbox{%
 \begin{tabularkv}[width=2.25in,height=0.75in,
    valign=center]{@{}l@{\extracolsep{\fill}}r@{}}
  top left& top right \\\interrowfill
  \multicolumn{2}{@{}c@{}}{bounding box}\\
  \interrowfill
  bottom left & bottom right
 \end{tabularkv}}
```

2.18 tabularx

The tabularx package by David Carlisle is used frequently, because it provides an easy way to adapt the width of the table to the width of the current row. The package defines the X column type, which stands for a p column of variable width depending on the width of the table to be specified by the user. The syntax is almost identical to a normal table, though the width of the table has to be given as well.

```
\begin{tabularx} [position] {table width}{column definition}
...&...&...\\
...&...&...\\
...
\end{tabularx}
```

You can combine the X column type arbitrarily with other standard or user-defined types. The main difference to the tabular* environment is that tabularx adjusts the column width whereas tabular* adjusts the space between the columns.

02-18-1

Text before the table, which spans the whole line to show that the table is that wide as well.

A bar next to the text can be created easily now. It can also span several paragraphs, but page breaks are not possible with tabularx (see ltxtable package).

Text after the table, which spans the whole line to show that the table is that wide as well.

```
\usepackage{tabularx}

Text before the table, which spans the whole line
show that the table is that wide as well.\par
\begin{tabularx}{\linewidth}{!{\vrule width 2pt}X
A bar next to the text can be created easily now.
\par\medskip It can also span several paragraphs,
but page breaks are not possible with
\texttt{tabularx} (see \texttt{ltxtable} package)
\end{tabularx}\par
Text after the table, which spans the whole line
show that the table is that wide as well.
```

All the X columns within a table have the same width, regardless of whether they are adjacent or separated by other column types, as shown here:

Text before the table, which spans the whole line to show that the table is that wide as well.

The width of this column is determined automatically.	This column is 1 cm wide.	The width of this column is also determined automatically.

Text after the table, which spans the whole line to show that the table is that wide as well.

```
\usepackage{tabularx}

Text before the table, which spans the whole line to
show that the table is that wide as well.\par
\begin{tabularx}{\linewidth}{|X | p{1cm} | X|}
The width of this column is determined automatically.
& This column is 1\,cm wide.
& The width of this column is also determined
  automatically.
\end{tabularx}\par
Text after the table, which spans the whole line to
show that the table is that wide as well.
```

02-18-2

However, you can adjust the X columns individually using \hsize by specifying a decimal fraction of the total width of the X columns. In the following example, the first X column is set to be 0.7 times the normal width and the second one 1.3 times it.

```
\usepackage{tabularx}

Text before the table, which spans the whole line to show that the table is
that wide as well.\par
\begin{tabularx}{\linewidth}{|>{\setlength\hsize{0.7\hsize}}X|p{1cm}|
                              >{\setlength\hsize{1.3\hsize}}X|}
The width of this column is determined automatically. & This column is 1\,cm wide.
& The width of this column is determined automatically.
\end{tabularx}\par
Text after the table, which spans the whole line to show that the table is
that wide as well.
```

Text before the table, which spans the whole line to show that the table is that wide as well.

The width of this column is deter- mined automati- cally.	This column is 1 cm wide.	The width of this column is determined automatically.

Text after the table, which spans the whole line to show that the table is that wide as well.

02-18-3

\hsize

With three X columns, the sum of all \hsize lengths has to add up to three, and so on.

In all these examples for tabularx, the justification of the text in narrow columns doesn't look good. In these situations, you should also use \raggedright or \RaggedRight from the ragged2e package by Martin Schröder; the latter saves the explicit \arraybackslash call.

02-18-4

Text before the table, which spans the whole line to show that the table is that wide as well.

The width of this column is determined automatically.	This column is 1 cm wide.	The width of this column is determined automatically.

Text after the table, which spans the whole line to show that the table is that wide as well.

```
\usepackage{tabularx,ragged2e}

Text before the table, which spans the
whole line to show that the table is
that wide as well.\par
\begin{tabularx}{\linewidth}{|
 >{\setlength\hsize{0.7\hsize}\RaggedRight}X|
 >{\RaggedRight}p{1cm}|
 >{\setlength\hsize{1.3\hsize}
   \RaggedRight}X|}
The width of this column is determined
automatically. & This column is 1\,cm
wide. & The width of this column is
determined automatically.
\end{tabularx}\par
Text after the table, which spans the
whole line to show that the table is
that wide as well.
```

All X columns correspond to the p column type, but you can transform them into a different type by redefining the assignment. In the following example we change from a p to a m column and reduce the font size. The output is a bit hard to understand at first glance; both X columns are centred vertically to each other and to the start of the middle p column.

02-18-5

Text before the table, which spans the whole line.

The width of this column is determined automatically.	This column is 1 cm wide.	The width of this column is determined automatically.

Text after the table, which spans the whole line.

```
\usepackage{tabularx,ragged2e}
\renewcommand\tabularxcolumn[1]{>{\small}m{#1}}

Text before the table, which spans the whole line.

\begin{tabularx}{\linewidth}{@{}
  >{\setlength\hsize{0.7\hsize}\RaggedRight}X |
  >{\RaggedRight}p{1cm} |
  >{\setlength\hsize{1.3\hsize}\RaggedRight}X@{}}
The width of this column is determined automatically.
& This column is 1\,cm wide.
& The width of this column is determined
  automatically.
\end{tabularx}\par
Text after the table, which spans the whole line.
```

Here are some points to bear in mind when using tabularx:

- tabularx typesets the table several times internally to determine the optimal width of the X columns. Therefore having many tabularx tables can slow down a LaTeX run significantly.
- You can use \verb and \verb* within the table, but the resulting horizontal spaces may be wrong.
- You can nest tabularx tables arbitrarily, but you must group the internal tables by enclosing them in {...}, \bgroup...\egroup, or \begingroup...\endgroup.

2.19 tabulary

The `tabulary` package by David Carlisle is the complement of the `tabularx` package by the same author. The only fixed specification is the table width; the columns are then calculated so that they all have the same height depending on this specification. The columns have to be of type L, R, C, or J. The first three correspond to the usual types of standard LaTeX and J to normal justification. The latter can be seen in Example 02-19-2, which shows three J columns that correspond to the normal p columns. But first an example using the other three types:

Text before the table, which spans the whole line.

The height of this column is determined automatically.	This column is of unknown width.	The height is also determined automatically.

Text after the table, which spans the whole line.

02-19-1

```
\usepackage{tabulary}

Text before the table, which spans the whole line.\par
\begin{tabulary}{\linewidth}{|L | C | R|}
The height of this column is determined
automatically.
& This column is of unknown width.
& The height is also determined
  automatically.
\end{tabulary}\par
Text after the table, which spans the whole line.
```

```
\usepackage{tabulary}

Text before the table, which will span the whole width of the line with an
additional linebreak but without sense.\par
\begin{tabulary}{\linewidth}{@{}J | J | J@{}}
The height of this column is determined automatically.
  & This column is ?\,cm wide, but how wide exactly is unknown.
  & The height of this column is determined automatically such that all columns
    have the same height for the given width.
\end{tabulary}\par
Text after the table, which will span the whole width of the line with an
additional linebreak but without sense.
```

Text before the table, which will span the whole width of the line with an additional linebreak but without sense.

02-19-2

The height of this column is determined automatically.	This column is ? cm wide, but how wide exactly is unknown.	The height of this column is determined automatically such that all columns have the same height for the given width.

Text after the table, which will span the whole width of the line with an additional linebreak but without sense.

This package uses the two lengths `\tymin` and `\tymax` internally so as not to let the widths of the columns become too small or too large. The default values are 10 pt and `2\textwidth`, but you can change them if appropriate. If you are using narrow columns, it is better to work with the standard l, r, or c column types anyway. These types can be combined arbitrarily with the types of tabulary.

2.20 threeparttable

The threeparttable package by Donald Arseneau lets you add captions and notes to tables. To achieve this, a standard tabular environment is put into a threeparttable environment, which works like table environment, but does not float.

If it should float, the table environment must be used *additionally*. The package allows the global options summarized in Table 2.7. They can be overwritten locally in the tablenotes environment.

Table 2.7: Summary of the package options for threeparttable.

name	*description*
para	All footnotes consecutively in a single paragraph.
flushleft	No left indent.
online	The argument of \item is typeset in normal font instead of vertically shifted.
normal	Assume default options of the package.

```
\begin{threeparttable} [position]
\caption{...}
\begin{tabular}...(or \begin{tabular*}...)
...\tnote{number} &...&...\\
...
\end{tabular} (or \end{tabular*})
\begin{tablenotes} [settings]
\item[number] text
...
\end{tablenotes}
\end{threeparttable}
```

The optional parameter *position* refers to the vertical alignment and can take one of the usual options: t (default), b, or c. For the tablenotes environment, the package options described above are possible as well. If inserted here, they override the corresponding global options. The package does not increase the numbers of footnotes automatically; you have to take care of this yourself.

The first of the following two examples uses the second footnote (\item) as a caption for the following ones. To make this caption appear in normal font size and bold, the \tnote command is redefined locally with \renewcommand.

```
\usepackage{threeparttable,array,booktabs,calc}

\begin{threeparttable}
\caption{Summary of the signs for the most important trigonometric
    functions.\tnote{1}}
\begin{tabular}{@{}rc*{6}{>{$}c<{$}}}\toprule
\emph{quadrant} & angle & \sin\tnote{a} & \cos\tnote{a} & \tan\tnote{b}
 & \mathrm{cot}\tnote{b} & \mathrm{sec}\tnote{c} & \mathrm{csec}\tnote{c} \\\midrule
   I & $0^\circ$ to $90^\circ$    & + & + & + & + & + & + \\
  II & $90^\circ$ to $180^\circ$  & + & - & - & - & - & + \\
 III & $180^\circ$ to $270^\circ$ & - & - & + & + & - & - \\
  IV & $270^\circ$ to $360^\circ$ & - & + & - & - & + & - \\\bottomrule
\end{tabular}
\begin{tablenotes}
  \item[1] Conversion to radian is easy.
  \begingroup% keep local
  \renewcommand\tnote[1]{\normalsize\bfseries#1}
  \item[range:] ~ \endgroup
  \item[a] \makebox[1.8em][r]{$-1$}      to $+1$
  \item[b] \makebox[1.8em][r]{$-\infty$} to $+\infty$
  \item[c] \makebox[1.8em][r]{$-\infty$} to $-1$ and $+1$ to $+\infty$
\end{tablenotes}
\end{threeparttable}
```

Table 1: Summary of the signs for the most important trigonometric functions.[1]

02-20-1

quadrant	angle	$\sin$ [a]	$\cos$ [a]	$\tan$ [b]	cot [b]	sec [c]	csec [c]
I	0° to 90°	+	+	+	+	+	+
II	90° to 180°	+	−	−	−	−	+
III	180° to 270°	−	−	+	+	−	−
IV	270° to 360°	−	+	−	−	+	−

[1] Conversion to radian is easy.

range:

[a] -1 to $+1$

[b] $-\infty$ to $+\infty$

[c] $-\infty$ to -1 and $+1$ to $+\infty$

```
\usepackage[para]{threeparttable}

\begin{threeparttable} \caption{Different gas analyses.}
\begin{tabular}[t]{r|c|c|c}\hline
               & P1               & P2\tnote{A} & P3\\\hline
decrease in pressure    & 0.149 & 0.494 & 0.199 \\
winding        & 0.146            & 0.480 & 0.240 \\
heat extraction & 0.164\tnote{a} & 0.508 & 0.209 \\\hline
\end{tabular}
\begin{tablenotes}[flushleft]
```

```
  \item[A] uncertain measurement \item[a] disturbance during measurement
\end{tablenotes}
\end{threeparttable}
```

02-20-2

Table 1: Different gas analyses.

	P1	P2[A]	P3
decrease in pressure	0.149	0.494	0.199
winding	0.146	0.480	0.240
heat extraction	0.164[a]	0.508	0.209

[A] uncertain measurement
[a] disturbance during measurement

Further commands that are of interest in threeparttable are shown in Table 2.8:

Table 2.8: Summary of the most important lengths and commands for threeparttable.

name	*description*
\TPTminimum	Minimal width of \caption (default 4 em).
\TPTrlap{*argument*}	Takes the margin of the table into account for footnotes in right-aligned columns.
\TPTtagStyle{*argument*}	Formatting of the label of \tnote (default {}).
\TPTnoteLabel{*argument*}	Formatting of the label of \item (default \tnote).
\TPTnoteSettings	Sets all defaults for tablenotes (list environment).

2.21 threeparttablex

The threeparttablex package by Lars Madsen is an extension of the threeparttable package, which is loaded as well by default. The aim of the package is to extend the functionality to support tables with a page break. threeparttablex allows the use of tablenotes together with longtable (cf. Section 4.1 on page 125). In addition to the functionality described in Section 2.20 on page 91, there are the following extensions:

- The ThreePartTable environment is a container for the new TableNotes and longtable environments.
- The TableNotes environment has the same functionality as the tablenotes environment from threeparttable, but must appear *before* the longtable environment.
- The \insertTableNotes command can also be used within longtable, unlike the TableNotes environment. \insertTableNotes uses the \multicolumn command.

```
\usepackage{longtable,threeparttablex}

\begin{ThreePartTable}
\begin{TableNotes}
\item[a] A remark to the table.
```

```
\item[b] This table is only a demo.
\end{TableNotes}
\begin{longtable}{@{}l c r p{1.5cm}@{}}
L & C & R & box\\\hline
\endfirsthead
\multicolumn{4}{@{}l}{\small\ldots\emph{continued}}\\\hline
L & C & R & box\\\hline
\endhead
\hline
\multicolumn{4}{r@{}}{\small\emph{continued on next page} \ldots}\\
\endfoot
\hline
\insertTableNotes
\endlastfoot
l & c & r & 1st row\\ l & c & r & 2nd row\\ l & c & r & 3rd row\\
l & c\tnote{a} & r & 4th row\\ l & c & r\tnote{b} & 5th row\\
l & c & r & 6th row\\ l & c & r & 7th row\\ l & c & r & 8th row\\
l & c & r & 9th row\\ l & c & r &10th row\\ l & c & r &11th row\\
l & c & r &12th row
\end{longtable}
\end{ThreePartTable}
```

threeparttablex demo

L	C	R	box
l	c	r	1st row
l	c	r	2nd row
l	c	r	3rd row
l	c[a]	r	4th row
l	c	r[b]	5th row
l	c	r	6th row
l	c	r	7th row
l	c	r	8th row
l	c	r	9th row
l	c	r	10th row
l	c	r	11th row

continued on next page ...

page 1

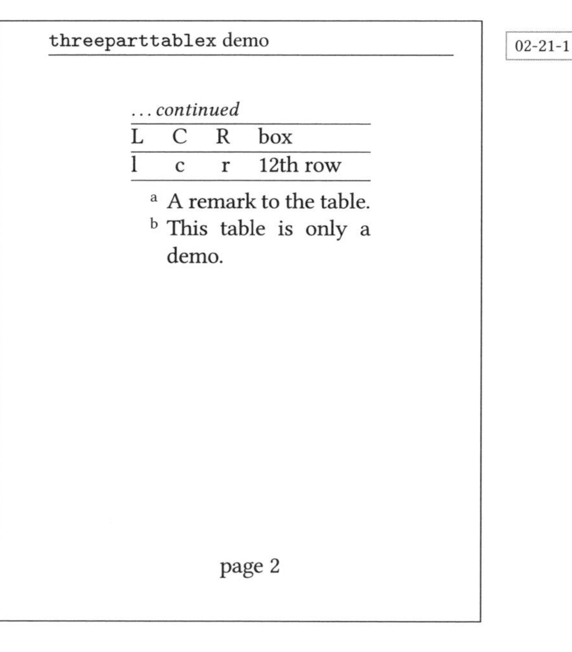

You can label the remarks within the TableNotes environment and then reference them with the \tnotex command (though to use this feature you must load the package with the referable option set). If you have the hyperref package loaded, use the starred version \tnotex* if you don't want these references to be converted into links.

```
\usepackage{longtable} \usepackage[referable]{threeparttablex}

\begin{ThreePartTable}
\begin{TableNotes}
\item[a]\label{tn:a} A remark to the table.
\item[b]\label{tn:b} This table is only a demo.
\end{TableNotes}
\begin{longtable}{@{}l c r p{1.5cm}@{}}
L & C & R & box\\\hline
\endfirsthead
\multicolumn{4}{@{}l}{\small\ldots\emph{continued}}\\\hline
L & C & R & box\\\hline
\endhead
\hline
\multicolumn{4}{r@{}}{\small\emph{continued on next page} \ldots}\\
\endfoot
\hline
\insertTableNotes
\endlastfoot
l & c & r & 1st row\\ l & c & r & 2nd row\\ l & c & r & 3rd row\\
l & c\tnotex{tn:a} & r & 4th row\\ l & c & r\tnotex{tn:b} & 5th row\\
l & c & r & 6th row\\ l & c & r & 7th row\\ l & c & r & 8th row\\
l & c & r & 9th row\\ l & c & r &10th row\\ l & c & r &11th row\\
l & c & r &12th row
\end{longtable}
\end{ThreePartTable}

The remarks~\ref{tn:a} and~\ref{tn:b} in the table\ldots.
```

02-21-2

threeparttablex demo

L	C	R	box
l	c	r	1st row
l	c	r	2nd row
l	c	r	3rd row
l	c[a]	r	4th row
l	c	r[b]	5th row
l	c	r	6th row
l	c	r	7th row
l	c	r	8th row
l	c	r	9th row
l	c	r	10th row
l	c	r	11th row

continued on next page ...

page 1

threeparttablex demo

... continued

L	C	R	box
l	c	r	12th row

[a] A remark to the table.
[b] This table is only a demo.

The remarks a and b in the table....

page 2

2.22 warpcol

ath mode

The warpcol package by Wayne A. Rochester provides an alternative to the dcolumn package (cf. Section 2.24 on page 98) to format columns of numbers. Like dcolumn, warpcol typesets the columns in math mode by default; so when adding captions in columns, you must switch to text mode, easily done by using the \multicolumn command. warpcol defines the P column type, which expects the formatting for decimal numbers in the form *Sx.y* as a parameter, where *S* stands for a negative sign, *x* for the number of digits of the whole number part, and *y* for the number of decimal places. This defines the basic width of the column, before any caption is added. In Example 02-22-1, the first column is formatted with P{3.1}, i.e. with three digits in front or the decimal point and one digit after. The second column is set to span the width of the sign, two whole number digits, and one decimal place.

column 1	*column 2*
123.4	−12.3
12.3	12.3
1.2	1.2

```
\usepackage{warpcol}

\begin{tabular}{P{3.1} P{-2.1}}\hline
\multicolumn{1}{c}{\emph{column 1}}
  & \multicolumn{1}{c}{\emph{column 2}}\\\hline
 123.4 & -12.3\\12.3 & 12.3\\1.2 & 1.2\\\hline
 \end{tabular}
```

02-22-1

It's a good idea to format column captions correctly regardless of their length, even if afterwards there is only a column of numbers. Usually, you'll set up the definition using a \multicolumn command and one of the three standard column types: l, c, or r. warpcol provides further support for the formatting through the following two commands:

\pcolbegin{*type*}{*argument*}	\pcolend

The first parameter of \pcolbegin expects one of the standard column types and the second one the definition of the format of the column of numbers. This is only of interest for a left- or right-aligned column, which could not be aligned correctly with the P column type. The following example illustrates the use of these commands:

```
\usepackage{warpcol}\newcolumntype{L}[1]{>{\pcolbegin{r}{#1}}l<{\pcolend}}
\newcolumntype{R}[1]{>{\pcolbegin{r}{#1}}r<{\pcolend}}

\begin{tabular}{@{} L{3.1}L{3.1}P{3.1}P{3.1}R{3.1}R{3.1} @{}} \hline
 \multicolumn{1}{l}{KT} & \multicolumn{1}{l}{long title}
   & \multicolumn{1}{c}{KT} & \multicolumn{1}{c}{long title}
   & \multicolumn{1}{r}{KT} & \multicolumn{1}{r}{long title}\\ \hline
 123.4 & 123.4 & 123.4 & 123.4 & 123.4 & 123.4 \\
  12.3 &  12.3 &  12.3 &  12.3 &  12.3 &  12.3 \\
   1.2 &   1.2 &   1.2 &   1.2 &   1.2 &   1.2 \\\hline
\end{tabular}
```

KT	long title	KT	long title	KT	long title
123.4	123.4	123.4	123.4	123.4	123.4
12.3	12.3	12.3	12.3	12.3	12.3
1.2	1.2	1.2	1.2	1.2	1.2

02-22-2

With \pcolbegin... \pcolend, you can left-align, right-align, or centre the columns of numbers arbitrarily.

02-22-3

left-aligned	right-aligned	centred
123.4	123.4	123.4
12.3	12.3	12.3
1.2	1.2	1.2

```
\usepackage{warpcol}

\begin{tabular}{@{}
    >{\pcolbegin{l}{3.1}}c<{\pcolend}P{3.1}
    >{\pcolbegin{c}{3.1}}c<{\pcolend} @{}}\hline
 \multicolumn{1}{@{}c}{left-aligned}
   & \multicolumn{1}{c}{right-aligned}
   & \multicolumn{1}{c@{}}{centred}\\ \hline
 123.4&123.4&123.4\\12.3&12.3&12.3\\1.2&1.2&1.2\\\hline
 \end{tabular}
```

When formatting the columns, you can pass anything as an argument that makes sense for a column of numbers. In the following example, the first column is formatted with the expression L{< 1.3}, which specifies a comparison operator, a space, one digit before the decimal point, and three digits after it. The second column is formatted as P{3\,3.2}: three digits, a space of \,, a further three digits, and two decimal places.

02-22-4

p	*cost (€)*
> 0.1	123 456.78
< 0.1	23 456.78
< 0.01	4 523.45
< 0.001	345.67

```
\usepackage{warpcol} \usepackage{eurosym}
\newcolumntype{L}[1]{>{\pcolbegin{l}{#1}}l<{\pcolend}}

\begin{tabular}{@{} L{< 1.3} P{3\,3.2} @{}}\hline
\multicolumn{1}{@{}c}{\emph{p}}
 & \multicolumn{1}{c@{}}{\emph{cost (\euro)}}\\\hline
 > 0.1  & 123\,456.78 \\ < 0.1   & 23\,456.78 \\
 < 0.01 &   4\,523.45 \\ < 0.001 &     345.67 \\\hline
\end{tabular}
```

2.23 widetable

The widetable package by Claudio Beccari is a combination of the tabular* and tabularx environments; it tries to adapt the width of *each* column to achieve the specified width.

```
\begin{widetable}{table width}{column definition}
...&...&...\\
\end{widetable}
```

The following three examples show the main difference between the longtable*, tabularx, and widetable environments; only the latter distributes the required space evenly over all columns.

```
\usepackage{tabularx,widetable}

\begin{tabular*}{\linewidth}{|l|c@{\kern\tabcolsep\vrule\extracolsep{\fill}}c|}\hline
column A & wider column B & longtable*\\\hline
\end{tabular*}\par\bigskip
\begin{tabularx}{\linewidth}{|l|X|X|}\hline
```

```
column A & wider column B & tabularx\\\hline
\end{tabularx}\par\bigskip
\begin{widetable}{\linewidth}{|l|c|c|}\hline
column A & wider column B & widetable\\\hline
\end{widetable}
```

column A	wider column B	longtable*

column A	wider column B	tabularx

column A	wider column B	widetable

02-23-1

2.24 dcolumn

The dcolumn package by David Carlisle provides formatting help for columns of numbers, which can be aligned at the decimal point or decimal comma. dcolumn defines the D column type for this:

D{*TEX separator*}{*output*}{*number of decimal places*}
D{*TEX separator*}{*output*}{*number left.number right*}

TEX separator — Corresponds to the separator within the TEX source and may only be a single character. Will usually be a dot (3.1412) or a comma (3,1242), but may also be a hyphen (3-1234).

output — Corresponds to the character that is to appear as the decimal separator in the output. May be any arbitrary mathematical sequence of characters, for example \cdot; however, it will usually be a dot or a comma.

number of decimal places — Defines the maximum number of decimal places. If the value is negative, the output is centred at the separator; otherwise it is right-aligned with the maximum number of decimal places.

number left.number right — Defines the maximum number of decimal places left and right of the separator. The two numbers may be separated by either a comma or a dot.

math mode

dcolumn always operates in math mode, so bear this in mind when inputting separator characters and selecting the font. This also means that you can't use the mathematical operator $ in the columns of the table; if you do, the decimal separator won't be determined correctly. The first example uses vertical lines to highlight the effect of the D column's third parameter.

```
\usepackage{dcolumn}

\begin{tabular}{| c | D{.}{,}{5} | D{,}{.}{-1} | }
\textit{name}& \textit{value} & \textit{standard form}\\\hline
 e & 2.71828 & 0,271828\cdot10^{1}\\ $\pi$ & 3.1416 & 0,31416\cdot10^{1}\\
 v & 0.21    & 0,21                \\    Q  & 0      & 0
\end{tabular}
```

02-24-1

name	*value*	*standard form*
e	2,71828	$0.271828 \cdot 10^1$
π	3,1416	$0.31416 \cdot 10^1$
v	0,21	0.21
Q	0	0

The centre column defines the dot as internal separator character, the comma as output character, and the maximum number of decimal places as 5. The third column defines the comma as internal separator, the dot as output, and a centred display in the table. However, the combination of centring with the standard form content of this third column is not advantageous for its layout, as there is too much content after the separator for it to look good to have the separator centred. Furthermore the "text" of the table caption for the two D columns is typeset in italics; math mode applies here, too. This has fatal consequences for the third column – the words are interpreted as a number and because there is no comma as a separator, it is assumed that all the letters are leading digits and the words are place to end immediately before the virtual separator character. The same applies to the centre column, only the effect is not so visible. The same table with modified cells looks much better:

```
\usepackage{dcolumn}

\begin{tabular}{| c | D{.}{,}{5} | D{,}{.}{-1} | }
\textit{name}& \multicolumn{1}{c|}{\textit{value}}
   & \multicolumn{1}{c|}{\textit{standard form}}\\\hline
 e   & 2.71828 & 0,271828\cdot10^{1}\\ $\pi$  & 3.1416  & 0,31416\cdot10^{1}\\
 v   & 0.21    & 0,21                \\    Q   & 0       & 0
\end{tabular}
```

02-24-2

name	*value*	*standard form*
e	2,71828	$0.271828 \cdot 10^1$
π	3,1416	$0.31416 \cdot 10^1$
v	0,21	0.21
Q	0	0

Now the centre column looks much better. For the right column, the centring at the decimal separator still makes it look bad because in the standard form content there is always only one leading digit. In cases like this, it would look better if a D column was not used at all but a normal left-aligned column used instead; however, an exception would be if you were using a font where not all of the digits had the same width. Of course, if you don't use a D column, you can't modify the separator automatically.

```
\usepackage{dcolumn}

\begin{tabular}{| c | D{.}{,}{5} | >{$}l<{$} | }
\textit{name}& \multicolumn{1}{c|}{\textit{value}}
   & \multicolumn{1}{c|}{\textit{standard form}}\\\hline
 e   & 2.71828 & 0,271828\cdot10^{1}\\ $\pi$  & 3.1416  & 0,31416\cdot10^{1}\\
 v   & 0.21    & 0,21                \\    Q    & 0       & 0
\end{tabular}
```

name	*value*	*standard form*
e	2,71828	$0,271828 \cdot 10^1$
π	3,1416	$0,31416 \cdot 10^1$
v	0,21	$0,21$
Q	0	0

02-24-3

Use the *left.right* notation for the selection of decimal places if either the maximum number of digits before and after the separator is approximately the same or you are getting problems with the formatting otherwise. In principle it is best to define a custom column type that references the D type. The following example shows several variants and their effect on the layout; the vertical lines have only been added to make the effects clearer.

```
\usepackage{dcolumn}
\newcolumntype{d}[1]{D{.}{.}{#1}}
\newcommand\mc[1]{\multicolumn{1}{c|}{#1}}
\newcommand\Mc[1]{\multicolumn{1}{|c|}{#1}}

\begin{tabular}{| d{-1}| d{1}| d{2}| d{3.2}| d{5.2}|}
\Mc{d\{-1\}}&\mc{d\{1\}}&\mc{d\{2\}}&\mc{d\{3.2\}}&\mc{d\{5.2\}}\\\hline
-13.02 & -13.02 & -13.02 & -13.02 & -13.02 \\
-13.02 & -13.02 & -13.02 & -13.02 & -13.02 \\
-13.02 & -13.02 & -13.02 & -13.02 & -13.02 \\
-13.02 & -13.02 & -13.02 & -13.02 & -13.02
\end{tabular}
```

d{-1}	d{1}	d{2}	d{3.2}	d{5.2}
−13.02	−13.02	−13.02	−13.02	−13.02
−13.02	−13.02	−13.02	−13.02	−13.02
−13.02	−13.02	−13.02	−13.02	−13.02
−13.02	−13.02	−13.02	−13.02	−13.02

02-24-4

2.25 rccol

The `rccol` package by Eckhart Guthöhrlein is an alternative to `dcolumn` for formatting columns of numbers. `rccol` supports the following package options:

`rounding`	Rounds numerical values to the number of digits specified by the column definition (default behaviour).
`norounding`	No rounding.
`comma`	Globally sets the comma as decimal separator (default behaviour). The option `german` has the same effect.
`point`	Globally sets the dot as decimal separator. The options `english` and `USenglish` have the same effect.

The package defines the `R` column type, which takes two mandatory parameters: one for the number of digits left of the decimal separator and the other one for the number of decimal places.

R{*integer digits*}{*decimal places*}
R - [TEX separator] [output] {*integer digits*}{*decimal places*}

By default the package expects the comma as decimal separator. If no comma is present, the formatting assumes that the entire number is an integer; dots are not recognized as separators unless the option is changed. This case can be seen in the last column of the following example; the "integer" is formatted according to the specification `{3}{2}` and the dot simply appended. This makes the number appear incorrectly and too far to the left in the column.

```
\usepackage{rccol}
\newcommand\mc[2]{\multicolumn{1}{#1}{\ttfamily#2}}

\begin{tabular}{| R{1}{5} | R{1}{6} @{$\cdot10^1$\hspace{\tabcolsep}} | c | R{3}{2} |}
\mc{|c|}{R\{1\}\{5\}} & \mc{c|}{R\{1\}\{6\}} & c & \mc{c|}{R\{3\}\{2\}}\\\hline
2,71828 & 0,271828 & $\pi$ & 314.16\\  0,21 & 0,21 & Q & 0.3\\
\end{tabular}
```

02-25-1

R{1}{5}	R{1}{6}	c	R{3}{2}
2,71828	$0{,}271828\cdot10^1$	π	31416,00.
0,21000	$0{,}210000\cdot10^1$	Q	03,00.

Setting `@{$\cdot10^1$\hspace{\tabcolsep}}` as the column separator makes it possible to display the exponents (`$\cdot10^1$`) and produce the usual column spacing (`\hspace{\tabcolsep}`). The `@` operator is especially suited to constructs like this. The `R` column type also takes two optional arguments, which you can use to control the decimal separator. If only one argument is given, it is used for both the input and output separator. If the minus sign is given (without parentheses), "–" is also taken into account when centring the number.

```
\usepackage{rccol} \newcommand\mc[2]{\multicolumn{1}{#1}{\ttfamily#2}}

\begin{tabular}{| R-{1}{4} | R{1}{6} @{$\cdot10^1$\hspace{\tabcolsep}}
    | c | R[.][,]{3}{2} |}
\mc{|c|}{R-\{1\}\{4\}} & \mc{c|}{R\{1\}\{6\}} & c & \mc{c|}{R[.][,]\{3\}\{2\}}\\\hline
-2,71828 & 0,271828 & $\pi$ & 314.16\\  -0,21 & 0,21 & Q & 0.3\\
\end{tabular}
```

R-{1}{4}	R{1}{6}	c	R[.][,]{3}{2}
−2,7183	0,271828·10^1	π	314,16
−0,2100	0,210000·10^1	Q	0,30

02-25-2

math mode

R columns are not automatically typeset in math mode; this does not apply for the minus sign though because the input is scanned for it. You must ensure that the numerical values are entered correctly; `rccol` accepts almost any combination of alphanumerical characters. You must also make sure that the last row ends with a `\\`. `rccol` automatically loads the packages `array` and `fltpoint`; both of these packages are usually contained in any current TEX distribution.

2.26 siunitx

The `siunitx` package by Joseph Wright is primarily intended to display SI units, but also offers support for formatting decimal numbers in tables. It provides the S column type to achieve this. Every entry in a cell is interpreted as a number by `siunitx`; captions or comments must either appear as part of a command or be enclosed in curly braces. Table 2.9 shows a summary of the parameters that are of interest for tables. All the other ones are described in the documentation of the package. [61]

`\sisetup{`*list of parameters*`}`

The parameters can be set as optional arguments when loading the package after the `\sisetup` command, or by passing them to the appropriate commands. The names of nearly all optional arguments changed from version 1.x of `siunitx` to the current version 2. However, if you prefer to use the old names, you can set the `load-configuration` argument to `version-1`.

Table 2.9: Some of the possible parameters of the `siunitx` package, when used for a table (*literal* stands for an arbitrary string).

name	*type*	*description*
`retain-zero-exponent`	Boolean	Allow 10^0.
`output-decimal-marker`	Symbol	Decimal symbol.
`group-separator`	Code	Space between the digits for large numbers.
`round-precision`	Number	Number of digits to output.
`exponent-base`	Literal	Base for exponential notation.
`exponent-product`	Literal	Multiplication symbol for exponential notation.
`round-mode`	Literal	Can be none or `places` for fixed point display.
`input-decimal-markers`	Literal	Decimal symbol for numbers.
`input-digits`	Literal	Number of digits for numbers.
`input-quotient`	Literal	Division symbol for numbers.
`input-exponent-markers`	Literal	Exponentiation symbol for numbers.
`input-ignore`	Literal	Number of characters to ignore.

continued...

... continued

name	*type*	*description*
input-product	Literal	Multiplication symbol for numbers.
input-signs	Literal	Sign symbol for numbers.
add-decimal-zero	List	Pad numbers with zeros.
explicit-sign	Literal	Sign symbol for numbers.
table-alignment	Type	Alignment of the table column, valid values are center, left, and right.
table-auto-round	Boolean	Switch to rounding numbers automatically to achieve the number of digits specified by table-format.
table-format	Number	Symbolic specifier for decimal numbers in table columns.
table-number-alignment	List	Alignment of S columns, valid values are center-decimal-marker, center, left, and right.
table-parse-only	Boolean	Do not align S columns at the decimal separator.
table-text-numbers	Type	Alignment of text in S columns, possible values are center, left, and right.
table-unit-alignment	Type	Alignment of unit s columns, possible values are center, left, and right (cf. Example 02-26-6 on page 106).
tight-spacing	Boolean	Reduce spacing by ±.
inter-unit-separator	Literal	Separator for units.
unit-value-separator	Literal	Space between number and unit.
use-xspace	Boolean	Use the \xspace command from the package of the same name after a unit.

2.26.1 Columns of numbers

Columns of numbers are aligned by default at the decimal point such that all dots in a column are aligned and centred (first column in the Example 02-26-1). This case corresponds to the parameter setting `table-number-alignment=center-decimal-marker`.

The second column in the following example is typeset with the keyword setting `table-number-alignment=center`, which first aligns the dots but then centres the column as a whole. The third and fourth column show right- and left-aligned columns, again with the dots aligned first and then the column aligned left or right as a whole. You can change the decimal point to be a comma through the `output-decimal-marker={,}` option.

```
\usepackage{siunitx,booktabs}

\sisetup{table-figures-integer=2,table-figures-decimal=4}
\begin{tabular}{S | % default column setting
               S[table-number-alignment=center] |
               S[table-number-alignment=right]  |
```

```
                S[table-number-alignment=left, output-decimal-marker={,}]}\toprule
\emph{default}&\emph{centred}&\emph{right-aligned}&\emph{left-aligned}\\\midrule
 2.3456 &  2.3456 &  2.3456 &  2.3456 \\
34.25   & 34.25   & 34.25   & 34.25   \\
 6.7835 &  6.7835 &  6.7835 &  6.7835 \\
90.473  & 90.473  & 90.473  & 90.473  \\\bottomrule
\end{tabular}
```

default	*centred*	*right-aligned*	*left-aligned*
2.3456	2.3456	2.3456	2,3456
34.25	34.25	34.25	34,25
6.7835	6.7835	6.7835	6,7835
90.473	90.473	90.473	90,473

02-26-1

The `table-format` option formats the column of numbers. The format for this option is *<number><decimal separator><number>*, for example `2.4`, which specifies two digits before the decimal separator and four digits after. The same applies for exponents: `2.2e1.1` takes four digits for the mantissa (2.2) and two digits for the exponent (1.1). The exponent will not have any digits after the decimal separator in the logarithmic notation. A sign in front of the format specification (as in the column definition of the second column in the following example) advises the package to take the possible presence of a sign in the input into account when determining alignment.

```
\usepackage[exponent-product=\cdot]{siunitx}  \usepackage{booktabs}

\sisetup{table-number-alignment=center}
\begin{tabular}{S[table-format=2.2e2]
                S[table-format=+2.2e2]
                S[table-format=2.2e1.1]
                S}\toprule
\emph{very large values} & \emph{very large values} &
\emph{very large values} & \emph{values}\\\midrule
  2.3e1   &   2.34e1  & +-2.34e1  &  +2.31 \\
-34.23e45 & -34.23e45 & -34.23e45 &  34.23 \\
-56.78    & -56.78    & -56.78    & -56.78 \\
  1.0e34  &   1.0e34  & +1.0e34   & +-1.0  \\\bottomrule
\end{tabular}
```

very large values	*very large values*	*very large values*	*values*
$2.3 \cdot 10^{1}$	$2.34 \cdot 10^{1}$	$\pm 2.34 \cdot 10^{1}$	2.31
$-34.23 \cdot 10^{45}$	$-34.23 \cdot 10^{45}$	$-34.23 \cdot 10^{45}$	34.23
-56.78	-56.78	-56.78	-56.78
$1.0 \cdot 10^{34}$	$1.0 \cdot 10^{34}$	$1.0 \cdot 10^{34}$	± 1.0

02-26-2

In the exponential notation, the format can be specified with the `table-sign-exponent` option. The value `true` causes the numbers to be aligned at the decimal separator as well as the decimal power, `false` causes the decimal power to appear immediately after the mantissa.

You can use the `table-auto-round` option to format numbers automatically through rounding or padding to achieve the number of digits specified by `table-format`. This option is ignored, however, if the column is also set to be centred at the decimal separator through `table-number-alignment=center-decimal-marker`, as shown in the following example:

02-26-3

column	*column*	*column*
1.2	1.200	1.2
1.234	1.235	1.234

```
\usepackage[exponent-product=\cdot]{siunitx}
\usepackage{booktabs}
\sisetup{table-format=1.3,table-alignment=center}

\begin{tabular}{%
  S
  S[table-auto-round]
  S[table-auto-round,
  table-number-alignment=center-decimal-marker]}\toprule
\emph{column} & \emph{column}
  & \emph{column} \\\midrule
1.2   & 1.2    & 1.2  \\
1.234 & 1.2345 & 1.234\\
\bottomrule
\end{tabular}
```

You can prevent numbers aligning at the decimal separator or the exponent by specifying `table-parse-only`; then the columns are aligned solely according to `table-number-alignment`.

02-26-4

centred	*left-aligned*	*right-aligned*
14.2	14.2	14.2
1.234 56	1.234 56	1.234 56
$1.2 \cdot 10^3$	$1.2 \cdot 10^3$	$1.2 \cdot 10^3$

```
\usepackage[exponent-product=\cdot]{siunitx}
\sisetup{table-parse-only}
\usepackage{booktabs}

\begin{tabular}{ S S[table-number-alignment=left]
  S[table-number-alignment=right]}\toprule
\emph{centred} & \emph{left-aligned}
  & \emph{right-aligned} \\\midrule
14.2    & 14.2    & 14.2 \\
1.23456 & 1.23456 & 1.23456\\
1.2e3   & 1.2e3   & 1.2e3\\\bottomrule
\end{tabular}
```

As with the `dcolumn` package (Section 2.24 on page 98), you can also align entries in a table even if they aren't purely numerical, for example `2.3456 ± 0.02` for a number with error margin. To do this, you need to define the following options appropriately: `group-separator` for the spacing between the digits, `output-decimal-marker` for the output decimal separator, `input-digits` for the digits and symbols of the input, and `input-decimal-markers` for the input decimal separator. If the format becomes very complex, it's a good idea to define a new column type based on S using `\newcolumntype`.

numbers
2.3456 ± 0.02
34.2345 ± 0.001
56.7835 ± 0.067
90.473 ± 0.021

```
\usepackage{siunitx}
\usepackage{booktabs}

\begin{tabular}{
  S[group-separator={},
  output-decimal-marker={\,\pm\,},
  input-digits={0123456789.},
  input-decimal-markers={+}]}\toprule
\emph{numbers}\\\midrule
 2.3456 + 0.02  \\
34.2345 + 0.001 \\
56.7835 + 0.067 \\
90.473  + 0.021 \\\bottomrule
\end{tabular}
```

02-26-5

2.26.2 Columns of numbers with units

As well as the S column type, there is the s type, which is used to format units and output them as a normal column with space `\tabcolsep` to the previous one.

value	*unit*
2.16×10^{-5}	$\mathrm{m^2\,s^{-1}}$
2.83×10^{-6}	$\mathrm{m^2\,s^{-1}}$
7.39×10^{3}	$\mathrm{Pa\,m^3\,mol^{-1}}$
1.0×10^{5}	Pa

```
\usepackage{siunitx}  \usepackage{booktabs}

\begin{tabular}{
  S[table-format=1.2e-1,table-alignment=center]
  s[table-unit-alignment=left]}\toprule
{\emph{value}} & \emph{unit}\\\midrule
2.16e-5 & \metre\squared\per\second    \\
2.83e-6 & \metre\squared\per\second    \\
7.39e3  & \pascal\cubic\metre\per\mole\\
1.0e5   & \pascal                      \\\bottomrule
\end{tabular}
```

02-26-6

Setting the column spacing to 5pt (`\kern5pt`) moves the unit closer to the value.

value	*unit*
2.16×10^{-5}	$\mathrm{m^2\,s^{-1}}$
2.83×10^{-6}	$\mathrm{m^2\,s^{-1}}$
7.39×10^{3}	$\mathrm{Pa\,m^3\,mol^{-1}}$
1.0×10^{5}	Pa

```
\usepackage{siunitx} \usepackage{booktabs}

\begin{tabular}{S[table-format=1.2e-1,
                  table-number-alignment=center]@{\kern5pt}
                s[table-unit-alignment=left]}\toprule
{\emph{value}} & \emph{unit}\\\midrule
2.16e-5 & \metre\squared\per\second    \\
2.83e-6 & \metre\squared\per\second    \\
7.39e3  & \pascal\cubic\metre\per\mole\\
1.0e5   & \pascal                      \\\bottomrule
\end{tabular}
```

02-26-7

If the unit is always the same, you can specify it in the column definition instead, but remember that then it must be enclosed in double curly braces `<{{...}}`!

02-26-8

no	*mass*	mass/10^3 kg
1	$4.56 \cdot 10^3$ kg	4.56
2	$2.40 \cdot 10^3$ kg	2.40
3	$1.345 \cdot 10^4$ kg	13.45
4	$4.5 \cdot 10^2$ kg	0.45

```
\usepackage[exponent-product=\cdot]{siunitx}
\usepackage{booktabs}
\sisetup{table-alignment=center}

\begin{tabular}{c
  S[table-format=1.3e1]<{{\,\si{\kilogram}}}
  S[table-format=2.2]}\toprule
\emph{no} & \multicolumn{1}{c}{\emph{mass}}
  & {mass/\SI{e3}{\kilogram}}\\\midrule
1 & 4.56e3  & 4.56  \\
2 & 2.40e3  & 2.40  \\
3 & 1.345e4 & 13.45 \\
4 & 4.5e2   & 0.45  \\\bottomrule
\end{tabular}
```

2.27 polytable

The polytable package by Andres Löh is a very particular application. It is especially helpful when you are formatting source code but can't use the standard listings package for source code listings. With polytable, you can assign symbolic names to individual columns and then refer to them.

```
\begin{pboxed}   ...  \end{pboxed}
\begin{ptboxed}  ...  \end{ptboxed}
\begin{pmboxed}  ...  \end{pmboxed}
\defaultcolumn{column type}          \nodefaultcolumn
\column{name}{type}                  \fromto{from}{to}{text}
\={from} [formatting]                \> [from] [formatting]        \< [from]
```

The term "boxed" does not denote a frame here, but that the rows are put into horizontal boxes of the natural width. For pboxed, this is done in paragraph mode, so this environment can therefore contain page breaks. For ptboxed, the rows are additionally put into a tabular environment, and for pmboxed into an array environment; with these environments, a page break is not possible. The commands known from the tabbing environment for setting tabs are redefined by the polytable package to work in the same way as the \fromto command.

Valid definitions for columns are for example \column{*foo*}{*r*} or \column{*bar*}{*l*}: the column with name *foo* is of type r (right-aligned) and *bar* of type l (left-aligned). With the \fromto command, you can typeset *text* starting at the *from* column (tab) across to the *to* column (tab). The *modus operandi* of polytable takes a bit of getting used to, but provides some advantages over the normal tabbing environment once it is understood. In the following example, the four columns A–D are defined; the width of the column results from the following tab. This is also the reason why the columns C and D are only defined in the second row – the entry would be too wide for the B column in the first row.

function fact(n: integer): integer;
begin
if $n > 1$ then
fact:= n * fact(n-1)
else
fact:= 1;
end;

```
\usepackage{polytable}

\begin{pboxed}
\column{A}{l}\column{B}{l}\column{C}{l}\column{D}{l}
\={A} function
  \>[B] \textbf{fact(n: integer)}: integer;\\
  \>[B] begin \>[C]\qquad \>[D]\qquad\\
    \={C} if $n>1$ then \\
      \={D} fact:= n * fact(n-1) \\
    \>[C] else \\ \>[D] fact:= 1; \\ \>[B] end;
\end{pboxed}
```

02-27-1

A more complex example can be found in the documentation of the package.

2.28 tabto

The tabto package by Donald Arseneau is available in two different versions, for plain TEX and for LATEX. Usually the LATEX version is shipped with a TEX distribution like TEX Live; therefore only the package named tabto can be found. The same package is called tabto-ltx on CTAN however. The package defines four new commands:

\tab	\tabto * {*length*}
\TabPositions{*pos1, pos2,... posn*}	\NumTabs{*number*}

The \tabto command lets you jump to a specific distance without explicitly having defined a tab there. If the jump to the specified place is not possible, a line break is inserted automatically to make it possible. Paragraph indents are considered accordingly.

A jump to 3 cm.
→
A long text at the beginning
jump to 3 cm.
→

```
\usepackage{tabto}

A\tabto{3cm}jump to 3\,cm.\\
\makebox[3cm][r]{$\rightarrow$}\\
A long text at the beginning
\tabto{3cm}jump to 3\,cm.\\
\makebox[3cm][r]{$\rightarrow$}
```

02-28-1

The starred version \tabto* places the tab regardless of the current position in the text; the text in the second line in the following example is overwritten twice. In both cases, a jump back to the specified position is performed, first to 3 cm, then to 1 cm.

A jump to 3 cm.
→
A long 1ext at the begjumpinto 3 cm.
→ →

```
\usepackage{tabto}

A\tabto*{3cm}jump to 3\,cm.\\
\makebox[3cm][r]{$\rightarrow$}\\
A long text at the beginning
\tabto*{3cm}jump to 3\,cm.%
\tabto*{1cm}1\,cm\\
\makebox[1cm][r]{$\rightarrow$}%
\makebox[2cm][r]{$\rightarrow$}
```

02-28-2

You can place tabs using the two commands \TabPositions and \NumTabs. In the first case, the argument is a comma-separated list of spaces; in the second case the argument is the number of tabs, which are then distributed evenly across the whole line. The jump to the next position is triggered through the \tab command. The spaces are always relative to the default left text margin.

02-28-3

A jump to 3 cm.
→
A long text at the beginning
line break!
0 1 cm 3 cm

```
\usepackage{tabto}

\TabPositions{1cm,3cm}
A\tab\tab jump to 3\,cm.\\
\makebox[3cm][r]{$\rightarrow$}\\
A long text at the beginning%
    \tab line break!\\
0\tab 1\,cm\tab 3\,cm
```

If a defined tab on the line is not possible with a \tab command because of the current position in the text, the tab is automatically replaced by a line break; the following text then starts at the beginning of the next line. The \NumTabs command is somewhat unclear; in theory the specified number defines the number of the tabs, but the first tab is placed at the beginning of the line at 0 pt and not reachable through \tab. Therefore \NumTabs{4} defines tabs at 0 pt, 0.25\linewidth, 0.5\linewidth, and 0.75\linewidth. Thus the following example produces a line break in the second line because a third tab within that single line was not possible.

02-28-4

1 2 3 end
1 2
3 end

```
\usepackage{tabto}

\NumTabs{4}
\tab1\tab2\tab3 \hfill end\par
\NumTabs{3}
\tab1\tab2\tab3 \hfill end
```

2.29 Tabbing

The Tabbing package by Jean-Pierre F. Drucbert lets you use accents within the Tabbing environment. This means that the \a workaround for the standard tabbing environment is not necessary (cf. Example 01-02-4 on page 14), but instead you have to give each tab command as an argument to the \TAB command. It is up to you to decide which method you find less cumbersome.

02-29-1

The example line can be “killed”
first café
second café
maître
crème brûlée

```
\usepackage{Tabbing}

\begin{Tabbing}
The \TAB{=}example line \TAB{=}can
  \TAB{=}be \TAB{=}``killed''\\
\TAB{>}first caf\'e\\
\TAB{>}\TAB{>}second caf\'e\\
\TAB{>}\TAB{>}\TAB{>}m\^aitre\\
\TAB{>}cr\`eme
    \TAB{>}\TAB{>}\TAB{>}br\^ul\'ee
\end{Tabbing}
```

Chapter 3

Colour in tables

With colour printers now widespread, using colours in tables is becoming more significant – they are an additional stylistic device to make tables more readable. This chapter covers the packages that support using colours in tables. If you want to use colour, always load the xcolor package; it is loaded by the colortbl package anyway and its support for selecting colours is much better.

3.1 colortbl

The colortbl package by David Carlisle stands for "colour table" and lets you add colour to tables in the form of coloured columns, rows, cells, or lines. The color package is required for that and is loaded automatically. The xcolor package extends the capabilities of this package by some additional commands. Further information can be found in Section 3.2 on page 116.

3.1.1 Columns

To colour columns, you must use the \columncolor command in the column definition of the table. The command has the following syntax:

```
\columncolor[colour model]{colour}[overhang left][overhang right]
```

The *colour model* denotes one of the models defined by the color or xcolor packages, for example rgb or cmyk (cf. Section 3.2 on page 116). For *colour*, you can use the predefined name of a colour, for example red, or the colour model's respective numerical values for a colour. You can use the two optional arguments, *overhang left* and *overhang right*, to make the column wider – this only refers to the colour though and does not affect the actual width of the column. If no overhang is specified, *both* values are set to \tabcolsep. If only *one* optional argument is given, it also automatically refers to *both*! Specifying [0pt] is identical to [0pt][0pt] (cf. Example 03-01-7 on page 114).

overhang

one	two	three
A	B	C

```
\usepackage{colortbl}
\definecolor{gray70}{gray}{0.7}
\definecolor{gray90}{gray}{0.9}

\begin{tabular}{>{\columncolor{gray70}}c
                >{\columncolor[rgb]{1,0,0}}c
                >{\columncolor{gray90}}c}
one & two & three\\ A    & B    & C
\end{tabular}
```

03-01-1

As can be seen from the above example, the whole width of the respective column is coloured; the overhang defined internally defaults to adding \tabcolsep to the left and right of the normal width. If in fact you only want to colour the actual width of the text in the column, set the overhangs to [0pt]. This is illustrated in the next example; the vertical lines have only been added to make the effect clearer.

one	two	three
A	B	C

```
\usepackage{colortbl}
\definecolor{gray70}{gray}{0.7}
\definecolor{gray90}{gray}{0.9}

\begin{tabular}{|>{\columncolor{gray70}[0pt]}c|
                 >{\columncolor[rgb]{1,0,0}[0pt]}c|
                 >{\columncolor{gray90}[0pt]}c|}
one & two & three\\ A    & B    & C
\end{tabular}
```

03-01-2

If a table is left- and right-aligned through @{}, you must take this into account for the columns: there must be no overhang on the left in the first column, and similarly on the right in the last column. This is shown in the following example:

one	two	three
A	B	C

```
\usepackage{colortbl}
\definecolor{gray70}{gray}{0.7}
\definecolor{gray90}{gray}{0.9}

\begin{tabular}{@{}>{\columncolor{gray70}[0pt][\tabcolsep]}c
                   >{\columncolor[rgb]{1,0,0}}c
                   >{\columncolor{gray90}[\tabcolsep][0pt]}c@{}}
one & two & three\\ A    & B    & C
\end{tabular}
```

03-01-3

3.1.2 Rows

Rows are always coloured after the columns have been coloured, i.e. the colour of a row overwrites the colour of the respective column. This results from the fact that coloured columns are specified in the header already. The `\rowcolor` command colours a whole row of a table, but you can also use the `\cellcolor` command to colour individual cells of a row (cf. Section 3.1.3 on the next page).

`\rowcolor` [colour model] {*colour*} [overhang left] [overhang right]

`\rowcolor` has the same syntax as `\columncolor`, but with different effects. `\rowcolor` must always be at the beginning of the first column of the particular row, and only affects that row. `\rowcolor` is in fact simply a concatenation of individual `\columncolor` or `\cellcolor` commands.

03-01-4

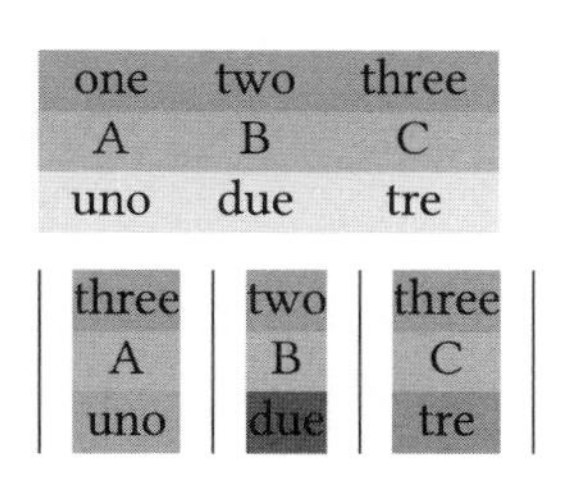

```
\usepackage[table]{xcolor}

\begin{tabular}{ccc}
\rowcolor[gray]{0.6}one & two & three\\
\rowcolor[gray]{0.7}A    & B    & C    \\
\rowcolor[gray]{0.9}uno  & due  & tre
\end{tabular}\\[6pt]
%
\begin{tabular}{|>{\columncolor{gray!70}[0pt]}c|
                 >{\columncolor[rgb]{1,0,0}[0pt]}c|
                 >{\columncolor{gray!90}[0pt]}c|}
\rowcolor[gray]{0.6}three & two & three\\
\rowcolor{cyan}      A    & B    & C    \\
                     uno  & due  & tre
\end{tabular}
```

03-01-5

one	two	three
A	B	C
uno	due	tre

one	two	three
A	B	C
uno	due	tre

one	two	three
A	B	C
uno	due	tre

```
\usepackage{colortbl}

\begin{tabular}{||@{}
  >{\columncolor[gray]{.7}[0pt][\tabcolsep]}ccc@{}||}
\rowcolor[gray]{0.6}one & two& three\\
\rowcolor{cyan} A & B & C\\ uno  & due  & tre
\end{tabular}\\[8pt]
\begin{tabular}{||@{}
  >{\columncolor[gray]{.7}[0pt][\tabcolsep]}ccc@{}||}
\rowcolor[gray]{0.6}[0pt]one & two& three\\
\rowcolor{cyan}[0pt] A & B & C\\ uno  & due  & tre
\end{tabular}\\[8pt]
\begin{tabular}{||@{}
  >{\columncolor[gray]{.7}[0pt][\tabcolsep]}cc
  >{\columncolor{white}[\tabcolsep][0pt]}c@{}||}
\rowcolor[gray]{0.6}one & two& three\\
\rowcolor{cyan} A & B & C\\ uno  & due  & tre
\end{tabular}
```

The optional arguments of \rowcolor don't refer to the left and right of the row, but as before to the columns, making them unusable for colouring rows effectively. In the first table of example 03-01-5 on the preceding page \rowcolor leads to a correct left margin, but incorrect right one; it doesn't take the final @ operator into account, but simply takes the internal value for the right overhang, which defaults to \tabcolsep. The second table shows that if the optional arguments of \rowcolor are used, it affects the individual columns as well. Only the third table shows the desired result – achieved by defining the third column with colour white and optional arguments [\tabcolsep][0pt], and using \rowcolor without an optional argument. The same would have to be done for the first column if it were not coloured.

3.1.3 Cells

In the order of colouring, cells are last. Therefore they overwrite any colours for columns and rows. In principle, the \cellcolor command is only a shortcut for the \multicolumn command, which assumes the current column type and sets a colour through \rowcolor.

\cellcolor [colour model] {*colour*}

Unlike the colour commands for columns and rows, \cellcolor doesn't have any optional arguments for the overhang, but assumes the current values. When colouring the first cell in a column, the \cellcolor command must come after any \rowcolor command.

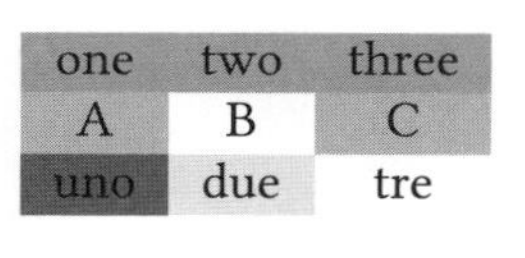

03-01-6

```
\usepackage{colortbl}

\begin{tabular}{ccc}
\rowcolor[gray]{0.6}one & two & three\\
\rowcolor[gray]{0.7}A    & \cellcolor{white}B & C \\
\rowcolor[gray]{0.9}\cellcolor{red}uno & due
   & \cellcolor{white}tre
\end{tabular}
```

one	two	three
A	B	C
uno	due	tre

03-01-7

```
\usepackage{colortbl}
\definecolor{gray70}{gray}{0.7}
\definecolor{gray90}{gray}{0.9}

\begin{tabular}{|>{\columncolor{gray70}[0pt]}c|
                 >{\columncolor[rgb]{1,0,0}[0pt]}c|
                 >{\columncolor{gray90}[0pt]}c|}
\rowcolor[gray]{0.6}one & two & \cellcolor{white}three\\
\rowcolor{cyan}      A    & \cellcolor{white}B    & C    \\
\cellcolor{white}uno      & due                   & tre
\end{tabular}
```

03-01-8

one	two	three
A	B	C
uno	due	tre

```
\usepackage{colortbl}
\definecolor{gray70}{gray}{0.7} \definecolor{gray90}{gray}{0.9}

\begin{tabular}{@{}>{\columncolor{gray70}[0pt][\tabcolsep]}c
                   >{\columncolor[rgb]{1,0,0}}c
                   >{\columncolor{gray90}[\tabcolsep][0pt]}c@{}}
                    \cellcolor{white}one & two & three\\
\rowcolor{cyan}     A    & \cellcolor{white}B    & C    \\
\rowcolor[gray]{0.9}uno & due  & \cellcolor{white}tre
\end{tabular}
```

3.1.4 Lines

Coloured vertical lines are the easiest ones to achieve – just replace the usual | operator with `!{\color{colour}\vline}`, inserting an appropriate value for the *colour*.

03-01-9

one	two	three
A	B	C
uno	due	tre

```
\usepackage{colortbl}

\begin{tabular}{!{\color[gray]{0.2}\vline}c
    !{\color[gray]{0.4}\vline}c!{\color[gray]{0.6}\vline}c
    !{\color[gray]{0.7}\vline} !{\color[gray]{0.9}\vline}}
  one & two & three\\ A & B & C \\
   uno & due  & tre
\end{tabular}
```

If you create double lines, the space between them remains white. If you want this space filled in, use a single thicker line of width 2`\arrayrulewidth`+`\doublerulesep` instead, as in the following example:

03-01-10

one	two	three
A	B	C
uno	due	tre

```
\usepackage{colortbl}
\newlength\Dicke\setlength\Dicke{2\arrayrulewidth}
\addtolength\Dicke{\doublerulesep}

\begin{tabular}{
    !{\color[gray]{0.2}\vline}!{\color[gray]{0.2}\vline}c
    !{\color[gray]{0.2}\vrule width \Dicke}c
    !{\color{red}\vline}!{\color{red}\vline}c
    !{\color{cyan}\vrule width \Dicke}}
 one & two & three\\ A & B & C \\ uno & due & tre
\end{tabular}
```

`colortbl` provides the following two commands:

`\arrayrulecolor` [colour model] {*colour*}
`\doublerulesepcolor` [colour model] {*colour*}

These set the colours globally for all line types; they may therefore occur anywhere. They only apply to lines after their declaration; if you insert them after the table header, they won't affect the colour of the vertical lines, as shown here:

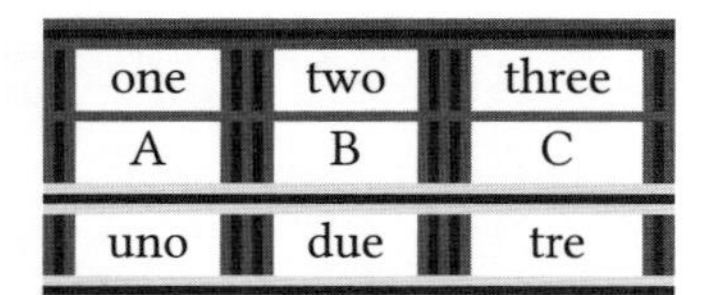


```
\usepackage{colortbl}
\setlength\arrayrulewidth{2pt}
\arrayrulecolor{red}\doublerulesepcolor{blue}

\begin{tabular}{||c|||c|||c||}\hline\hline
  one & two & three\\\hline\arrayrulecolor[gray]{0.9}
  A     &   B  & C     \\\hline\hline
   uno & due   & tre \\\hline\hline
\end{tabular}
```

03-01-11

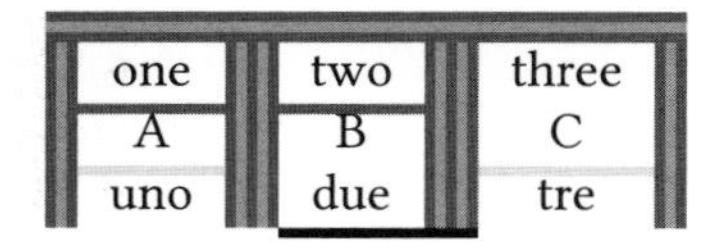


```
\usepackage{colortbl}
\setlength\arrayrulewidth{2pt}
\arrayrulecolor{red}\doublerulesepcolor[gray]{0.6}

\begin{tabular}{||c|||c|||c||}\hline\hline
 one& two& three\\\cline{1-2}\arrayrulecolor[gray]{0.9}
 A   &    B& C   \\\cline{1-1}\cline{3-3}\arrayrulecolor{black}
 uno& due& tre\\\cline{2-2}
\end{tabular}
```

03-01-12

The example above shows that corners don't always look great, especially when using `\cline`. The `hhline` package works better here.

3.2 xcolor

The main difference between the `xcolor` package by Uwe Kern and the `color` package by David Carlisle is that the latter always activates the option `dvipsnames` if one of the drivers `dvips`, `oztex`, or `xdvi` is chosen. This can cause problems if the document is compiled with `pdftex`, which will report undefined colours. This is why `xcolor` expects the user to explicitly specify the option `dvipsnames` if the corresponding predefined colours are to be used.

`\usepackage[`*dvipsnames,prologue*`]{`*xcolor*`}`

The `colortbl` package, described in Section 3.1 on page 111, is loaded automatically by `xcolor` if the package option `table` is given (cf. Table 3.1).

Table 3.1: Summary of the package options of xcolor.

option	*description*
`natural`	(default) Uses all colours within their model, except RGB (converted to rgb), HSB (converted to hsb), and Gray (converted to gray).
`rgb`	Converts all colours into the rgb model.
`cmy`	Converts all colours into the cmy model.
`cmyk`	Converts all colours into the cmyk model.
`hsb`	Converts all colours into the hsb model.
`gray`	Converts all colours into the gray model.

continued...

... continued

option	*description*
RGB	Converts all colours into the RGB model and then into the rgb model.
HTML	Converts all colours into the HTML model and then into the rgb model.
HSB	Converts all colours into the HSB model and then into the hsb model.
Gray	Converts all colours into the Gray model and then into the gray model.
dvipsnames	Loads the predefined DVIPS colours.
svgnames	Loads the predefined SVG colours.
prologue	Writes the list of colour names (dvipsnames) in the PostScript header; this is important when creating documents through DVIPS.
table	Loads the colortbl package to enable coloured table rows.
hyperref	Support for hyperref.
showerrors	(default) Outputs a message for undefined colours.
hideerrors	Only outputs an error message if an undefined colour is used, and sets it to black.

xcolor extends the functionality of colortbl especially when colouring alternate table rows with different colours. The other advantage primarily concerns the definition of colours; this is not specific to tables however and also applies to other uses. The colour models that are supported by the current version of xcolor are summarized in Table 3.2.

Table 3.2: Supported colour models (L, M, N are natural numbers).

name	*base colours*	*parameter range*	*default*
rgb	red, green, blue	$[0,1]$	
cmy	cyan, magenta, yellow	$[0,1]$	
cmyk	cyan, magenta, yellow, black	$[0,1]$	
hsb	hue, saturation, brightness	$[0,1]$	
gray	gray	$[0,1]$	
RGB	Red, Green, Blue	$\{0,1,\dots,L\}$	$L = 255$
HTML	RRGGBB	$\{000000,\dots,FFFFFF\}$	
HSB	Hue, Saturation, Brightness	$\{0,1,\dots,M\}$	$M = 240$
Gray	Gray	$\{0,1,\dots,N\}$	$N = 15$
wave	lambda (nm)	$[363,814]$	

In principle there is no difference between colouring the individual cells of a table or matrix.

$$\underline{A} = \left(\begin{array}{ccc} A & B & C \\ A & BBB & C \\ A & B & C \end{array}\right)$$

03-02-1

```
\usepackage[table]{xcolor}

\[ \underline{A} =
  \left(\begin{array}{c>{\columncolor{magenta}}cc}
  A & B & C\\
\rowcolor{cyan} A & \cellcolor{white} BBB & C\\
  A & B & C
  \end{array}\right) \]
```

Using the \columncolor, \rowcolor, and \cellcolor commands, you can achieve any arbitrary combination of colours. An alternative to using \cellcolor is to define an individual cell with \multicolumn and then use \columncolor for it. The syntax of the three colour commands in \xcolor is the same as for the ones from colortbl, though \xcolor also defines three additional commands for colouring rows with alternating colours.

\columncolor [colour model] {*colour*} [overhang left] [overhang right]
\rowcolor [colour model] {*colour*} [overhang left] [overhang right]
\cellcolor[*colour model*]{*colour*}
\rowcolors * [command] {*start row*}{*colour – odd row*}{*colour – even row*}
\showrowcolors
\hiderowcolors

The optional argument of \rowcolors lets you execute the usual commands that are valid here, for example \hline or \noalign{...}. The advantage of the optional argument is that the execution of these commands can be suppressed for rows for which \rowcolors is not active by using the starred version (cf. Example 03-02-7 on page 121). For alternating coloured and uncoloured rows, you can leave one of the arguments for the colour of the odd and even rows empty.

table 1		
A	BBB	C
A	B	C

table 2		
A	BBB	C
A	B	C

03-02-2

```
\usepackage[table]{xcolor}

\rowcolors{1}{}{blue!30}
\begin{tabular}{|ccc|}\hline
  \multicolumn{3}{|c|}{table 1}\\\hline
  A & BBB & C\\\hline  A & B & C\\\hline
\end{tabular}  \par\bigskip
\rowcolors*[\hline]{1}{}{blue!30}
\begin{tabular}{|ccc|}
  \multicolumn{3}{|c|}{table 2}\\ \hiderowcolors
  A & BBB & C\\ A & B & C\\
\end{tabular}
```

The following example shows an application of the simple colour commands for rows, columns, and cells. As the individual cells only contain mathematical content, we have used an array environment.

```
\usepackage[table]{xcolor} \definecolor{umbra}{rgb}{0.8,0.8,0.5}
\newcommand*\zero{\multicolumn{1}{>{\columncolor{white}}c}{0}}
\newcommand*\colCell[2]{\multicolumn{1}{>{\columncolor{#1}}c}{#2}}

\[ \left[\,
\begin{array}{*{5}{>{\columncolor[gray]{0.95}}c}}
  h_{k,1,0}(n) & h_{k,1,1}(n) & h_{k,1,2}(n) & \zero & \zero \\
  h_{k,2,0}(n) & h_{k,2,1}(n) & h_{k,2,2}(n) & \zero & \zero \\
  h_{k,3,0}(n) & h_{k,3,1}(n) & h_{k,3,2}(n) & \zero & \zero \\
  h_{k,4,0}(n) & \colCell{umbra}{h_{k,4,1}(n)} & h_{k,4,2}(n) & \zero & \zero \\
  \zero & h_{k,1,0}(n-1) & h_{k,1,1}(n-1) & h_{k,1,2}(n-1) & \zero \\
  \zero & h_{k,2,0}(n-1) & h_{k,2,1}(n-1) & h_{k,2,2}(n-1) & \zero \\
  \zero & h_{k,3,0}(n-1) & h_{k,3,1}(n-1) & h_{k,3,2}(n-1) & \zero \\
  \zero & \colCell{umbra}{h_{k,4,0}(n-1)} & h_{k,4,1}(n-1) & h_{k,4,2}(n-1) & \zero \\
  \zero & \zero & h_{k,1,0}(n-2) & h_{k,1,1}(n-2) & h_{k,1,2}(n-2)\\
  \rowcolor[gray]{0.75}\zero&\zero& h_{k,2,0}(n-2) & h_{k,2,1}(n-2) & h_{k,2,2}(n-2)\\
  \zero & \zero & h_{k,3,0}(n-2) & h_{k,3,1}(n-2) & h_{k,3,2}(n-2)\\
  \zero & \zero & h_{k,4,0}(n-2) & h_{k,4,1}(n-2) & h_{k,4,2}(n-2)
\end{array} \,\right]_{12\times 5} \]
```

03-02-3

$$\left[\,\begin{array}{ccccc}
h_{k,1,0}(n) & h_{k,1,1}(n) & h_{k,1,2}(n) & 0 & 0 \\
h_{k,2,0}(n) & h_{k,2,1}(n) & h_{k,2,2}(n) & 0 & 0 \\
h_{k,3,0}(n) & h_{k,3,1}(n) & h_{k,3,2}(n) & 0 & 0 \\
h_{k,4,0}(n) & h_{k,4,1}(n) & h_{k,4,2}(n) & 0 & 0 \\
0 & h_{k,1,0}(n-1) & h_{k,1,1}(n-1) & h_{k,1,2}(n-1) & 0 \\
0 & h_{k,2,0}(n-1) & h_{k,2,1}(n-1) & h_{k,2,2}(n-1) & 0 \\
0 & h_{k,3,0}(n-1) & h_{k,3,1}(n-1) & h_{k,3,2}(n-1) & 0 \\
0 & h_{k,4,0}(n-1) & h_{k,4,1}(n-1) & h_{k,4,2}(n-1) & 0 \\
0 & 0 & h_{k,1,0}(n-2) & h_{k,1,1}(n-2) & h_{k,1,2}(n-2) \\
0 & 0 & h_{k,2,0}(n-2) & h_{k,2,1}(n-2) & h_{k,2,2}(n-2) \\
0 & 0 & h_{k,3,0}(n-2) & h_{k,3,1}(n-2) & h_{k,3,2}(n-2) \\
0 & 0 & h_{k,4,0}(n-2) & h_{k,4,1}(n-2) & h_{k,4,2}(n-2)
\end{array}\,\right]_{12\times 5}$$

For an alternating colouring of the rows, you must call the \rowcolors command *before* the table, with the appropriate arguments.

```
\usepackage[table]{xcolor} \definecolor{umbra}{rgb}{0.8,0.8,0.5}
\newcommand*\zero{\multicolumn{1}{>{\columncolor{white}}c}{0}}

\[ \left[\, \rowcolors{1}{umbra}{blue!10}
\begin{array}{*{5}{c}}
  h_{k,1,0}(n) & h_{k,1,1}(n) & h_{k,1,2}(n) & \zero & \zero\\
  h_{k,2,0}(n) & h_{k,2,1}(n) & h_{k,2,2}(n) & \zero & \zero\\
  h_{k,3,0}(n) & h_{k,3,1}(n) & h_{k,3,2}(n) & \zero & \zero\\
  h_{k,4,0}(n) & h_{k,4,1}(n) & h_{k,4,2}(n) & \zero & \zero\\
  \zero & h_{k,1,0}(n-1) & h_{k,1,1}(n-1) & h_{k,1,2}(n-1) & \zero\\
  \zero & h_{k,2,0}(n-1) & h_{k,2,1}(n-1) & h_{k,2,2}(n-1) & \zero\\
  \zero & h_{k,3,0}(n-1) & h_{k,3,1}(n-1) & h_{k,3,2}(n-1) & \zero\\
```

```
  \zero & h_{k,4,0}(n-1) & h_{k,4,1}(n-1) & h_{k,4,2}(n-1) & \zero\\
  \zero & \zero & h_{k,1,0}(n-2) & h_{k,1,1}(n-2) & h_{k,1,2}(n-2)\\
  \zero & \zero & h_{k,2,0}(n-2) & h_{k,2,1}(n-2) & h_{k,2,2}(n-2)\\
  \zero & \zero & h_{k,3,0}(n-2) & h_{k,3,1}(n-2) & h_{k,3,2}(n-2)\\
  \zero & \zero & h_{k,4,0}(n-2) & h_{k,4,1}(n-2) & h_{k,4,2}(n-2)
\end{array} \,\right]_{12\times 5} \]
```

$$\left[\begin{array}{ccccc}
h_{k,1,0}(n) & h_{k,1,1}(n) & h_{k,1,2}(n) & 0 & 0\\
h_{k,2,0}(n) & h_{k,2,1}(n) & h_{k,2,2}(n) & 0 & 0\\
h_{k,3,0}(n) & h_{k,3,1}(n) & h_{k,3,2}(n) & 0 & 0\\
h_{k,4,0}(n) & h_{k,4,1}(n) & h_{k,4,2}(n) & 0 & 0\\
0 & h_{k,1,0}(n-1) & h_{k,1,1}(n-1) & h_{k,1,2}(n-1) & 0\\
0 & h_{k,2,0}(n-1) & h_{k,2,1}(n-1) & h_{k,2,2}(n-1) & 0\\
0 & h_{k,3,0}(n-1) & h_{k,3,1}(n-1) & h_{k,3,2}(n-1) & 0\\
0 & h_{k,4,0}(n-1) & h_{k,4,1}(n-1) & h_{k,4,2}(n-1) & 0\\
0 & 0 & h_{k,1,0}(n-2) & h_{k,1,1}(n-2) & h_{k,1,2}(n-2)\\
0 & 0 & h_{k,2,0}(n-2) & h_{k,2,1}(n-2) & h_{k,2,2}(n-2)\\
0 & 0 & h_{k,3,0}(n-2) & h_{k,3,1}(n-2) & h_{k,3,2}(n-2)\\
0 & 0 & h_{k,4,0}(n-2) & h_{k,4,1}(n-2) & h_{k,4,2}(n-2)
\end{array}\right]_{12\times 5}$$

03-02-4

The following two examples show again the use of the \rowcolors command and also the meaning of the starred version. They also demonstrate the use of the rownum counter, which saves the number of the respective row internally. The rows 8-10 are not coloured; \hiderowcolors and \showrowcolors were used here. The \multicolumn command can also be used to prevent colouring of individual cells. The \arrayrulecolor command from colortbl changes the colour of the lines at any time in the table. We defined the \No command in the examples to save space; the first row of the table uses the substitution \number\rownum for comparison purposes.

column 1	row 1
column 1	row 2
column 1	row 3
column 1	row 4
column 1	row 5
column 1	row 6
column 1	row 7
column 1	row 8
column 1	row 9
column 1	row 10
column 1	row 11
column 1	row 12
column 1	row 13

```
\usepackage[table]{xcolor}

\rowcolors[\hline]{3}{green!25}{yellow!50}
\arrayrulecolor{red!75!gray}\newcommand*\No{\number\rownum}
\begin{tabular}{ll}
 column 1 & row \number\rownum\\
 column 1 & row \No\\ column 1 & row \No\\
 column 1 & row \No\\\arrayrulecolor{black}
 column 1 & row \No\\ column 1 & row \No\\
 \rowcolor{blue!25} column 1 & row \No\\
\hiderowcolors% prevent colouring
 column 1 & row \No\\ column 1 & row \No\\
 column 1 & row \No\\
\showrowcolors% colouring: activate!
 column 1 & row \No\\ column 1 & row \No\\
\multicolumn{1}{>{\columncolor{red!40}}l}{column 1}
   & row \number\rownum\\
\end{tabular}
```

03-02-5

The use of the starred version of \rowcolors now discards the optional argument if the respective row is before the start row of \rowcolors or between \hiderowcolors and \showrowcolors. Without the starred version, the optional argument is considered for *every* row.

03-02-6

column 1	row 1
column 1	row 2
column 1	row 3
column 1	row 4
column 1	row 5
column 1	row 6
column 1	row 7
column 1	row 8
column 1	row 9
column 1	row 10
column 1	row 11
column 1	row 12
column 1	row 13

```
\usepackage[table]{xcolor}
\newcommand*\No{\number\rownum}

\rowcolors*[\hline]{3}{green!25}{yellow!50}
\arrayrulecolor{red!75!gray}
\begin{tabular}{ll}
 column 1 & row \number\rownum\\
 column 1 & row \No\\ column 1 & row \No\\
 column 1 & row \No\\\arrayrulecolor{black}
 column 1 & row \No\\ column 1 & row \No\\
 \rowcolor{blue!25}
 column 1 & row \No\\ column 1 & row \No\\
 \hiderowcolors
 column 1 & row \No\\ column 1 & row \No\\
 \showrowcolors
 column 1 & row \No\\ column 1 & row \No\\
 \multicolumn{1}{>{\columncolor{red!40}}l}{column 1}
    & row \No\\
\end{tabular}
```

For colouring rows, you can also use colour series. They can be defined through the \definecolorseries command and incremented through the \rowcolors command and the argument {*CS!!+*}. Further information can be found in the manual of the xcolor package. [29]

03-02-7

1
2
3
4
5
6
7
8
9
10
11
12
13

```
\usepackage[table]{xcolor}
\usepackage{array}
\newcommand*\No{\makebox[1cm]{%
  \textcolor{CL!!+}{\number\rownum}}}

\definecolorseries{CS}{rgb}{last}{yellow}{blue}
\definecolorseries{CL}{rgb}{last}{blue}{yellow}
\resetcolorseries[13]{CS}
\resetcolorseries[13]{CL}
\rowcolors[\hline]{1}{CS!!+}{CS!!+}
\begin{tabular}{c}
\No\\ \No\\ \No\\ \No\\ \No\\
\No\\ \No\\ \No\\ \No\\ \No\\
\No\\ \No\\ \No
\end{tabular}
```

3.3 TEXnicalities

The colortbl package provides the \arrayrulecolor{*colour*} command; its effect is global. Each change of the line colour therefore affects all following line commands, regardless of whether \arrayrulecolor is called locally within a group. The second line typeset with \hline in the following example is therefore red, as the first \Chline command changed the colour globally.

Egypt	30.06.1995
Albania	08.09.2000
Angola	23.11.1996
Argentina	01.01.1995
Antilles	21.01.1996

03-03-1

```
\usepackage[table]{xcolor}
\newcommand\Chline[1]{\arrayrulecolor{#1}\hline}

\begin{tabular}{@{}ll@{}}\\\hline
Egypt     & 30.06.1995 \\\Chline{red}
Albania   & 08.09.2000 \\\hline
Angola    & 23.11.1996 \\\Chline{blue}
Argentina & 01.01.1995 \\\Chline{red!40}
Antilles  & 21.01.1996 \\\hline\hline
\end{tabular}
```

However, we can define the new command to reset the colour to the default value (black) so that changes are not global anymore, as in the following example:

marching band	AN	9.80
presentation	AN	8.66
commity	AN	13.31

03-03-2

```
\usepackage[table]{xcolor}
\newcommand\Chline[1]{\arrayrulecolor{#1}%
  \hline\arrayrulecolor{black}}
\newcommand\Ccline[2]{\arrayrulecolor{#1}%
  \cline{#2}\arrayrulecolor{black}}

\begin{tabular}{l r r}\\\Chline{blue}
marching band & AN & 9.80\\\hline
presentation  & AN & 8.66\\\Ccline{red}{1-2}
commity       & AN & 13.31\\\Ccline{blue}{2-3}
\end{tabular}
```

beamer When using the beamer class, you must pass the option table to the xcolor package, which is loaded by beamer by default, either through the class option of the document class or with the \PassOptionsToPackage command before loading the document class.

```
\documentclass[xcolor=table]{beamer}
\usetheme{Malmoe} \useoutertheme{sidebar} \usecolortheme{dove}
\newcommand\Chline[1]{\arrayrulecolor{#1}\hline\arrayrulecolor{black}}

\begin{frame}{Example}{Coloured lines}
\begin{center}\Large
\begin{tabular}{l >{\columncolor{red!30}}r r}\\\Chline{blue}
\rowcolor{magenta!40} \emph{Name} & \emph{Type} & \emph{Value}\\\Chline{blue}
marching band & AN & 9.80\\\Chline{red}  presentation & AN & 8.66\\\Chline{green}
commity       & AN &13.31\\\Chline{blue} food         & AN &11.01\\\hline
\end{tabular}
\end{center}
\end{frame}
```

03-03-3

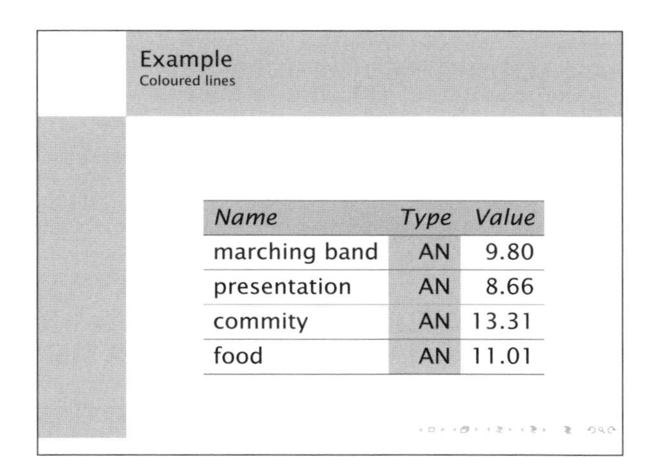

Name	Type	Value
marching band	AN	9.80
presentation	AN	8.66
commity	AN	13.31
food	AN	11.01

The following example shows the relations between the RGB and CMYK notation and the German so-called traffic colours, which are used for the traffic signs.

```
\usepackage[table]{xcolor}\usepackage{ragged2e}% see preamble -> CTAN!
```

```
\begin{tabular}{>{\Centering}p{1.75cm}>{\columnncolor{cyan}}c>{\columnncolor{magenta}}c
    >{\columnncolor{yellow}}c>{\columnncolor{black}}c >{\Centering}p{2.5cm}
>{\columnncolor{red}}c>{\columnncolor{green}}c>{\columnncolor{blue}}c >{\Centering}p{1.75cm}}
CMYK & C & M & Y & \color{white}K & name & R & G & \color{white}B & RGB\\\hline
\TZeile{RAL1023}{0}{10}{90}{0}{traffic yellow}{100}{90}{10} & \cellcolor[rgb]{1,0.9,0.1}\\
\TZeile{RAL2009}{5}{70}{100}{0}{traffic orange}{95}{30}{0} & \cellcolor[rgb]{0.95,0.3,0}\\
\TZeile{RAL3020}{0}{100}{100}{10}{traffic red}{90}{0}{0} & \cellcolor[rgb]{0.9,0,0}\\
\TZeile{RAL4006}{50}{100}{0}{10}{traffic purple}{40}{0}{90} & \cellcolor[rgb]{0.4,0,0.9}\\
\TZeile{RAL5017}{100}{20}{5}{40}{traffic blue}{0}{40}{55} & \cellcolor[rgb]{0,0.4,0.55}\\
\TZeile{RAL6024}{90}{10}{80}{10}{traffic green}{0}{80}{10} & \cellcolor[rgb]{0,0.8,0.1}\\
\TZeile{RAL7042}{30}{10}{20}{40}{traffic grey A}{30}{50}{40} & \cellcolor[rgb]{0.3,0.5,0.4}\\
\TZeile{RAL7043}{30}{10}{20}{80}{traffic grey B}{0}{10}{0} & \cellcolor[rgb]{0,0.1,0}\\
\TZeile{RAL9016}{3}{0}{0}{0}{traffic white}{97}{100}{100} & \cellcolor[rgb]{0.97,1,1}\\
\TZeile{RAL9017}{100}{90}{100}{95}{traffic black}{0}{0}{0} & \cellcolor[rgb]{0,0,0}
\end{tabular}
```

03-03-4

CMYK	C	M	Y	K	name	R	G	B	RGB
	0	10	90	0	RAL1023 traffic yellow	100	90	10	
	5	70	100	0	RAL2009 traffic orange	95	30	0	
	0	100	100	10	RAL3020 traffic red	90	0	0	
	50	100	0	10	RAL4006 traffic purple	40	0	90	
	100	20	5	40	RAL5017 traffic blue	0	40	55	
	90	10	80	10	RAL6024 traffic green	0	80	10	
	30	10	20	40	RAL7042 traffic grey A	30	50	40	
	30	10	20	80	RAL7043 traffic grey B	0	10	0	
	3	0	0	0	RAL9016 traffic white	97	100	100	
	100	90	100	95	RAL9017 traffic black	0	0	0	

```
\usepackage{array,booktabs,ragged2e}
\usepackage[table]{xcolor}      \definecolor{gold}{rgb}{.99,1,.9}
\definecolor{lgrey}{gray}{.95} \definecolor{lblue}{rgb}{.92,.97,1}
\newcolumntype{C}[1]{>{\columncolor{#1}[0pt][\tabcolsep]\Centering$}c<{$}}
\newcolumntype{M}[2]{>{\columncolor{#1}[2\tabcolsep][0pt]\Centering$}m{#2}<{$}}

\begin{tabular}{@{}C{yellow!40}*{10}{>{$}m{12pt}<{$}}M{lgrey}{14pt}M{lgrey}{12pt}@{}}\toprule
\rowcolor{blue!40}Tabelle&\mathsf{1}&\mathsf{2}&\mathsf{3}&\mathsf{4}&\mathsf{5}&\mathsf{6}
  &\mathsf{7} &\mathsf{8}&\mathsf{9}&\mathsf{10}&Y_{t}  &Z_{t}\\\midrule
0 &\circ&\circ&\circ&\circ&\circ  &\circ  &\circ&\ast   &\circ  &\circ&1&\mbox{---} \\
1 &\circ&\circ&\circ&\circ&\circ  &\circ  &\circ&\dagger&\ast   &\circ&1&1\\
2 &\circ&\circ&\circ&\circ&\ast   &\ast   &\circ&\dagger&\dagger&\circ&2&2\\
3 &\circ&\circ&\circ&\circ&\dagger&\ast   &\circ&\dagger&\dagger&\circ&1&0\\
4 &\circ&\circ&\circ&\circ&\dagger&\dagger&\circ&\dagger&\dagger&\circ&0&0\\\bottomrule
\end{tabular}
```

Tabelle	1	2	3	4	5	6	7	8	9	10	Y_t	Z_t
0	$\circ$	$\circ$	$\circ$	$\circ$	$\circ$	$\circ$	$\circ$	$\ast$	$\circ$	$\circ$	1	—
1	$\circ$	$\circ$	$\circ$	$\circ$	$\circ$	$\circ$	$\circ$	$\dagger$	$\ast$	$\circ$	1	1
2	$\circ$	$\circ$	$\circ$	$\circ$	$\ast$	$\ast$	$\circ$	$\dagger$	$\dagger$	$\circ$	2	2
3	$\circ$	$\circ$	$\circ$	$\circ$	$\dagger$	$\ast$	$\circ$	$\dagger$	$\dagger$	$\circ$	1	0
4	$\circ$	$\circ$	$\circ$	$\circ$	$\dagger$	$\dagger$	$\circ$	$\dagger$	$\dagger$	$\circ$	0	0

03-03-5

When using the booktabs package, it's also easy to create coloured lines:

```
\usepackage[table]{xcolor}
\usepackage{booktabs} \arrayrulecolor{red}

\begin{tabular}{@{}llr@{}}\toprule
\multicolumn{2}{c}{Item}\\\cmidrule(r){1-2}\morecmidrules\cmidrule(r){1-2}
Animal & Description & Price (\$)\\\arrayrulecolor{blue}\cmidrule(r){1-1}
        \cmidrule[2pt](l{1em}r{1em}){2-2}\cmidrule(l){3-3}
Gnat   & per gram    & 13.65 \\              & each      &  0.01 \\\addlinespace[2ex]
Gnu    & stuffed     & 92.50 \\\midrule  Emu & stuffed   & 33.33 \\\specialrule{2pt}{1ex}{1ex}
Armadillo & frozen &  8.99 \\\arrayrulecolor{green}\bottomrule
\end{tabular}
```

Item		
Animal	Description	Price ($)
Gnat	per gram	13.65
	each	0.01
Gnu	stuffed	92.50
Emu	stuffed	33.33
Armadillo	frozen	8.99

03-03-6

Chapter 4

Multi-page tables

Multi-page tables have to be handled differently. They can't be part of a floating environment because these don't allow page breaks but, on the other hand, multi-page tables also contain captions that are typeset differently to the ones in the standard LaTeX `table` environment. This chapter looks at some of the packages that can handle multi-page tables. There is no single, best package for longer tables, but `longtable` is the most popular as it is easy to use.

4.1 longtable

The `longtable` package offers many possibilities for creating tables spanning several pages. The syntax corresponding to the normal `tabular` environment is the easiest case:

```
\begin{longtable}[HPos]{column definition}
...&...&...\\
...&...&...
\end{longtable}
```

Specification of an optional argument for vertical alignment within a line doesn't make sense for `longtable` as it is *always* typeset as a separate paragraph. So in contrast to the `tabular` environment, only the horizontal alignment is important: the possible values for *HPos* are `l`, `c` (default), and `r`.

left centred right

left	centred	right	box
l	c	r	p{1.7cm}

left	centred	right	box
l	c	r	p{1.7cm}

left	centred	right	box
l	c	r	p{1.7cm}

```
\usepackage{longtable}

left \hfill centred \hfill right

\begin{longtable}{|l|c|r|p{1.7cm}|}\hline
left & centred & right & box\\\hline
l & c & r & p\{1.7cm\}\\\hline
\end{longtable}
% right-aligned
\begin{longtable}[r]{|l|c|r|p{1.7cm}|}\hline
left & centred & right & box\\\hline
l & c & r & p\{1.7cm\}\\\hline
\end{longtable}
% left-aligned
\begin{longtable}[l]{|l|c|r|p{1.7cm}|}\hline
left & centred & right & box\\\hline
l & c & r & p\{1.7cm\}\\\hline
\end{longtable}
```

04-01-1

4.1.1 Page break

automatic page break

A page break for `longtable` is by definition only possible *after* a table row (cf. Example 04-01-2), not within a row. It is either inserted automatically or you can force one by inserting `\newpage` (cf. Example 04-01-5 on page 129). You can also prevent a potential page break at the end of a row by inserting `\\*` or `\nopagebreak`.

The resulting layout can look bad, especially when you have uneven columns or rows, as demonstrated in Example 04-01-2. This table consists of only three rows, but the height of the third row is very large in comparison to the other two. The page break therefore has to be inserted after just two rows because the third (last) row wouldnit fit onto the page. In such extreme cases, only manual intervention helps. In this example, a page break after the last but five line of *text* or thereabouts within the third *table* row would make sense. In principle, you could terminate the table row here and start a new one, so that a page break would be inserted inbetween; however, then the last line of the third row would not be justified, as shown in Example 04-01-3 on the facing page.

```
\usepackage{array,longtable}

\begin{longtable}{@{} l c r p{2.5cm} @{}}
l & c & r & 1st row\\\hline
l & c & r & 2nd row\\\hline
l & c & r & A row with a lot of text that results in a page break after just the
    second table row because the text included in the third line is too
    high to fit on the first page. Pagebreaks are only possible between
    table lines and not inside a cell \ldots
\end{longtable}
```

04-01-2

Page break demo

l	c	r	1st row
l	c	r	2nd row

page 1

Page break demo

l	c	r	A row with a lot of text that results in a page break after just the second table row because the text included in the third line is too high to fit on the first page. Pagebreaks are only possible between table lines and not inside a cell ...

page 2

```
\usepackage{array,longtable}

\begin{longtable}{@{}l c r p{2.5cm}@{}}
l & c & r & 1st row\\\hline  l & c & r & 2nd row\\\hline
l & c & r & A row with a lot of text that results in a page break after just the
    second table row because the text included in the third line is too
    high to fit on the first page.\\% inserted
 & & & Pagebreaks are only possible between table lines and not inside a cell \ldots
\end{longtable}
```

04-01-3

Page break demo

l	c	r	1st row
l	c	r	2nd row
l	c	r	A row with a lot of text that results in a page break after just the second table row because the text included in the third line is too high to fit on the first page.

page 1

Page break demo

Pagebreaks are only possible between table lines and not inside a cell ...

page 2

So the last row of text on the first page doesn't appear to have been filled correctly before the page break, due to the manual insertion of a new row to allow the page break. However, there is a small trick with which we can stretch the last row so that manual breaks remain invisible in the output.

```
\newcommand\NewLine{\setlength\parfillskip{0pt}\tabularnewline}}
```

The \NewLine command sets the \parfillskip length to 0 pt before the end of the row of the table so that the final cell's paragraph is not filled with whitespace and appears left and right justified. There is no difference now to the table without this manual page break in the output. The change is made within the table cell, which therefore doesn't overwrite other definitions; all table cells are put into a group such that all changes remain local. If two or more columns have long text in the last row, requiring two or more cells to be split across the page break, you must insert the \NewLine command for each column/cell that needs the last line of its paragraph justified.

```
\usepackage{array,longtable}
\newcommand\NewLine{\setlength\parfillskip{0pt}\tabularnewline}

\begin{longtable}{@{} l c r p{2.5cm} @{}}
l & c & r & 1st row\\\hline
l & c & r & 2nd row\\\hline
l & c & r & A row with a lot of text that results in a page break after just the
    second table row because the text included in the third line is too
    high to fit on the first page.\NewLine% inserted
  &   &   & Pagebreaks are only possible between complete
    table lines and not inside a cell \ldots
\end{longtable}
```

Page break demo

l	c	r	1st row
l	c	r	2nd row
l	c	r	A row with a lot of text that results in a page break after just the second table row because the text included in the third line is too high to fit on the first page.

page 1

Page break demo

			Pagebreaks are only possible between complete table lines and not inside a cell ...

page 2

04-01-4

After a table row, you can use the normal \newpage command at any time to force a page break: \newpage

```
\usepackage{longtable}

\begin{longtable}{@{}l c r p{1.5cm}@{}}
L & C & R & box\\\hline
l & c & r & 1st row\\ l & c & r & 2nd row\\ l & c & r & 3rd row\\
l & c & r & 4th row\\ l & c & r & 5th row\\ l & c & r & 6th row\\
\newpage
l & c & r & 7th row\\ l & c & r & 8th row\\ l & c & r & 9th row\\
l & c & r &10th row\\ l & c & r &11th row\\ l & c & r &12th row
\end{longtable}
```

04-01-5

newpage demo

L	C	R	box
l	c	r	1st row
l	c	r	2nd row
l	c	r	3rd row
l	c	r	4th row
l	c	r	5th row
l	c	r	6th row

page 1

newpage demo

l	c	r	7th row
l	c	r	8th row
l	c	r	9th row
l	c	r	10th row
l	c	r	11th row
l	c	r	12th row

page 2

4.1.2 Horizontal and vertical spacing

Table 4.1 on the next page shows a summary of the length parameters that can be used to change the horizontal and vertical spacing of a `longtable`. The defaults depend both on the package, and also on the used document class, which may define custom values. The values given in the table are the ones that are generally valid, where `\bigskipamount` is equal to `12.0pt plus 4.0pt minus 4.0pt` and `\fill` is equal to `0.0pt plus 1.0fill` here. It is important to assign a dynamic length to at least one of the horizontal or vertical spacings so that the table can be typeset correctly within the text.

We recommend that you only set the horizontal spacings manually if none of the options seem sensible – they are equivalent to the values shown in Table 4.2 on the following page. \LTleft \LTright

The arrangement demonstrated here only works as long as the width of the table is not larger than the width of the current text line. For wider tables, it has to be saved first into a

Table 4.1: The horizontal and vertical margin lengths of a longtable.

name	*description*	*default*
\LTleft	space between the table and the left text area	\fill
\LTright	space between the table and the right text area	\fill
\LTpre	space between the table and the upper text area	\bigskipamount
\LTpost	space between the table and the lower text area	\bigskipamount

box as a default tabular to get the width of the tabular with \wd\myTabBox. This length can then be used accordingly to set the length \LTleft, defined internally by longtable. The table is left-aligned by default, but this method makes other alignments possible as well (cf. Example 04-01-6).

Table 4.2: Relationship between the optional argument of the longtable environment and the horizontal lengths \LTleft and \LTright.

option value	\LTleft	\LTright
l	0 pt	\fill
c	\fill	\fill
r	\fill	0 pt

left centred right

left	centred	right	box
l	c	r	p{1.5cm}

right-aligned

left	centred	right	box
l	c	r	p{1.5cm}

centred

left	centred	right	box
l	c	r	p{1.5cm}

```
\usepackage{longtable,calc}

left \hfill centred \hfill right
\setlength\LTleft{0pt}
\begin{longtable}{|l|c|r|p{1.5cm}|}\hline
left & centred & right & box\\\hline
l & c & r & p\{1.5cm\}\\\hline
\end{longtable}
\setlength\LTleft{\fill}\setlength\LTright{0pt}
\hfill right-aligned
\begin{longtable}{|l|c|r|p{1.5cm}|}\hline
left & centred & right & box\\\hline
l & c & r & p\{1.5cm\}\\\hline
\end{longtable}
\setlength\LTleft{\fill}\setlength\LTright{\fill}
\centerline{centred}
\begin{longtable}{|l|c|r|p{1.5cm}|}\hline
left & centred & right & box\\\hline
l & c & r & p\{1.5cm\}\\\hline
\end{longtable}
```

04-01-6

\LTpre
\LTpost

Usually, you won't need to change the space before and after a longtable; the default of \bigskipamount should be sufficient already. Furthermore, the spacing is not defined to be symmetrical before and after the table, as can be seen from the following example, which means changing the spacing is not as simple as just modifying \LTpre and \LTpost by the same amount. Different values must be chosen, depending on whether the text is typeset with a paragraph indent (\parindent) or a paragraph space (\parskip), and whether with or without table caption. The example shows, for one paragraph spacing, first the default values and then modified values for \LTpre and \LTpost.

04-01-7

A line of text before the table.

left	centred	right	box
l	c	r	p{1.5cm}

A line of text after the table.

A line of text before the table.

left	centred	right	box
l	c	r	p{1.5cm}

A line of text after the table.

```
\usepackage{longtable}

A line of text before the table.
\begin{longtable}{|l|c|r|p{1.5cm}|}\hline
left & centred & right & box\\\hline
l & c & r & p\{1.5cm\}\\\hline
\end{longtable}
A line of text after the table.\par
A line of text before the table.
\setlength\LTpre{0pt}%
\setlength\LTpost{0pt}%
\begin{longtable}{|l|c|r|p{1.5cm}|}\hline
left & centred & right & box\\\hline
l & c & r & p\{1.5cm\}\\\hline
\end{longtable}
A line of text after the table.
```

4.1.3 Headers and footers

The general syntax for a `longtable` environment is somewhat more involved than for a normal table. Captions can be placed above or below the table; for further explanation on captions see Section 4.1.4. Here it is only important to note that depending on the arrangement, you can incorporate these captions in the header or footer so that they would therefore be repeated on every page. All four specifications of `\endfirsthead`, `\endhead`, `\endlastfoot`, and `\endfoot` are optional and the order may be arbitrary: they only have to be given before the table rows.

```
\begin{longtable}[HPos]{column definition}
\caption*[LOT]{text}\\
⟨definitions first table header⟩...
\endfirsthead
⟨definitions other table headers⟩...
\endhead
⟨definitions other table footers⟩...
\endfoot
⟨definitions last table footer⟩...
\endlastfoot
...&...&...\\% the tabular lines
\caption*[LOT]{text}\\
\end{longtable}
```

If the specification of a `\endfirsthead` or `\endlastfoot` is missing, they are automatically assigned with the values of `\endhead` and `\endfoot`. If you only need the table to have a first header row and a last footer row, you don't need to use this extended functionality at all; it can be created with normal table rows.

```
\usepackage{longtable}

\begin{longtable}{@{}l c r p{1.5cm}@{}}
L & C & R & box\\\hline
\endfirsthead
\multicolumn{4}{@{}l}{\small\ldots\emph{continued}}\\\hline L& C& R& box\\\hline
\endhead
\hline
\multicolumn{4}{r@{}}{\small\emph{continued on the next page} \ldots}\\
\endfoot
\hline
\endlastfoot
l & c & r & 1st row\\ l & c & r & 2nd row\\ l & c & r & 3rd row\\
l & c & r & 4th row\\ l & c & r & 5th row\\ l & c & r & 6th row\\
l & c & r & 7th row\\ l & c & r & 8th row\\ l & c & r & 9th row\\
l & c & r &10th row\\ l & c & r &11th row\\ l & c & r &12th row\\
l & c & r &13th row\\ l & c & r &14th row\\ l & c & r &15th row
\end{longtable}
```

04-01-8

Header and footer demo

L	C	R	box
l	c	r	1st row
l	c	r	2nd row
l	c	r	3rd row
l	c	r	4th row
l	c	r	5th row
l	c	r	6th row
l	c	r	7th row
l	c	r	8th row
l	c	r	9th row
l	c	r	10th row
l	c	r	11th row

continued on the next page ...

page 1

Header and footer demo

... continued

L	C	R	box
l	c	r	12th row
l	c	r	13th row
l	c	r	14th row
l	c	r	15th row

page 2

4.1.4 Table captions

The syntax for the `\caption` was given in the `longtable` environment definition on page 131.

- ▷ The starred version suppresses the numbering and therefore an entry in the list of tables (lot).
- ▷ If the optional argument is empty (`\caption[]{...}`), no entry is made into the list of tables (lot).

▷ A single optional argument is added to the list of tables (lot). This is the normal behaviour.

In general, using \caption in conjunction with longtable is equivalent to using \multicolumn, because the table caption is a part of the environment and not a separate paragraph as it would be using the "normal" \caption command. Therefore the line has to be terminated with \\ or \tabularnewline.

```
\usepackage{longtable}

\begin{longtable}{@{}l c r p{1.5cm}@{}}
\caption{table caption}\label{tab:l1}\\
L & C & R & box\\\hline
\endfirsthead
\multicolumn{4}{@{}l}{\small\ldots\emph{continued}}\\\hline
L & C & R & box\\\hline
\endhead
\hline
\multicolumn{4}{r@{}}{\small\emph{continued on the next page} \ldots}\\
\endfoot
\hline
\endlastfoot
l & c & r & 1st row\\ l & c & r & 2nd row\\ l & c & r & 3rd row\\
l & c & r & 4th row\\ l & c & r & 5th row\\ l & c & r & 6th row\\
l & c & r & 7th row\\ l & c & r & 8th row\\ l & c & r & 9th row\\
l & c & r &10th row\\ l & c & r &11th row\\ l & c & r &12th row
\end{longtable}
As shown in Table~\ref{tab:l1}, \ldots
```

04-01-9

\caption demo

Table 1: table caption

L	C	R	box
l	c	r	1st row
l	c	r	2nd row
l	c	r	3rd row
l	c	r	4th row
l	c	r	5th row
l	c	r	6th row
l	c	r	7th row
l	c	r	8th row
l	c	r	9th row

continued on the next page ...

page 1

\caption demo

... continued

L	C	R	box
l	c	r	10th row
l	c	r	11th row
l	c	r	12th row

As shown in Table 1, ...

page 2

As the \caption command is in principle part of the table, it can also be inserted into the header or footer, so that they appear repeatedly without incrementing the internal table counter. In this context it is important that a \label command should only occur once, either in the first header, in the last footer, or alternatively somewhere within the actual table. Otherwise you may get the error message: "multiply defined labels".

\label

```
\usepackage{longtable}

Text without sense before the now inserted \texttt{longtable}.

\begin{longtable}{@{}l c r p{1.5cm}@{}}
L & C & R & box\\\hline
\endfirsthead
\multicolumn{4}{@{}l}{\small\ldots\emph{continued}}\\\hline
L & C & R & box\\\hline
\endhead
\hline
\multicolumn{4}{r@{}}{\small\emph{continued on the next page} \ldots}\\
\caption{table caption}\\
\endfoot
\hline
\\[-2ex]
\caption{table caption}
\endlastfoot
l & c & r & 1st row\\ l & c & r & 2nd row\\ l & c & r & 3rd row\\
l & c & r & 4th row\\ l & c & r & 5th row\\ l & c & r & 6th row\\
l & c & r & 7th row\\ l & c & r & 8th row\\ l & c & r & 9th row\\
l & c & r &10th row\\ l & c & r &11th row\\ l & c & r &12th row\\
\end{longtable}
```

\caption demo

Text without sense before the now inserted longtable.

L	C	R	box
l	c	r	1st row
l	c	r	2nd row
l	c	r	3rd row
l	c	r	4th row
l	c	r	5th row
l	c	r	6th row
l	c	r	7th row

continued on the next page ...

Table 1: table caption

page 1

\caption demo

... *continued*

L	C	R	box
l	c	r	8th row
l	c	r	9th row
l	c	r	10th row
l	c	r	11th row
l	c	r	12th row

Table 1: table caption

page 2

04-01-10

When table captions are set below the table, you can sometimes get differing spaces above the caption if lines are used in one place and not in the other. This was catered for in Example 04-01-10 by inserting a new row for the last table caption and at the same time reducing the space resulting from this by `\\[-2ex]`. You can alter the width of the table caption using the `\LTcapwidth` length. The default is 4 inches, or the width of the enclosing `\parbox`, which is part of the `\multicolumn`:

\LTcapwidth

```
\multicolumn{⟨n⟩}{c}{\parbox{\LTcapwidth}{⟨text⟩}}
```

⟨*n*⟩ is the automatically determined number of columns of the `longtable` and ⟨*text*⟩ is the normal caption.

```
\usepackage{longtable} \setlength\LTcapwidth{1in}% <-- change length

Text without sense before the now inserted \texttt{longtable}.
\begin{longtable}{@{}l c r p{1.5cm}@{}}
L & C & R & box\\\hline
\endfirsthead
\multicolumn{4}{@{}l}{\small\ldots\emph{continued}}\\\hline
L & C & R & box\\\hline
\endhead
\hline
\multicolumn{4}{r@{}}{\small\emph{continued on the next page} \ldots}
\endfoot
\endlastfoot% empty last footer, no line after caption
l & c & r &1st row\\l & c & r & 2nd row\\l & c & r & 3rd row\\l & c & r & 4th row\\
l & c & r &5th row\\l & c & r & 6th row\\l & c & r & 7th row\\l & c & r & 8th row\\
l & c & r &9th row\\l & c & r &10th row\\l & c & r &11th row\\l & c & r &12th row\\\hline
\caption{Table caption with 1\,inch width}\label{tab:14}
\end{longtable}
```

04-01-11

\caption demo

Text without sense before the now inserted `longtable`.

L	C	R	box
l	c	r	1st row
l	c	r	2nd row
l	c	r	3rd row
l	c	r	4th row
l	c	r	5th row
l	c	r	6th row
l	c	r	7th row
l	c	r	8th row

continued on the next page ...

page 1

\caption demo

... continued

L	C	R	box
l	c	r	9th row
l	c	r	10th row
l	c	r	11th row
l	c	r	12th row

Table 1: Table caption with 1 inch width

page 2

```
\usepackage{longtable}
\usepackage[labelfont=bf]{caption}

\setlength\LTcapwidth{2.75cm}% <--- change length
\begin{longtable}{@{}l c r p{1.5cm}@{}}
\caption{Table caption with 2.75\,cm width.\label{tab:14}}\\[5pt]
L & C & R & box\\\hline
l & c & r & 1st row\\ l & c & r & 2nd row\\ l & c & r & 3rd row\\
l & c & r & 4th row\\ l & c & r & 5th row\\ l & c & r & 6th row\\
l & c & r & 7th row\\ l & c & r & 8th row\\ l & c & r & 9th row\\
l & c & r &10th row\\ l & c & r &11th row\\ l & c & r &12th row\\\hline
\end{longtable}
```

\caption demo

Table 1: Table caption with 2.75 cm width.

L	C	R	box
l	c	r	1st row
l	c	r	2nd row
l	c	r	3rd row
l	c	r	4th row
l	c	r	5th row
l	c	r	6th row
l	c	r	7th row
l	c	r	8th row

page 1

\caption demo

l	c	r	9th row
l	c	r	10th row
l	c	r	11th row
l	c	r	12th row

page 2

04-01-12

4.1.5 Footnotes

In a `longtable` environment, you can use the normal `\footnote` command. It also continues the normal footnote counting. If you want a different counting used within the table, you must set the counter before starting the table, for example using `\setcounter`{*footnote*}{*0*} to reset to zero. After the table, you must then set the counter back to the number it had reached if the old counter will be used in the text again. As the footnotes appear at the bottom of the page together with the normal footnotes, changing the counting is not really useful.

```
\usepackage{longtable}

A demo\footnote{line of text} for footnotes.
\begin{longtable}{@{}l c r p{1.5cm}@{}}
L\footnote{caption} & C & R & box\\\hline
l & c\footnote{first row, second column} & r & 1st row
```

```
\\ l & c & r\footnote{second row, third column} & 2nd row\\
l & c & r & 3rd row\\ l & c & r & 4th row\\ l & c & r & 5th row
\\ l & c & r & 6th row\\ l & c & r & 7th row\\
l & c & r & 8th row\footnote{eighth row, last column}\\ l & c & r & 9th row\\
l & c & r &10th row\\ l\footnote{eleventh row, first column} & c & r &11th row\\\hline
\end{longtable}
A demo\footnote{line of text} for footnotes.
```

04-01-13

\caption demo

A demo[1] for footnotes.

L[2]	C	R	box
l	c[3]	r	1st row
l	c	r[4]	2nd row
l	c	r	3rd row
l	c	r	4th row
l	c	r	5th row
l	c	r	6th row

[1]line of text
[2]caption
[3]first row, second column
[4]second row, third column

page 1

\caption demo

l	c	r	7th row
l	c	r	8th row[5]
l	c	r	9th row
l	c	r	10th row
l[6]	c	r	11th row

A demo[7] for footnotes.

[5]eighth row, last column
[6]eleventh row, first column
[7]line of text

page 2

4.1.6 TEXnicalities...

\LTchunksize

To determine the width of the table, the package writes the required information about the individual columns in the .aux file and therefore needs at least two LaTeX runs; an exception is a "short" longtable without a page break. The number of table rows that TeX reads and evaluates to determine the width of the columns at one time is determined by \LTchunksize and defaults to 20. If this value is larger than the number of table rows, TeX needs fewer runs to determine the width. The default value is relatively small, which means that if you set up a large number of individual headers or footers, TeX struggles to compute the table sensibly. On modern computers, the value of \LTchunksize can be increased tenfold without any problems. The following example shows two pages of a table that have been produced after only one LaTeX run. The log file contains a corresponding note:

```
Package longtable Warning: Column widths have changed
(longtable)                in table 1 on input line 39.
Package longtable Warning: Table widths have changed. Rerun LaTeX.
[7] (./3-1-13.aux)
LaTeX Warning: Label(s) may have changed. Rerun to get cross-references right.
```

The .aux file now contains the largest width of each of the individual columns and in which chunk it was found:

```
\gdef \LT@i {\LT@entry
    {2}{17.11958pt}\LT@entry
    {2}{29.75977pt}\LT@entry
    {2}{25.31984pt}\LT@entry
    {1}{48.67912pt}}
```

The largest width of the first three columns was in the second chunk and the width of the fourth column was fixed anyway with p{1.5cm} – its width was determined at the beginning (chunk 1) already. In a consecutive run, LaTeX reads these values and typesets the table, which now has the correct column widths on each page. Only the result after the first run is shown below for space reasons. \LTchunksize was deliberately set to the value 7 to illustrate the effect. The first chunk consists of the table caption and the following six rows. The first three columns in the second chunk are wider; but TeX only notices this after the page break. The table would be typeset correctly after another LaTeX run.

```
\usepackage{longtable} \setcounter{LTchunksize}{7}\setlength\LTcapwidth{2.75cm}
```

```
\begin{longtable}{@{}l c r p{1.5cm}@{}}
\caption{Table caption with 2.75\,cm width.\label{tab:14}}\\[5pt]
L & C & R & box\\\hline  l & c & r & 1st\\ ll & c & r & 2nd\\ l & c & r & 3rd\\
l & c & r & 4th\\ lll & c & rr & 5th\\ l & cc & r & 6th\\ l & c & r & 7th\\
llll & c & rrr & 8th row \\ l & ccc & r & 9th row \\ l & c & r &10th row\\
llll & c & rrrr &11th row\\ l & cccc & r &12th row\\\hline
\end{longtable}
This example was only run once through \LaTeX. This is the reason why the
table isn't typeset correctly.
```

\LTchunksize demo

Table 1: Table caption with 2.75 cm width.

L	C	R	box
l	c	r	1st
ll	c	r	2nd
l	c	r	3rd
l	c	r	4th
lll	c	rr	5th
l	cc	r	6th
l	c	r	7th
llll	c	rrr	8th row

page 1

\LTchunksize demo

l	ccc	r	9th row
l	c	r	10th row
llll	c	rrrr	11th row
l	cccc	r	12th row

This example was only run once through LaTeX. This is the reason why the table isn't typeset correctly.

page 2

04-01-14

You can't use the \nofiles option in conjunction with longtable, as it would prevent the output of the auxiliary files and thus the output of the auxiliary information, which longtable requires for calculating the width of the table. When using the \multicolumn command, several LaTeX runs may be necessary until TeX has determined the correct width. Further information on this can be found in the package documentation. [17]

.aux file

\multicolumn

You can use the \kill command to delete an example row that has been used to determine the table columns. Example rows, discussed in the tabbing environment (cf. Section 1.2 on page 12), can sometimes be helpful when creating centred or right-aligned columns of a fixed width.

```
\usepackage{longtable}

\begin{longtable}{@{}l c r p{1.5cm}@{}}
L & XXXX & right & p \kill
L & C & R & box\\\hline
l & c & r & 1st\\ ll & c & r & 2nd\\ l & c & r & 3rd\\
l & c & r & 4th\\ lll & c & rr & 5th\\ l & cc & r & 6th\\
l & c & r & 7th\\ llll & c & rrr & 8th row\\ l & ccc & r & 9th row\\
l & c & r &10th row\\ llll & c & rrrr &11th row\\ l & cccc & r &12th row\\\hline
\end{longtable}
```

04-01-15

\kill demo

L	C	R	box
l	c	r	1st
ll	c	r	2nd
l	c	r	3rd
l	c	r	4th
lll	c	rr	5th
l	cc	r	6th
l	c	r	7th
llll	c	rrr	8th row
l	ccc	r	9th row
l	c	r	10th row
llll	c	rrrr	11th row

page 1

\kill demo

l	cccc	r	12th row

page 2

4.2 ltablex

The ltablex package by Anil K. Goel extends the tabularx environment with possible page breaks. In contrast to the similar ltxtable package (cf. Section 4.3 on page 141), no external files are required; the table can be used in the usual manner. Captions are possible, too.

```
\begin{tabularx}{table width}{column definition}
\caption * {text}\\
...&...&...\\
...&...&...\\
...\\
\end{tabularx}
```

The package works similarly to the well-known longtable (cf. Section 4.1 on page 125) package, and therefore needs at least two LaTeX runs to determine the correct width of the columns.

```
\usepackage{ltablex}
\usepackage{ragged2e}

\begin{tabularx}{\linewidth}{@{}>{\ttfamily}l>{\RaggedRight}X@{}}
\caption{File extensions.}\\
aux &  (auxiliary) Auxiliary file, contains links etc. \\
bbl &  (bibliography) Auxiliary file, contains the entries for the bibliography.\\
bib &  (bibtex) Contains the literature database.\\
blg &  (bibliography log) Contains the output of a Bib\TeX\ run.\\
cfg &  (config) Configuration file.\\
clo &  (class options) Definitions for the document class and the corresponding
    class options.\\
cls &  (class) Document class file.\\
\end{tabularx}
```

\ltablex demo

Table 1: file extensions

aux	(auxiliary) Auxiliary file, contains links etc.
bbl	(bibliography) Auxiliary file, contains the entries for the bibliography.
bib	(bibtex) Contains the literature database.
blg	(bibliography log) Contains the output of a BibTeX run.

page 1

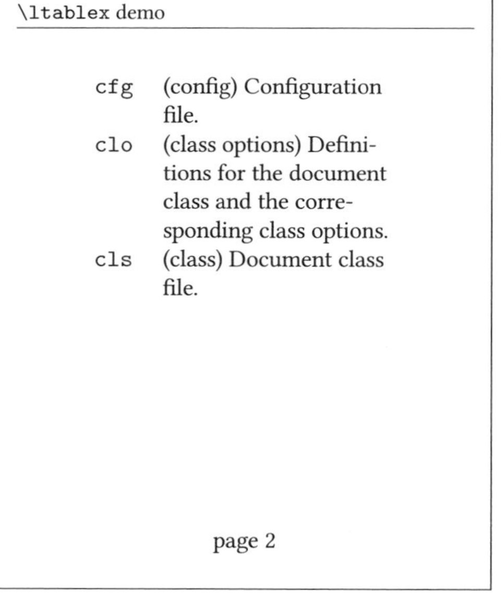

04-02-1

The specification of headers and footers is the same as for the longtable package (cf. Section 4.1.3 on page 131).

```
\usepackage{ltablex,ragged2e}

\begin{tabularx}{\linewidth}{@{}>{\ttfamily}l>{\RaggedRight}X@{}}
\caption*{File extensions.}\\
.ext & description\\\hline
\endfirsthead
\multicolumn{2}{@{}l}{\ldots\ \small continued}\\\hline
.ext & description\\\hline
\endhead
\hline
\multicolumn{2}{r@{}}{\small continued\ldots}\\
\endfoot
\hline
\endlastfoot
aux &  (auxiliary) Auxiliary file, contains links etc. \\
bbl &  (bibliography) Auxiliary file, contains the entries for the bibliography.\\
bib &  (bibtex) Contains the literature database.\\
blg &  (bibliography log) Contains the output of a Bib\TeX\ run.\\
cfg &  (config) Configuration file.\\
clo &  (class options) Definitions for the document class and the corresponding
    class options.\\
\end{tabularx}
```

04-02-2

\ltablex demo

file extensions

.ext	description
aux	(auxiliary) Auxiliary file, contains links etc.
bbl	(bibliography) Auxiliary file, contains the entries for the bibliography.
bib	(bibtex) Contains the literature database.

continued...

page 1

\ltablex demo

... continued

.ext	description
blg	(bibliography log) Contains the output of a BibTeX run.
cfg	(config) Configuration file.
clo	(class options) Definitions for the document class and the corresponding class options.

page 2

4.3 ltxtable

The ltxtable package by David Carlisle unites the features of tabularx and longtable, hence the name of the package. In contrast to those packages, the table has to be saved as an external file; the easiest way to achieve this is through the filecontents environment.

foo bar baz

```
%% LaTeX2e file 'demoFile.tex'
%% generated by the 'filecontents' environment
%% from source '04-03-1' on 2009/12/26.
%%
bar
```

```
\begin{filecontents}{demoFile.tex}
bar
\end{filecontents}
\usepackage{verbatim}
% End Preamble

foo \input{demoFile.tex} baz

\small\verbatiminput{demoFile.tex}
```

04-03-1

```
\begin{filecontents*}{file name}
...
\end{filecontents*}
```

filecontents environment

This is written during the TeX run and can be read back in immediately afterwards. The starred version suppresses the output of commented lines (cf. Example 04-03-1). The filecontents environment may only be used in the preamble and not in the text body and never overwrites existing files. You should also load the filecontents package of the same name; this saves having to delete the external file if the contents change.

You can't use the filecontents environment at the current position in the text; this is a restriction for longer documents – it is harder to keep the overview over the text. If you have several such tables, use separate files and read them through \input{*file*} in the preamble or make a completely separate file without using the filecontents environment.

The syntax of a "tabularx-longtable" is also a combination of the two. The outer form corresponds to tabularx and the inner to longtable. The file is read through the \LTXtable command. In Example 04-03-2, the file is saved as part of the preamble and written to disk during the LaTeX run.

```
\LTXtable{table width}{file name}
```

```
\usepackage{ltxtable,filecontents,ragged2e}
\begin{filecontents}{LTXtab0.tex}
\begin{longtable}{@{}>{\ttfamily}l>{\RaggedRight}X@{}}
\caption{File extensions and their meaning.}\\
aux &  (auxiliary) Auxiliary file, contains links etc. \\
bbl &  (bibliography) Auxiliary file, contains the entries for the bibliography.\\
bib &  (bibtex) Contains the literature database.\\
blg &  (bibliography log) Contains the output of a Bib\TeX\ run.\\
cfg &  (config) Configuration file.\\
clo &  (class options) Definitions for the document class and the corresponding
    class options.\\
cls &  (class) Document class file.\\
\end{longtable}
\end{filecontents}
```

```
\rule{1cm}{0.5pt}\hfill text width\hfill\rule{1cm}{0.5pt}

\LTXtable{\linewidth}{LTXtab0}

\rule{1cm}{0.5pt}\hfill text width\hfill\rule{1cm}{0.5pt}
```

04-03-2

\LTXtable demo

text width

Table 1: File extensions and their meaning.

aux	(auxiliary) Auxiliary file, contains links etc.
bbl	(bibliography) Auxiliary file, contains the entries for the bibliography.
bib	(bibtex) Contains the literature database.

page 1

\LTXtable demo

blg	(bibliography log) Contains the output of a BibTEX run.
cfg	(config) Configuration file.
clo	(class options) Definitions for the document class and the corresponding class options.
cls	(class) Document class file.

text width

page 2

The external file is identical to a `longtable` apart from being able to use the X column type as well. The behaviour of footnotes is significantly different however; they are still possible, but require special attention. *footnote*

- ▷ Within the normal `longtable` environment, the footnote symbols must be set with `\footnotemark` (cf. Example 04-03-3); they are counted as usual. If you want it to start at one in the table, you must reset the footnote counter before the table starts.
- ▷ Outside the table, i.e. *after* inserting it into the text through `\ltablex`, the footnote counter must be decreased by the number of inserted `\footnotemarks`; four in Example 04-03-3 – `\addtocounter{`*footnote*`}{`*-4*`}`.
- ▷ The actual footnotes are specified through `\stepcounter{`*footnote*`}\footnotetext{`*text*`}`.
  The counter must be incremented manually through `\stepcounter`. The number of the footnote could also be specified through the optional argument `\footnotetext` [number] `{`*text*`}`, but this needs to be changed manually every time a new footnote is inserted before the table because the numbering changes.
- ▷ The footnotes always appear *after* the table, i.e. potentially several pages after the corresponding number.

```
\usepackage{ltxtable,filecontents}
\begin{filecontents}{LTXtab1.tex}
\begin{longtable}{@{}>{\ttfamily}l>{\raggedright\arraybackslash}X@{}}
aux \footnotemark&  (auxiliary) Auxiliary file, contains links, refs, etc. \\
bbl \footnotemark&  (bibliography) Auxiliary file, contains the
                    entries for the bibliography.\\
cfg &  (config) Configuration file.\\
clo \footnotemark&  (class options) Definition file for the document class
                    and the corresponding class options.\\
cls \footnotemark&  (class) Document class file, e.g. \texttt{book.cls}.\\
\end{longtable}
\end{filecontents}
\rule{1cm}{0.5pt}\hfill text width\footnote{start}\hfill\rule{1cm}{0.5pt}

\LTXtable{\linewidth}{LTXtab1}
\addtocounter{footnote}{-4}
\stepcounter{footnote}\footnotetext{auxiliary}%
\stepcounter{footnote}\footnotetext{bibliography}
\stepcounter{footnote}\footnotetext{class options}%
\stepcounter{footnote}\footnotetext{class}
\vfill
\rule{1cm}{0.5pt}\hfill text width\footnote{foo}\hfill\rule{1cm}{0.5pt}
```

\footnote demo

text width[1]

aux [2]	(auxiliary) Auxiliary file, contains links, refs, etc.
bbl [3]	(bibliography) Auxiliary file, contains the entries for the bibliography.
cfg	(config) Configuration file.
clo [4]	(class options) Definition file for the document class and the corresponding class options.

[1] start

page 1

\footnote demo

cls [5]	(class) Document class file, e.g. book.cls.

text width[6]

[2] auxiliary
[3] bibliography
[4] class options
[5] class
[6] foo

page 2

04-03-3

4.4 stabular

The `stabular` package by Sigitas Tolušis is part of the `sttools` and extends the internal LaTeX `tabular` and `array` environments so that they may contain a page break. Additionally, two similar environments and two new commands are defined. The two environments have the same syntax as the ones in standard LaTeX, but are prefixed with an "s".

```
\begin{stabular}
...
\end{stabular}
\begin{stabular*}{width}
...
\end{stabular*}
\emptyrow [length]        \tabrow{Text} [height]
```

The `\emptyrow` command creates an empty table row of height zero with optional line feed (vertical space after the row); `\tabrow` creates a row of normal height of the argument, but also with optional line feed. Both commands must be last in a table row; the argument of `\tabrow` is usually only used to determine the height of the respective table row. Line breaks with an optional `\hline` are of course allowed afterwards.

To make the effect of the `\emptyrow` and `\tabrow` commands obvious, both have been used with and without optional line feed in the following example. The non-existent line feed results in row 2 "missing".

04-04-1

1st	table row 1
3rd	table row 3
5th	table row 5
text	
7th	table row 7
text	
9th	table row 9

```
\usepackage{stabular}

\begin{stabular}{lc}\\\hline
1st & table row 1 \\\hline
\emptyrow\hline
3rd & table row 3 \\\hline
\emptyrow[10pt]\hline
5th & table row 5 \\\hline
\tabrow{text}\hline
7th & table row 7 \\\hline
\tabrow{text}[5pt]\hline
9th & table row 9 \\\hline
\end{stabular}
```

```
\usepackage{stabular}

A normal \texttt{stabular} environment, containing a page break, which cannot be
centred.

% the following \texttt{center} environment only demonstrates that it has no
% effect on \texttt{stabular}.
\begin{center}
```

```
\begin{stabular}{@{}p{0.55\linewidth} r@{}}
\emph{country} & \emph{entry}\\\hline
Egypt     & 30.06.1995\\ Albania & 08.09.2000 \\
Angola      & 23.11.1996\\ Antigua and Barbuda& 01.01.1995 \\
Antilles    & 21.01.1996\\ Arab Emirates & 10.04.1996 \\
Argentina & 01.01.1995\\ Armenia & 05.02.2003\\Australia & 01.01.1995\\
Bahrain     & 01.01.1995\\ Bangladesh & 01.01.1995\\Barbados& 01.01.1995\\
Belgium     & 01.01.1995\\ Belize & 01.01.1995 \\
\end{stabular}
\end{center}
```

stabular demo

A normal stabular environment, containing a page break, which cannot be centred.

country	*entry*
Egypt	30.06.1995
Albania	08.09.2000
Angola	23.11.1996
Antigua and Barbuda	01.01.1995
Antilles	21.01.1996
Arab Emirates	10.04.1996
Argentina	01.01.1995
Armenia	05.02.2003
Australia	01.01.1995
Bahrain	01.01.1995

page 1

stabular demo

Bangladesh	01.01.1995
Barbados	01.01.1995
Belgium	01.01.1995
Belize	01.01.1995

page 2

04-04-2

The example clearly shows some advantages and disadvantages of the stabular environment. Its simplicity to use is an advantage: the only difference to the standard LaTeX environment is the "s" prefix. However, being unable to centre the environment and to define intermediate headers and footers are disadvantages. The reason is the internal definition of the environment; it doesn't write its contents into a box to be able to determine the width of the table. This can't be rectified by using a minipage because that may not contain a page break. Through some trial and error and an empty p column, an according left indentation can be achieved, as can be seen in the following example. The first (empty) column is defined by p{1.5em}.

```
\usepackage{stabular}

A normal \texttt{stabular} environment, containing a page break, which cannot be
centred automatically.

\begin{stabular}{@{}p{1.5em}@{} p{0.55\linewidth} r@{}}
```

```
& \emph{country} & \emph{entry}\\\cline{2-3}
& Egypt     & 30.06.1995\\ & Albania & 08.09.2000 \\
& Angola     & 23.11.1996\\ & Antigua and Barbuda& 01.01.1995 \\
& Antilles    & 21.01.1996\\ & Arab Emirates & 10.04.1996 \\
& Argentina & 01.01.1995\\ & Armenia & 05.02.2003\\& Australia & 01.01.1995\\
& Bahrain     & 01.01.1995\\ & Bangladesh & 01.01.1995\\& Barbados& 01.01.1995\\
& Belgium     & 01.01.1995\\ & Belize & 01.01.1995 \\
\end{stabular}
```

04-04-3

stabular demo

A normal stabular environment, containing a page break, which cannot be centred automatically.

country	*entry*
Egypt	30.06.1995
Albania	08.09.2000
Angola	23.11.1996
Antigua and Barbuda	01.01.1995
Antilles	21.01.1996
Arab Emirates	10.04.1996
Argentina	01.01.1995
Armenia	05.02.2003
Australia	01.01.1995
Bahrain	01.01.1995

page 1

stabular demo

Bangladesh	01.01.1995
Barbados	01.01.1995
Belgium	01.01.1995
Belize	01.01.1995

page 2

A table across the whole width of the page is no problem; the stabular* environment is similar to tabular*. However, in these cases it actually makes more sense to use the tabularx environment or the \LTXtable command, as they increase the width of the column while the starred version of stabular just increases the space between two columns (cf. Section 1.1 on page 5).

```
\usepackage{stabular}

A normal \texttt{stabular} environment, containing a page break, which will
extend across the whole width of the page.

\begin{stabular*}{\linewidth}{@{}p{0.55\linewidth} @{\extracolsep{\fill}} r@{}}
\emph{country} & \emph{entry}\\\hline
Egypt     & 30.06.1995\\ Albania & 08.09.2000 \\
Angola     & 23.11.1996\\ Antigua and Barbuda& 01.01.1995 \\
Antilles    & 21.01.1996\\ Arab Emirates & 10.04.1996 \\
Argentina & 01.01.1995\\ Armenia & 05.02.2003\\Australia & 01.01.1995\\
Bahrain     & 01.01.1995\\ Bangladesh & 01.01.1995\\Barbados& 01.01.1995\\
```

```
Belgium     & 01.01.1995\\ Belize & 01.01.1995 \\
\end{stabular*}
```

stabular* demo

A normal stabular environment, containing a page break, which will extend across the whole width of the page.

country	*entry*
Egypt	30.06.1995
Albania	08.09.2000
Angola	23.11.1996
Antigua and Barbuda	01.01.1995
Antilles	21.01.1996
Arab Emirates	10.04.1996
Argentina	01.01.1995
Armenia	05.02.2003
Australia	01.01.1995

page 1

stabular* demo

Bahrain	01.01.1995
Bangladesh	01.01.1995
Barbados	01.01.1995
Belgium	01.01.1995
Belize	01.01.1995

page 2

04-04-4

If, for some reason, you can't use either of the other packages for tables with page breaks, but headers and footers are required on each page, you can insert them *after* typesetting the table. In the example above, "Australia" was in the last row on the first page; therefore it can be replaced by a footer.[1]

```
\usepackage{stabular}

A normal \texttt{stabular} environment, containing a page break, which will
extend across the whole width of the page.

\begin{stabular*}{\linewidth}{@{}p{0.55\linewidth} @{\extracolsep{\fill}} r@{}}
\emph{country} & \emph{entry}\\\hline
Egypt          & 30.06.1995\\ Albania            & 08.09.2000\\
Angola         & 23.11.1996\\ Antigua and Barbuda& 01.01.1995\\
Antilles       & 21.01.1996\\ Arab Emirates      & 10.04.1996\\
Argentina      & 01.01.1995\\ Armenia            & 05.02.2003\\\hline
\multicolumn{2}{r@{}}{\small\emph{continued}\ldots}\\
% page break
\multicolumn{2}{@{}l}{\ldots\small\emph{continued}}\\\hline
Australia      & 01.01.1995\\ Bahrain            & 01.01.1995\\
Bangladesh     & 01.01.1995\\ Barbados           & 01.01.1995\\
Belgium        & 01.01.1995\\ Belize             & 01.01.1995\\
\end{stabular*}
```

[1] Such "handicraft work" should only be done with final versions of a document.

04-04-5

stabular* demo

A normal stabular environment, containing a page break, which will extend across the whole width of the page.

country	*entry*
Egypt	30.06.1995
Albania	08.09.2000
Angola	23.11.1996
Antigua and Barbuda	01.01.1995
Antilles	21.01.1996
Arab Emirates	10.04.1996
Argentina	01.01.1995
Armenia	05.02.2003

continued...

page 1

stabular* demo

... continued

Australia	01.01.1995
Bahrain	01.01.1995
Bangladesh	01.01.1995
Barbados	01.01.1995
Belgium	01.01.1995
Belize	01.01.1995

page 2

4.5 supertabular

The main difference between the supertabular package by Johannes Braams and Theo Jurriens and the longtable package (cf. Section 4.1 on page 125) is the syntax; for a supertabular, all captions, headers, and footers have to be specified *outside* the actual table. supertabular can be loaded with the options listed in Table 4.3.

name	*meaning*
errorshow	Does not write additional information into the log file (default).
pageshow	Outputs information on the determined page breaks.
debugshow	Every row that is output is also added to the log.

Table 4.3: Summary of the package options of supertabular.

The new supertabular and supertabular* environments have the same syntax as the general tabular and tabular* environments. The mpsupertabular and mpsupertabular* environments behave similarly to the environments without the "mp" prefix, which stands for minipage. The "mp" versions have the advantage that footnotes are definitely counted and output page-wise; cf. Section 4.5.4 on page 155.

```
\begin{supertabular}{column definition}
...
\end{supertabular}
\begin{supertabular*}{table width}{column definition}
...
\end{supertabular*}

\begin{mpsupertabular}{column definition}
...
\end{mpsupertabular}
\begin{mpsupertabular*}{table width}{column definition}
...
\end{mpsupertabular*}
```

```
\usepackage[pageshow]{supertabular}

\begin{center}\begin{supertabular}{@{}l r@{}}
\emph{country} & \emph{entry}\\\hline
Egypt              & 30.06.1995 \\ Albania             & 08.09.2000 \\
Angola             & 23.11.1996 \\ Antigua and Barbuda & 01.01.1995 \\
Antilles           & 21.01.1996 \\ Arab Emirates       & 10.04.1996 \\
Argentina          & 01.01.1995 \\ Armenia             & 05.02.2003 \\
Australia          & 01.01.1995 \\ Bahrain             & 01.01.1995 \\
Bangladesh         & 01.01.1995 \\ Barbados            & 01.01.1995 \\
Belgium            & 01.01.1995 \\ Belize              & 01.01.1995 \\
Benin              & 22.02.1996 \\
\end{supertabular}\end{center}
```

supertabular demo

country	*entry*
Egypt	30.06.1995
Albania	08.09.2000
Angola	23.11.1996
Antigua and Barbuda	01.01.1995
Antilles	21.01.1996
Arab Emirates	10.04.1996
Argentina	01.01.1995
Armenia	05.02.2003
Australia	01.01.1995
Bahrain	01.01.1995

page 1

supertabular demo

Bangladesh	01.01.1995
Barbados	01.01.1995
Belgium	01.01.1995
Belize	01.01.1995
Benin	22.02.1996

page 2

04-05-1

The last row of the table *must* be terminated with a line end command, either \\ or \tabularnewline; otherwise TEX will give an error message. The example above already shows a disadvantage of the supertabular environment; the parts of the table can have different widths on different pages. In contrast to the longtable environment, no information is written to the .aux file that could be evaluated for the following pages. To avoid this effect, either insert a header or footer or use the starred version. The starred version has the advantage that the ltxtable package (cf. Section 4.3 on page 141) does not have to be used, but the disadvantage that the corresponding column has to be filled manually (cf. Section 1.1 on page 3). To achieve this, the array package must be loaded in this case because otherwise the column separator ! is unknown and the \extracolsep command can't be used.

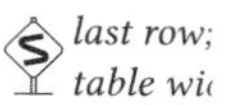


```
\usepackage{array,supertabular}

\begin{supertabular*}{\linewidth}{@{}l!{\extracolsep{\fill}} r@{}}
\emph{country} & \emph{entry}\\\hline
Egypt              & 30.06.1995 \\ Albania             & 08.09.2000 \\
Angola             & 23.11.1996 \\ Antigua and Barbuda & 01.01.1995 \\
Antilles           & 21.01.1996 \\ Arab Emirates       & 10.04.1996 \\
Argentina          & 01.01.1995 \\ Armenia             & 05.02.2003 \\
Australia          & 01.01.1995 \\ Bahrain             & 01.01.1995 \\
Bangladesh         & 01.01.1995 \\ Barbados            & 01.01.1995 \\
Belgium            & 01.01.1995 \\ Belize              & 01.01.1995 \\
Benin              & 22.02.1996 \\
\end{supertabular*}
```

04-05-2

supertabular demo

country	*entry*
Egypt	30.06.1995
Albania	08.09.2000
Angola	23.11.1996
Antigua and Barbuda	01.01.1995
Antilles	21.01.1996
Arab Emirates	10.04.1996
Argentina	01.01.1995
Armenia	05.02.2003
Australia	01.01.1995
Bahrain	01.01.1995

page 1

supertabular demo

Bangladesh	01.01.1995
Barbados	01.01.1995
Belgium	01.01.1995
Belize	01.01.1995
Benin	22.02.1996

page 2

4.5.1 Page break

`supertabular` determines the remaining space on the page after each row and inserts a page break if required. In some cases this is not optimal, however, as shown in the previous examples. You can use the `\shrinkheight` command to increase or decrease the comparison value for the page. The command *must* be at the beginning of a row and may be given arbitrary lengths and units. In the following example, the page is extended by three lines at the beginning of the table (first row) already to achieve a better page break. If this value were further decreased, however, an empty page would occur as TeX would move the block, which would then be too large, to the next page. A positive value assigned to `\shrinkheight` would instead shrink the page so that the page break would occur earlier.

`\shrinkheight{`*length*`}`

```
\usepackage{array,supertabular}

\begin{supertabular*}{\linewidth}{@{}l!{\extracolsep{\fill}} r@{}}
\emph{country} & \emph{entry}\\\hline   \shrinkheight{-3\normalbaselineskip}
Egypt               & 30.06.1995 \\ Albania              & 08.09.2000 \\
Angola              & 23.11.1996 \\ Antigua and Barbuda  & 01.01.1995 \\
Antilles            & 21.01.1996 \\ Arab Emirates        & 10.04.1996 \\
Argentina           & 01.01.1995 \\ Armenia              & 05.02.2003 \\
Australia           & 01.01.1995 \\ Bahrain              & 01.01.1995 \\
Bangladesh          & 01.01.1995 \\ Barbados             & 01.01.1995 \\
Belgium             & 01.01.1995 \\ Belize               & 01.01.1995 \\
Benin               & 22.02.1996 \\
\end{supertabular*}
```

supertabular demo

country	*entry*
Egypt	30.06.1995
Albania	08.09.2000
Angola	23.11.1996
Antigua and Barbuda	01.01.1995
Antilles	21.01.1996
Arab Emirates	10.04.1996
Argentina	01.01.1995
Armenia	05.02.2003
Australia	01.01.1995
Bahrain	01.01.1995
Bangladesh	01.01.1995
Barbados	01.01.1995
Belgium	01.01.1995

page 1

supertabular demo

Belize	01.01.1995
Benin	22.02.1996

page 2

04-05-3

4.5.2 Headers and footers

All specifications must be done *before* the table itself. The following commands can be used:

`\tablefirsthead{`*definition*`}`	`\tablehead{`*definition*`}`
`\tabletail{`*definition*`}`	`\tablelasttail{`*definition*`}`

All *definitions* must correspond to at least one table row each and may contain a `\hline` in the simplest case. If `\tablefirsthead` or `\tablelasttail` are not defined, they are automatically substituted by `\tablehead` and `\tabletail` respectively.

```
\usepackage{supertabular}

\tablefirsthead{\hline \emph{country} & \emph{entry}\\\hline}
\tablehead{\emph{country} & \emph{entry}\\\hline}
\tabletail{\hline \multicolumn{2}{r@{}}{continued \ldots}\\}
\tablelasttail{\hline}
\begin{center} \begin{supertabular}{@{}p{0.55\linewidth} r@{}}
Egypt            & 30.06.1995 \\ Albania             & 08.09.2000 \\
Angola           & 23.11.1996 \\ Antigua and Barbuda & 01.01.1995 \\
Antilles         & 21.01.1996 \\ Arab Emirates       & 10.04.1996 \\
Argentina        & 01.01.1995 \\ Armenia             & 05.02.2003 \\
Australia        & 01.01.1995 \\ Bahrain             & 01.01.1995 \\
Bangladesh       & 01.01.1995 \\ Barbados            & 01.01.1995 \\
Belgium          & 01.01.1995 \\ Belize              & 01.01.1995 \\
Benin            & 22.02.1996 \\
\end{supertabular} \end{center}
```

04-05-4

supertabular demo

country	*entry*
Egypt	30.06.1995
Albania	08.09.2000
Angola	23.11.1996
Antigua and Barbuda	01.01.1995
Antilles	21.01.1996
Arab Emirates	10.04.1996
Argentina	01.01.1995
Armenia	05.02.2003
Australia	01.01.1995
	continued ...

page 1

supertabular demo

country	*entry*
Bahrain	01.01.1995
Bangladesh	01.01.1995
Barbados	01.01.1995
Belgium	01.01.1995
Belize	01.01.1995
Benin	22.02.1996

page 2

4.5.3 Table captions

There are three different commands to add captions:

\tablecaption [LOT entry] {*text*}   \topcaption [LOT entry] {*text*}
\bottomcaption [LOT entry] {*text*}

The optional argument *LOT entry* replaces the default entry of *text* into the table of contents (.toc) if used. When using \tablecaption, the document class determines the position of the label by specifying either \@topcaptionfalse or \@topcaptiontrue. This specification can be overwritten at any time, however, by using one of the other two commands, which force the caption to be above or below the table, respectively. The caption package also supports the supertabular package.

```
\usepackage{supertabular} \usepackage[labelfont=bf]{caption}

\tablecaption{Demonstration of a table caption.}
\tablefirsthead{\hline \emph{country} & \emph{entry}\\\hline}
\tablehead{\emph{country} & \emph{entry}\\\hline}
\tabletail{\hline \multicolumn{2}{r@{}}{continued \ldots}\\}  \tablelasttail{\hline}
\begin{center}\begin{supertabular}{@{}p{0.55\linewidth} r@{}}
Egypt          & 30.06.1995\\ Albania     & 08.09.2000\\Angola          & 23.11.1996\\
Antigua and Barbuda& 01.01.1995\\Antilles& 21.01.1996\\Arab Emirates & 10.04.1996\\
Argentina      & 01.01.1995\\ Armenia    & 05.02.2003\\Australia       & 01.01.1995\\
Bahrain        & 01.01.1995\\ Bangladesh & 01.01.1995\\Barbados        & 01.01.1995\\
Belgium        & 01.01.1995\\ Belize     & 01.01.1995\\Benin           & 22.02.1996\\
\end{supertabular}\end{center}
```

04-05-5

supertabular demo

Table 1: Demonstration of a table caption.

country	*entry*
Egypt	30.06.1995
Albania	08.09.2000
Angola	23.11.1996
Antigua and Barbuda	01.01.1995
Antilles	21.01.1996
Arab Emirates	10.04.1996
Argentina	01.01.1995

continued ...

page 1

supertabular demo

country	*entry*
Armenia	05.02.2003
Australia	01.01.1995
Bahrain	01.01.1995
Bangladesh	01.01.1995
Barbados	01.01.1995
Belgium	01.01.1995
Belize	01.01.1995
Benin	22.02.1996

page 2

4.5.4 Footnotes

If you use footnotes within the normal supertabular environment, they appear as a symbol in the table, but the text of the footnote is missing. Therefore \footnotemark and \footnotetext have to be used separately again, as shown in Example 04-03-3 on page 143.

```
\usepackage{supertabular}

\tablefirsthead{\hline \emph{country} & \emph{entry}\\\hline}
\tablehead{\emph{country} & \emph{entry}\\\hline}
\tabletail{\hline \multicolumn{2}{r@{}}{continued \ldots}\\}
\tablelasttail{\hline}
Text\footnote{before the text} and footnote.
\begin{center}\begin{supertabular}{@{}p{0.55\linewidth} r@{}}
Egypt\footnotemark  & 30.06.1995 \\ Albania   & 08.09.2000\\Angola  & 23.11.1996\\
Antigua and Barbuda & 01.01.1995 \\ Antilles\footnotemark & 21.01.1996 \\
Arab Emirates       & 10.04.1996 \\ Argentina & 01.01.1995\\Armenia & 05.02.2003\\
Australia           & 01.01.1995 \\ Bahrain   & 01.01.1995 \\
Bangladesh          & 01.01.1995 \\ Barbados  & 01.01.1995 \\
Belgium             & 01.01.1995 \\ Belize\footnotemark & 01.01.1995 \\
\end{supertabular}\addtocounter{footnote}{-3}
\stepcounter{footnote}\footnotetext{first footnote}
\stepcounter{footnote}\footnotetext{second footnote}
\stepcounter{footnote}\footnotetext{third footnote}
\end{center}
Text\footnote{after the text} and footnote.
```

04-05-6

supertabular demo

Text[1] and footnote.

country	*entry*
Egypt[2]	30.06.1995
Albania	08.09.2000
Angola	23.11.1996
Antigua and Barbuda	01.01.1995
Antilles[3]	21.01.1996
Arab Emirates	10.04.1996
Argentina	01.01.1995
Armenia	05.02.2003
	continued ...

[1]before the text

page 1

supertabular demo

country	*entry*
Australia	01.01.1995
Bahrain	01.01.1995
Bangladesh	01.01.1995
Barbados	01.01.1995
Belgium	01.01.1995
Belize[4]	01.01.1995

Text[5] and footnote.

[2]first footnote
[3]second footnote
[4]third footnote
[5]after the text

page 2

This has the disadvantage that the footnotes all appear together after the table, which can be bad for large tables where there are several pages between footnote mark and corresponding text. It is better therefore to use the mpsupertabular environment as long as no other footnotes (apart from the table footnotes) appear on the first or last page of the table. Within the minipage, the footnotes are typeset with a footnote rule immediately after the table and are counted with letters. As can be seen in the following example, this results in a clear differentiation, but the appearance is unsatisfactory. The footnotes immediately before and after the table should be removed.

```
\usepackage{supertabular}

\tablefirsthead{\hline \emph{country} & \emph{entry}\\\hline}
\tablehead{\emph{country} & \emph{entry}\\\hline}
\tabletail{\hline \multicolumn{2}{r@{}}{continued \ldots}\\} \tablelasttail{\hline}
Text\footnote{before the text} and footnote.\par\bigskip
\begin{mpsupertabular}{@{}p{0.55\linewidth} r@{}}
Egypt\footnote{first foonote}& 30.06.1995 \\ Albania  & 08.09.2000 \\
Angola            & 23.11.1996 \\ Antigua and Barbuda & 01.01.1995 \\
Antilles\footnote{second footnote}& 21.01.1996 \\ Arabian Emirates & 10.04.1996 \\
Argentina         & 01.01.1995 \\ Armenia             & 05.02.2003 \\
Australia         & 01.01.1995 \\ Bahrain             & 01.01.1995 \\
Bangladesh        & 01.01.1995 \\ Barbados            & 01.01.1995 \\
Belgium           & 01.01.1995 \\ Belize\footnote{third footnote} & 01.01.1995 \\
\end{mpsupertabular}\par\bigskip
Text\footnote{after the text} and footnote.
```

supertabular demo

Text[1] and footnote.

[1]before the text

page 1

supertabular demo

country	*entry*
Egypt[a]	30.06.1995
Albania	08.09.2000
Angola	23.11.1996
Antigua and Barbuda	01.01.1995
Antilles[b]	21.01.1996
Arabian Emirates	10.04.1996
Argentina	01.01.1995
	continued ...

[a]first foonote
[b]second footnote

page 2

supertabular demo

country	*entry*
Armenia	05.02.2003
Australia	01.01.1995
Bahrain	01.01.1995
Bangladesh	01.01.1995
Barbados	01.01.1995
Belgium	01.01.1995
Belize[a]	01.01.1995

[a]third footnote

Text[2] and footnote.

[2]after the text

page 3

04-05-7

```
\usepackage{supertabular}

\tablefirsthead{\hline \emph{country} & \emph{entry}\\\hline}
\tablehead{\emph{country} & \emph{entry}\\\hline}
\tabletail{\hline \multicolumn{2}{r@{}}{continued \ldots}\\}
\tablelasttail{\hline}
```

```
Text without footnote.\par\medskip
\begin{mpsupertabular*}{\linewidth}{@{}p{0.55\linewidth} @{\extracolsep{\fill}} r@{}}
Egypt\footnote{first footnote} & 30.06.1995 \\ Albania & 08.09.2000 \\
Angola          & 23.11.1996 \\ Antigua and Barbuda& 01.01.1995 \\
Antilles\footnote{second footnote}& 21.01.1996 \\ Arabische Emirate & 10.04.1996 \\
Argentina       & 01.01.1995 \\ Armenia              & 05.02.2003 \\
Australia       & 01.01.1995 \\ Bahrain              & 01.01.1995 \\
Bangladesh      & 01.01.1995 \\ Barbados             & 01.01.1995 \\
Belgium         & 01.01.1995 \\ Belize\footnote{third footnote} & 01.01.1995 \\
\end{mpsupertabular*}\par\medskip
Text without footnote.
```

04-05-8

supertabular demo

Text without footnote.

country	*entry*
Egypt[a]	30.06.1995
Albania	08.09.2000
Angola	23.11.1996
Antigua and Barbuda	01.01.1995
Antilles[b]	21.01.1996
Arabische Emirate	10.04.1996
Argentina	01.01.1995

continued ...

[a]first footnote
[b]second footnote

page 1

supertabular demo

country	*entry*
Armenia	05.02.2003
Australia	01.01.1995
Bahrain	01.01.1995
Bangladesh	01.01.1995
Barbados	01.01.1995
Belgium	01.01.1995
Belize[a]	01.01.1995

[a]third footnote

Text without footnote.

page 2

4.6 xtab

The xtab package by Peter Wilson is an extension of the supertabular package (cf. Section 4.6). It is meant to provide better functionality especially regarding page breaks. The syntax is in principle the same as for the environments from supertabular. The use of the xtabular and xtabular* environments is otherwise completely identical to the usual tabular and tabular* environments. The mpxtabular and mpxtabular* environments are likewise similar to the environments without the mp prefix, which stands for minipage. This has the advantage that footnotes can be counted and output per page, cf. Section 4.5.4 on page 155.

```
\begin{xtabular}{column definition}
...
\end{xtabular}
\begin{xtabular*}{table width}{column definition}
...
\end{xtabular*}
\begin{mpxtabular}{column definition}
...
\end{mpxtabular}
\begin{mpxtabular*}{table width}{column definition}
...
\end{mpxtabular*}
```

```
\usepackage{xtab}

\begin{center}\begin{xtabular}{@{}l r@{}}
\emph{country} & \emph{entry}\\\hline
Egypt          & 30.06.1995\\ Albania    & 08.09.2000\\Angola          & 23.11.1996\\
Antigua and Barbuda & 01.01.1995\\Antilles& 21.01.1996\\Arab Emirates & 10.04.1996\\
Argentina      & 01.01.1995\\ Armenia    & 05.02.2003\\Australia       & 01.01.1995\\
Bahrain        & 01.01.1995\\ Bangladesh & 01.01.1995\\Barbados        & 01.01.1995\\
Belgium        & 01.01.1995\\ Belize     & 01.01.1995\\Benin           & 22.02.1996\\
\end{xtabular}\end{center}
```

xtab demo

country	*entry*
Egypt	30.06.1995
Albania	08.09.2000
Angola	23.11.1996
Antigua and Barbuda	01.01.1995
Antilles	21.01.1996
Arab Emirates	10.04.1996
Argentina	01.01.1995

page 1

xtab demo

Armenia	05.02.2003
Australia	01.01.1995
Bahrain	01.01.1995
Bangladesh	01.01.1995
Barbados	01.01.1995
Belgium	01.01.1995
Belize	01.01.1995
Benin	22.02.1996

page 2

04-06-1

last row
table width

The last row of the table *must* be terminated with a line end command, either `\\` or `\tabularnewline`; otherwise you will get an error message. The example above already shows one of the disadvantages of the `xtab` package; the parts of the table can have different widths on different pages. In contrast to the `longtable` environment, no information is written to the .aux file that could be evaluated for the following pages. To avoid this effect, either insert a header or footer or use the starred version. The starred version has the advantage that the `ltxtable` package (cf. Section 4.3 on page 141) does not have to be used, but the disadvantage that the corresponding column has to be filled manually (cf. Section 1.1 on page 3). To achieve this, the `array` package must be loaded because otherwise the column operator `!` is unknown and the `\extracolsep` command can't be used.

```
\usepackage{array,xtab}

\begin{xtabular*}{\linewidth}{@{}l!{\extracolsep{\fill}} r@{}}
\emph{country} & \emph{entry}\\\hline
Egypt              & 30.06.1995 \\ Albania              & 08.09.2000 \\
Angola             & 23.11.1996 \\ Antigua and Barbuda  & 01.01.1995 \\
Antilles           & 21.01.1996 \\ Arab Emirates        & 10.04.1996 \\
Argentina          & 01.01.1995 \\ Armenia              & 05.02.2003 \\
Australia          & 01.01.1995 \\ Bahrain              & 01.01.1995 \\
Bangladesh         & 01.01.1995 \\ Barbados             & 01.01.1995 \\
Belgium            & 01.01.1995 \\ Belize               & 01.01.1995 \\
Benin              & 22.02.1996 \\
\end{xtabular*}
```

04-06-2

xtabular demo

country	*entry*
Egypt	30.06.1995
Albania	08.09.2000
Angola	23.11.1996
Antigua and Barbuda	01.01.1995
Antilles	21.01.1996
Arab Emirates	10.04.1996
Argentina	01.01.1995

page 1

xtabular demo

Armenia	05.02.2003
Australia	01.01.1995
Bahrain	01.01.1995
Bangladesh	01.01.1995
Barbados	01.01.1995
Belgium	01.01.1995
Belize	01.01.1995
Benin	22.02.1996

page 2

4.6.1 Page break

`xtabular` determines the remaining space on the page after each row and inserts a page break if required. In some cases this is not optimal, however, as shown in the previous example. You can use the `\shrinkheight` command to increase or decrease the comparison value for the page.

`\shrinkheight{`*length*`}`

The command *must* be at the beginning of a row and may be given arbitrary lengths and units. In the following example, the page is extended by three lines at the beginning of the table (first row) already to achieve a better page break. If this value were further decreased, however, an empty page would occur as TeX would move the block, which would then be too large, to the next page. A positive value assigned to `\shrinkheight` would instead shrink the page so that the page break would occur earlier.

```
\usepackage{array,xtab}

\begin{xtabular*}{\linewidth}{@{}l!{\extracolsep{\fill}} r@{}}
\emph{country} & \emph{entry}\\\hline
\shrinkheight{-3.1\normalbaselineskip}
Egypt              & 30.06.1995 \\ Albania              & 08.09.2000 \\
Angola             & 23.11.1996 \\ Antigua and Barbuda  & 01.01.1995 \\
Antilles           & 21.01.1996 \\ Arab Emirates        & 10.04.1996 \\
Argentina          & 01.01.1995 \\ Armenia              & 05.02.2003 \\
Australia          & 01.01.1995 \\ Bahrain              & 01.01.1995 \\
Bangladesh         & 01.01.1995 \\ Barbados             & 01.01.1995 \\
Belgium            & 01.01.1995 \\ Belize               & 01.01.1995 \\
Benin              & 22.02.1996 \\
\end{xtabular*}
```

xtabular demo

country	*entry*
Egypt	30.06.1995
Albania	08.09.2000
Angola	23.11.1996
Antigua and Barbuda	01.01.1995
Antilles	21.01.1996
Arab Emirates	10.04.1996
Argentina	01.01.1995
Armenia	05.02.2003
Australia	01.01.1995

page 1

xtabular demo

Bahrain	01.01.1995
Bangladesh	01.01.1995
Barbados	01.01.1995
Belgium	01.01.1995
Belize	01.01.1995
Benin	22.02.1996

page 2

04-06-3

4.6.2 Headers and footers

All specifications must be done *before* the table itself. The following commands can be used:

\tablefirsthead{*definition*}	\tabletail{*definition*}
\tablehead{*definition*}	\tablelasttail{*definition*}

All *definitions* must correspond to at least one table row each and may contain a \hline in the simplest case. If \tablefirsthead or \tablelasttail are not defined, they are automatically substituted by \tablehead and \tabletail respectively.

```
\usepackage[table]{xcolor} \usepackage{xtab}

\tablefirsthead{\hline \emph{country} & \emph{entry}\\\hline}
\tablehead{\emph{country} & \emph{entry}\\\hline}
\tabletail{\hline \multicolumn{2}{r@{}}{continued \ldots}\\}
\tablelasttail{\hline}
\begin{center}
\begin{xtabular}{@{}p{0.55\linewidth} r@{}}
Egypt                & 30.06.1995 \\ Albania              & 08.09.2000 \\
Angola               & 23.11.1996 \\ Antigua and Barbuda  & 01.01.1995 \\
Antilles             & 21.01.1996 \\ Arab Emirates        & 10.04.1996 \\
Argentina            & 01.01.1995 \\ Armenia              & 05.02.2003 \\
Australia            & 01.01.1995 \\ Bahrain              & 01.01.1995 \\
Bangladesh           & 01.01.1995 \\ Barbados             & 01.01.1995 \\
Belgium              & 01.01.1995 \\ Belize               & 01.01.1995 \\
Benin                & 22.02.1996 \\
\end{xtabular}
\end{center}
```

04-06-4

xtabular demo

country	*entry*
Egypt	30.06.1995
Albania	08.09.2000
Angola	23.11.1996
Antigua and Barbuda	01.01.1995
	continued ...

page 1

xtabular demo

country	*entry*
Antilles	21.01.1996
Arab Emirates	10.04.1996
Argentina	01.01.1995
Armenia	05.02.2003
Australia	01.01.1995
Bahrain	01.01.1995
	continued ...

page 2

4.6.3 Table captions

The `xtab` package also has three different commands to set captions:

```
\tablecaption [LOT entry] {text}        \topcaption [LOT entry] {text}
\bottomcaption [LOT entry] {text}
```

The optional argument *LOT entry* substitutes the default entry of *text* into the table of contents if used. When using `\tablecaption`, the document class determines the position of the label by specifying either `\@topcaptionfalse` or `\@topcaptiontrue`. This specification can be overwritten at any time, however, by using one of the other two commands, which force the caption to be above or below the table, respectively. The `caption` package supports the `xtab` package with all its functionality.

```
\usepackage{xtab}  \usepackage[labelfont=bf]{caption}
```

```
\tablecaption{Demonstration of a table caption.}
\tablefirsthead{\hline \emph{country} & \emph{entry}\\\hline}
\tablehead{\emph{country} & \emph{entry}\\\hline}
\tabletail{\hline \multicolumn{2}{r@{}}{continued \ldots}\\}
\tablelasttail{\hline}
\begin{xtabular}{@{}p{0.55\linewidth} r@{}}
Egypt          & 30.06.1995\\ Albania     & 08.09.2000\\Angola          & 23.11.1996\\
Antigua and Barbuda & 01.01.1995\\Antilles& 21.01.1996\\Arab Emirates & 10.04.1996\\
Argentina      & 01.01.1995\\ Armenia    & 05.02.2003\\Australia       & 01.01.1995\\
Bahrain        & 01.01.1995\\ Bangladesh & 01.01.1995\\Barbados        & 01.01.1995\\
Belgium        & 01.01.1995\\ Belize     & 01.01.1995\\Benin           & 22.02.1996\\
\end{xtabular}
```

04-06-5

xtabular demo

Table 1: Demonstration of a table caption.

country	*entry*
Egypt	30.06.1995
Albania	08.09.2000
	continued ...

page 1

xtabular demo

country	*entry*
Angola	23.11.1996
Antigua and Barbuda	01.01.1995
Antilles	21.01.1996
Arab Emirates	10.04.1996
Argentina	01.01.1995
Armenia	05.02.2003
	continued ...

page 2

4.6.4 Footnotes

In principle, Section 4.5.4 on page 155 applies here as well. Again you have to use the footnote commands \footnotemark and \footnotetext, as already shown in Example 04-03-3 on page 143.

```
\usepackage{xtab}

\tablefirsthead{\hline \emph{country} & \emph{entry}\\\hline}
\tablehead{\emph{country} & \emph{entry}\\\hline}
\tabletail{\hline \multicolumn{2}{r@{}}{continued \ldots}\\}
\tablelasttail{\hline}
Text\footnote{before the table} and footnote.\par
\begin{xtabular}{@{}p{0.55\linewidth} r@{}}
Egypt\footnotemark  & 30.06.1995 \\ Albania            & 08.09.2000 \\
Angola              & 23.11.1996 \\ Antigua and Barbuda & 01.01.1995 \\
Antilles\footnotemark& 21.01.1996 \\ Arab Emirates      & 10.04.1996 \\
Argentina           & 01.01.1995 \\ Armenia            & 05.02.2003 \\
Australia           & 01.01.1995 \\ Bahrain            & 01.01.1995 \\
Bangladesh          & 01.01.1995 \\ Barbados           & 01.01.1995 \\
Belgium             & 01.01.1995 \\ Belize\footnotemark & 01.01.1995 \\
\end{xtabular}
\addtocounter{footnote}{-3}
\stepcounter{footnote}\footnotetext{first footnote}
\stepcounter{footnote}\footnotetext{second footnote}
\stepcounter{footnote}\footnotetext{third footnote}
Text\footnote{after the table} and footnote.
```

04-06-6

xtabular demo

Text[1] and footnote.

country	*entry*
Egypt[2]	30.06.1995
Albania	08.09.2000
Angola	23.11.1996
Antigua and Barbuda	01.01.1995

continued ...

[1]before the table

page 1

xtabular demo

country	*entry*
Antilles[3]	21.01.1996
Arab Emirates	10.04.1996
Argentina	01.01.1995
Armenia	05.02.2003
Australia	01.01.1995
Bahrain	01.01.1995

continued ...

page 2

This has the disadvantage that the footnotes all appear together at the end of the table – for long tables, there can be several pages between the footnote mark and the footnote text. It is better therefore to use the mpxtabular environment as long as no other footnotes (apart from the table footnotes) appear on the first or last page of the table. Within the minipage, the footnotes are typeset with their own footnote rule immediately after the table and are counted with letters. As shown in the following example, this provides a clear distinction, but the the appearance is unsatisfactory. The footnotes immediately before or after the table should be omitted.

```
\usepackage{xtab}

\tablefirsthead{\hline \emph{country} & \emph{entry}\\\hline}
\tablehead{\emph{country} & \emph{entry}\\\hline}
\tabletail{\hline \multicolumn{2}{r@{}}{continued \ldots}\\}
\tablelasttail{\hline}
Text\footnote{before the table} and footnote.
\begin{center}
\begin{mpxtabular}{@{}p{0.55\linewidth} r@{}}
Egypt\footnote{first footnote}  & 30.06.1995 \\ Albania               & 08.09.2000 \\
Angola                 & 23.11.1996 \\ Antigua and Barbuda  & 01.01.1995 \\
Antilles\footnote{second footnote}& 21.01.1996 \\ Arab Emirates        & 10.04.1996 \\
Argentina              & 01.01.1995 \\ Armenia              & 05.02.2003 \\
Australia              & 01.01.1995 \\ Bahrain              & 01.01.1995 \\
Bangladesh             & 01.01.1995 \\ Barbados             & 01.01.1995 \\
Belgium                & 01.01.1995 \\ Belize\footnote{third footnote} & 01.01.1995 \\
\end{mpxtabular}
\end{center}
Text\footnote{after the table} and footnote.
```

xtabular demo

Text[1] and footnote.

country	*entry*
Egypt[a]	30.06.1995
Albania	08.09.2000
Angola	23.11.1996
	continued ...

[a]first footnote

[1]before the table

page 1

xtabular demo

country	*entry*
Antigua and Barbuda	01.01.1995
Antilles[a]	21.01.1996
Arab Emirates	10.04.1996
Argentina	01.01.1995
Armenia	05.02.2003
Australia	01.01.1995
	continued ...

[a]second footnote

page 2

04-06-7

```
\usepackage{xtab}

\tablefirsthead{\hline \emph{country} & \emph{entry}\\\hline}
\tablehead{\emph{country} & \emph{entry}\\\hline}
\tabletail{\hline \multicolumn{2}{r@{}}{continued \ldots}\\}
\tablelasttail{\hline}
Text without footnote.

\medskip
\begin{mpxtabular*}{\linewidth}{@{}p{0.55\linewidth} @{\extracolsep{\fill}} r@{}}
Egypt\footnote{first footnote}  & 30.06.1995 \\ Albania              & 08.09.2000 \\
Angola                 & 23.11.1996 \\ Antigua and Barbuda  & 01.01.1995 \\
Antilles\footnote{second footnote}& 21.01.1996 \\ Arab Emirates        & 10.04.1996 \\
Argentina              & 01.01.1995 \\ Armenia              & 05.02.2003 \\
Australia              & 01.01.1995 \\ Bahrain              & 01.01.1995 \\
Bangladesh             & 01.01.1995 \\ Barbados             & 01.01.1995 \\
Belgium                & 01.01.1995 \\ Belize\footnote{third footnote} & 01.01.1995 \\
\end{mpxtabular*}

\medskip
Text without footnote.
```

04-06-8

xtabular demo

Text without footnote.

country	*entry*
Egypt[a]	30.06.1995
Albania	08.09.2000
Angola	23.11.1996
	continued ...

[a]first footnote

page 1

xtabular demo

country	*entry*
Antigua and Barbuda	01.01.1995
Antilles[a]	21.01.1996
Arab Emirates	10.04.1996
Argentina	01.01.1995
Armenia	05.02.2003
Australia	01.01.1995
	continued ...

[a]second footnote

page 2

4.6.5 TEXnicalities

The page break can be controlled through the `\shrinkheight` command to achieve a better breakdown into pages. The command *must* be called after the first row of the table with a length as parameter. A positive length decreases the amount of space available on a page and a negative value increases it. In general you should use multiples of `\normalbaselineskip` for the value, as within the table \baselineskip is set to 0 pt internally. The following example is identical to Example 04-06-5 on page 162 apart from the removal of footnotes and the use of the \shrinkheight command.

```
\shrinkheight{length}
```

```
\usepackage{xtab} \usepackage[labelfont=bf]{caption}

\tablecaption{Demonstration of a table caption.}
\tablefirsthead{\hline \emph{country} & \emph{entry}\\\hline}
\tablehead{\emph{country} & \emph{entry}\\\hline}
\tabletail{\hline \multicolumn{2}{r@{}}{continued \ldots}\\}
\tablelasttail{\hline}
\begin{center}
\begin{xtabular}{@{}p{0.55\linewidth} r@{}}
Egypt                & 30.06.1995 \\\shrinkheight{-7\normalbaselineskip}
Albania              & 08.09.2000 \\
Angola               & 23.11.1996 \\ Antigua and Barbuda  & 01.01.1995 \\
Antilles             & 21.01.1996 \\ Arab Emirates       & 10.04.1996 \\
Argentina            & 01.01.1995 \\ Armenia             & 05.02.2003 \\
Australia            & 01.01.1995 \\ Bahrain             & 01.01.1995 \\
Bangladesh           & 01.01.1995 \\ Barbados            & 01.01.1995 \\
Belgium              & 01.01.1995 \\ Belize              & 01.01.1995 \\
\end{xtabular}
\end{center}
```

04-06-9

xtabular demo

Table 1: Demonstration of a table caption.

country	*entry*
Egypt	30.06.1995
Albania	08.09.2000
Angola	23.11.1996
Antigua and Barbuda	01.01.1995
Antilles	21.01.1996
Arab Emirates	10.04.1996
Argentina	01.01.1995
Armenia	05.02.2003

continued ...

page 1

xtabular demo

country	*entry*
Australia	01.01.1995
Bahrain	01.01.1995
Bangladesh	01.01.1995
Barbados	01.01.1995
Belgium	01.01.1995
Belize	01.01.1995

page 2

The length for \shrinkheight depends on the internal calculation of the required vertical space. Specifying a multiple of \normalbaselineskip is not the same as saying "7 more lines" – it is just trial and error to find the correct setting.

Chapter 5

Tips and tricks

This chapter describes various tips and tricks that have not been listed so far or are not directly supported by one package. Some of the tricks have been taken from the usual TeX mailing lists and newsgroups. In these cases, the respective author is given.

5.1 Tables – general

trick

At the beginning of a table row, TeX searches internally for specific primitive commands that affect the formatting, for example `\span`, `\omit`, and `\noalign`. This can lead to error messages if the first column's column type is defined to change the encoding for that column. While searching for specific commands in the row, TeX expands the commands in the first column, and only then considers the column type, with its explicit change of encoding. In the following example by Bernd Raichle, the `\relax` command prevents the following `\textepsilon` from the `tipa` package from being expanded.

```
\usepackage[T3,T1]{fontenc}
\usepackage[latin1]{inputenc}
\usepackage{array,dcolumn,tabularx,textcomp,ragged2e}
\usepackage[noenc]{tipa}
\newcolumntype{C}{>{\Centering}X}

\begin{tabularx}{0.85\linewidth}%
  {|>{\tipaencoding}c|l|>{\RaggedRight}X|D{.}{.}{-1}|}\hline
 \multicolumn{1}{|c|}{Sound} & \multicolumn{1}{c|}{Examples}
 & \multicolumn{1}{C|}{Place and manner of articulation}
 & \multicolumn{1}{C|}{Occurrence frequency (\%)} \\\hline
\relax\textepsilon & lait, jouet, merci & front, half-open & 5.3 \\\hline
\end{tabularx}
```

Sound	Examples	Place and manner of articulation	Occurrence frequency (%)
ɛ	lait, jouet, merci	front, half-open	5.3

05-01-1

tip If your table contains empty or not completely filled rows and makes use of vertical lines, you must list all columns, or a vertical line will be missing:

foo	bar	baz
foo		
foo	bar	baz

foo	bar	baz
foo		
foo	bar	baz

```
\begin{tabular}{|c|c|c|}\hline
foo & bar & baz\\
foo \\
foo & bar & baz\\\hline
\end{tabular}\par\medskip

\begin{tabular}{|c|c|c|}\hline
foo & bar & baz\\
foo & & \\
foo & bar & baz\\\hline
\end{tabular}\par\medskip
```

05-01-2

trick At the end of a row in a table, you can insert arbitrary vertical space by using the optional argument of \\. However, if a horizontal line is added as well, the processing order of TeX "first line feed, then line" leads to an unsatisfactory result. The TeX \noalign command lets you insert vertical material at the end of a row such that the horizontal line is drawn first and then the vertical line feed is inserted.

Egypt	30.06.1995
Albania	08.09.2000
Angola	23.11.1996
Argentina	01.01.1995
Antilles	21.01.1996

```
\begin{tabular}{@{}ll@{}}\\\hline
Egypt     & 30.06.1995 \\[10pt]\hline
Albania     & 08.09.2000 \\
    \hline\noalign{\vspace{10pt}}
Angola      & 23.11.1996 \\
    \hline\noalign{\vspace{15pt}}
Argentina   & 01.01.1995 \\
Antilles    & 21.01.1996
\end{tabular}
```

05-01-3

trick A longtable usually requires several runs because it writes information about the current width in the .aux file and reads it back in. To reference this width, for example to typeset the caption or surrounding text with the same width as the table, you can use this trick by Heiko Oberdiek. The code for setting the length \LongTableWidth is in the preamble, which is not visible here.

05-01-4

Table 1: Caption for a longtable ....

Hello	world and some more
foo	bar

Here we have text with the same width as the longtable.

```
\usepackage{longtable}
\newlength\LongtableWidth% Siehe Beispielcode

\begin{longtable}{|ll|}
\caption{Caption for a \texttt{longtable}\dotfill}\\
Hello & world and some more\\
foo   & bar
\end{longtable}
\begin{center}
\begin{minipage}{\LongtableWidth}
Here we have text with the same width as
the \texttt{longtable}.
\end{minipage}
\end{center}
```

If a table should be read through the \input command, the entire table should be contained *tip* in the external file. Otherwise, problems may occur. Here is an example:

```
\begin{tabular}{ c c }
\input{table rows}
\end{tabular}
```

This sequence generates the following error message if the first row of the external file *table rows* contains a \multicolumn command:

```
! Misplaced \omit.
\multispan ->\omit
                    \@multispan
l.1 \multicolumn{2}{c}{A}
                          \\
?
```

This can be prevented by putting \begin{tabular} and \end{tabular} into the file as well:

05-01-5

A	
a	b
a	b

```
\begin{filecontents*}{table.tex}
\begin{tabular}{c c}
\multicolumn{2}{c}{A}\\
a & b\\ a & b
\end{tabular}
\end{filecontents*}

\input{table}
```

5.2 tabbing environments

trick The problem with filling the space to the next tab within a `tabbing` environment with `\dotfill` or `\hrulefill` is that the fill won't be visible; this is because it is put inside a box of natural width, which in the case of these two commands is 0 pt. Heiko Oberdiek suggested a `\rtab` command to be used instead of `\>`; alternatively, the internal `\@rtab` command can be overwritten with `\rtab` so that `\>` behaves the same way as `\rtab`. Both options are illustrated here:

blabla blabla
bla blabla

blabla . . . blabla
bla_____blabla

blabla . . . blabla
bla_____blabla

```
% see preamble in example for \rtab

\begin{tabbing}
blablabla \= \kill \\
blabla \dotfill \> blabla\\% no effect!
bla\hrulefill \> blabla    % no effect!
\end{tabbing}
\begin{tabbing}
blablabla \=\kill\\blabla\dotfill\rtab blabla\\bla\hrulefill\rtab blabla
\end{tabbing}
\makeatletter\let\@rtab\rtab\makeatother
\begin{tabbing}
blablabla \=\kill\\blabla\dotfill\> blabla\\bla\hrulefill\>blabla
\end{tabbing}
```

05-02-1

5.3 Two-column mode

tip The only environment that lets you typeset tables across columns in `\twocolumn` mode is `supertabular` from the package of the same name (cf. Section 4.5 on page 149). When using the `multicol` package, you can't use `\twocolumn` mode anymore, and have to use the `tabbing` environment instead.

twocolumn-Demo

twocolumn mode

L	Z	R
l	c	r
l	c	r
l	c	r
l	c	r
l	c	r
l	c	r
l	c	r

l	c	r
l	c	r
l	c	r
l	c	r
l	c	r

Seite 1

```
\usepackage{supertabular}

\twocolumn[\centering%
  \texttt{twocolumn} mode\bigskip]
\begin{supertabular}{l c r }\hline
L & Z & R \\\hline
l & c & r \\ l & c & r \\ l & c & r \\
l & c & r \\ l & c & r \\ l & c & r \\
l & c & r \\ l & c & r \\ l & c & r \\
l & c & r \\ l & c & r \\ l & c & r \\
\end{supertabular}
```

05-03-1

The `tabbing` environment has the disadvantage that it is always left-aligned, but the advantage that it can be used either in `\twocolumn` mode or within the `multicols` environment. *tip*

05-03-2

twocolumn-demo

`twocolumn` mode

L Z R	l c r
l c r	l c r
l c r	l c r
l c r	
l c r	
l c r	
l c r	
l c r	
l c r	
l c r	

Seite 1

```
\twocolumn[\centering%
  \texttt{twocolumn} mode\bigskip]
\begin{tabbing}
L \=Z  \=R \kill
L \>Z \>R \\
l \>c \>r \\ l \>c \>r \\ l \>c \>r \\
l \>c \>r \\ l \>c \>r \\ l \>c \>r \\
l \>c \>r \\ l \>c \>r \\ l \>c \>r \\
l \>c \>r \\ l \>c \>r \\ l \>c \>r \\
\end{tabbing}
```

05-03-3

twocolumn-Demo

`multicols` mode

L Z R	l c r
l c r	l c r
l c r	l c r
l c r	l c r
l c r	l c r
l c r	l c r
l c r	

Normal one-column text.

Seite 1

```
\usepackage{multicol}

\subsection*{\texttt{multicols} mode}
\begin{multicols}{2}
\begin{tabbing}
L \=Z  \=R \kill
L \>Z \>R \\
l \>c \>r \\ l \>c \>r \\ l \>c \>r \\
l \>c \>r \\ l \>c \>r \\ l \>c \>r \\
l \>c \>r \\ l \>c \>r \\ l \>c \>r \\
l \>c \>r \\ l \>c \>r \\ l \>c \>r \\
\end{tabbing}
\end{multicols}\par
Normal one-column text.
```

5.4 Table captions

When typesetting a table that crosses a page break, it is possible that the break could be inserted between the table caption and the following table. To avoid this, you must ensure that the remaining space on the page when you start the table is sufficient for the caption *tip* and at least three table rows. Donald Arseneau created the \need command, which checks whether there is sufficient space left on the page and inserts a page break straightaway if not.

\need{*length*}

You could also extend the definition of the corresponding table environment to integrate the \need command. The following two examples show the first two pages of a document; in the first example, the standard behaviour without the \need command is shown and in the second one, the behaviour with the command. The choice of size for the required length takes some experience to assess exactly, but \need{*6\normalbaselineskip*} will usually succeed in preventing a page break between table caption and body.

```
\usepackage{supertabular}
\newcommand\demoText{In theory, the definition of the table environment could be
extended to integrate the \protect\texttt{\textbackslash need} command. These two
examples show the first two pages of a document, where the first page has
(without \protect\texttt{\textbackslash need}) or does not have (with
\protect\texttt{\textbackslash need}) a page break.}

\section{A table}
\demoText  \begin{center}
\tablecaption{Caption.}
\tablehead{\hline column1 & column2 \\}
\begin{supertabular}{|cl|cl|}\hline
  yyy & xxx \\\hline yyy & xxx \\\hline yyy & xxx \\\hline
\end{supertabular}  \end{center}
```

need-demo

1 A table

In theory, the definition of the table environment could be extended to integrate the \need command. These two examples show the first two pages of a document, where the first page has (without \need) or does not have (with \need) a page break.

Table 1: Caption.

page 1

need-demo 1 A TABLE

column1	column2
yyy	xxx
yyy	xxx
yyy	xxx

page 2

05-04-1

```
\usepackage{supertabular}
\makeatletter
\newcommand\need[1]{\par \penalty-100 \begingroup % preserve \dimen@
  \dimen@\pagegoal \advance\dimen@-\pagetotal % space left
  \ifdim #1>\dimen@ % not enough space left
%     only do \vfil if some space left on page
      \ifdim\dimen@>\z@ \vskip -\pagedepth plus 1fil \fi
      \break
  \fi \endgroup}
\makeatother

\section{A table}
\demoText% see other example
\need{6\normalbaselineskip}
\begin{center}
\tablecaption{Caption.}
\tablehead{\hline column1 & column2 \\}
\begin{supertabular}{|cl|cl|}\hline
  yyy & xxx \\\hline yyy & xxx \\\hline yyy & xxx \\\hline
\end{supertabular}
\end{center}
```

05-04-2

need demo

1 A table

In theory, the definition of the table environment could be extended to integrate the \need command. These two examples show the first two pages of a document, where the first page has (without \need) or does not have (with \need) a page break.

page 1

need demo *1 A TABLE*

Table 1: Caption.

column1	column2
yyy	xxx
yyy	xxx
yyy	xxx

page 2

5.5 Math mode

trick

The typesetting of columns of numbers aligned at the decimal separator is actually done internally by treating the decimal separator as column separator and separating the integer part and the decimal places into two columns. However, as individual table rows are always typeset as separate groups to keep the definitions local, this means that definitions before a D column are not known anymore when the decimal places (in the second internal column) are typeset. The following trick enables you to typeset all digits in a different font; this example by Heiko Oberdiek sets the digits in sans-serif.

test	test1.0	test1.2	test3.1
test	1	1,22	333,1
test	2	3,44	444,1

0123456789

```
\usepackage{dcolumn}
\makeatletter \newcolumntype{s}[1]{%
  >{\DC@{.}{\sf\aftergroup\sf,}{#1}\sf}l<{\DC@end}}
\makeatother

\sffamily
\begin{tabular}{ l s{1.0} s{1.2} s{3.1} }
test & \multicolumn{1}{l}{test1.0} &
       \multicolumn{1}{l}{test1.2} &
       \multicolumn{1}{l}{test3.1} \\\hline
test & 1 & 1.22 & 333.1\\ test & 2 & 3.44 & 444.1
\end{tabular}\par\medskip
$\mathsf{0123456789}$
```

05-05-1

tip If you want to display content of D columns centred at the decimal separator through -1 and with a constant added, you can't use the `.` column type or the < operator – for example `\newcolumntype{a}{.<{+6240}}` in the following example. This column type is used to format the second column of the table; it results in +6240 being appended first and then the number being centred on the decimal separator. The resulting space on the left of the second column is too large.

Using the internal commands `\DC@` for the beginning and `\DC@end`, you can first centre the number and after that append a constant, as seen in the example for the columns *S5* (column type b) and *S6* (column type B).

```
\usepackage{dcolumn}
\makeatletter \newcolumntype{.}{D{.}{.}{-1}} \newcolumntype{a}{.<{+6240}}
\newcolumntype{b}{>{\DC@{.}{.}{-1}}c<{\DC@end+6240}}
\newcolumntype{B}{>{\DC@{.}{.}{-1}}c<{\DC@end+25530}}
\newcommand\interval[1]{\multicolumn{1}{c}{#1}}  \makeatother

\begin{tabular}{@{}la..bB@{}}
 \interval{S1}&\interval{S2}&\interval{S3}&\interval{S4}&\interval{S5}&\interval{S6}\\
 99.0\,\% & 14.40& 438& 5256& 375.60&182.70\\99.9\,\% & 1.59& 44 & 526 & 37.60&18.30\\
 99.99\,\%&  0.15& 4.4& 0.53& 3.76 & 1.83
\end{tabular}
```

S1	S2	S3	S4	S5	S6
99.0 %	14.40 + 6240	438	5256	375.60 +6240	182.70 +25530
99.9 %	1.59 + 6240	44	526	37.60+6240	18.30+25530
99.99 %	0.15 + 6240	4.4	0.53	3.76+6240	1.83+25530

05-05-2

5.6 Excel and OpenOffice files

In general, there are always problems converting Excel or OpenOffice files into a LaTeX-compatible format. It is only successful for files whose cells don't contain arithmetics and can therefore be saved in csv format (comma separated values). Such files can then be read and processed with the `datatool` package, usually without problems (cf. Section 2.8). You can convert tables with arithmetics into tables without such operations in Excel and OpenOffice through copy and paste and "insert values"; then you can convert these to csv format and use the `datatool` package for them too.

tip There is a software tool on CTAN by Joachim Marder and George Pearson that provides an extension for Excel on Windows to support arithmetic for the output. It only supports versions up to and including Excel 97, however (`http://www.dante.de/CTAN//support/excel2latex/`). The `exceltex` package by Hans-Peter Doerr offers another way and is a combination of a normal LaTeX package and an external Perl program of the same name. The table is not converted before, but read from within a LaTeX document; you can specify the region to be used. The actual conversion is done by the Perl script, which has to be called between two LaTeX runs.

```
latex example
exceltex example
latex example
```

The Perl program exceltex requires the Perl module `Spreadsheet::ParseExcel`, which is available on CPAN `http://search.cpan.org/~szabgab/Spreadsheet-ParseExcel-0.32/lib/Spreadsheet/ParseExcel.pm`. The `exceltex` package isn't available in TeXLive 2007; it must be installed separately. The Perl program must be executable. The package supports reading individual cells or several rows:

```
\inccell{xls file!sheet!cell}
\inctab{xls file!sheet!first cell!last cell}
```

5-06-1

Reading of a cell: Nadine Haßemer

```
\usepackage{exceltex}

Reading of a cell:
\inccell{test.xls!Zeugnisliste!C3}
\inccell{test.xls!Zeugnisliste!D3}
```

```
\usepackage{exceltex,booktabs}

Reading of a table:\par\setlength\tabcolsep{2pt}
\begin{tabular}{@{} *{16}{l} @{}}\toprule
given name & surname & DOB & \multicolumn{13}{c@{}}{subjects}\\
        &           &       &D &U &T &E &F &L &G &K &M &P &C &B &S\\\midrule
\inctab{test.xls!Zeugnisliste!C2!R5}\bottomrule
\end{tabular}
```

05-06-2

Reading of a table:

given name	surname	DOB	D	U	T	E	F	L	G	K	M	P	C	B	S
			subjects												
Victoria	Hoene	06.08.80				x					x				
Nadine	Haßemer	18.12.78	x				x								
So-Young	Lee	20.07.80									x			x	
Sebastian	Weigmann	12.06.79										x	x		

exceltex also creates subdirectories with the file names followed by `-excltx`. The individual entries are saved into these files with, for example, the following content: `\textcolor[rgb]{0, 0, 0}{Nadine}`.

Additional information can be taken from the package description, especially regarding the further functionality of the Perl program. The documentation can't be displayed through texdoc (cf. Section 7 on page 213), however, because the name is not the same as the package name.

```
\usepackage{exceltex,booktabs} \ttfamily

\begin{tabular}{@{} *{8}{r} @{}}\toprule
\multicolumn{8}{c}{Courses}\\\midrule

\inctab{test.xls!Tabelle1!G2!N19}\bottomrule

\end{tabular}
```

05-06-

Courses							
DE-1	de-1	DE-2	de-2	DE-3	de-3	DE-4	de-4
Mu-1	mu-1	Mu-2	mu-2	Mu-3	mu-3	Mu-4	mu-4
Ku-1	ku-1	Ku-2	ku-2	Ku-3	ku-3	Ku-4	ku-4
E1-1	e1-1	E1-2	e1-2	E1-3	e1-3	E1-4	e1-4
F2-1	f2-1	F2-2	f2-2	F2-3	f2-3	F2-4	f2-4
L3-1	l3-1	L3-2	l3-2	L3-3	l3-3	L3-4	l3-4
	tü-1		tü-2		tü-3		tü-4
	ds-1		ds-2		ds-3		ds-4
	pw-1		pw-2		pw-3		pw-4
GE-1	ge-1	GE-2	ge-2	GE-3	ge-3	GE-4	ge-4
	phil-1		phil-2		phil-3		phil-4
MA-1	ma-1	MA-2	ma-2	MA-3	ma-3	MA-4	ma-4
PH-1	ph-1	PH-2	ph-2	PH-3	ph-3	PH-4	ph-4
CH-1	ch-1	CH-2	ch-2	CH-3	ch-3	CH-4	ch-4
BI-1	bi-1	BI-2	bi-2	BI-3	bi-3	BI-4	bi-4
	in-1		in-2		in-3		in-4
SP-1	sp-1	SP-2	sp-2	SP-3	sp-3	SP-4	sp-4
EK-1		EK-2		EK-3		EK-4	

Chapter 6

Examples

This chapter lists different examples that were taken from the usual newsgroups and mailing lists. The respective author is listed as well. Almost all examples have been adapted to meet the author's ideas of good typography – usually only the contents of the cells are the same as in the original. Most of the examples have been taken from [50], the standard literature for the typography of tables on CTAN.

Table 6.1: Summary of the authors of the individual examples.

author	*example(s)*
Uwe Borchert	03-03-4
Jean-Côme Charpentier	06-00-1, 06-00-8
Christiane Geiger	06-00-26
Morten Høgholm	05-05-2
Stefan Junge	06-00-28, 06-00-41
Kai-Martin Knaak	06-00-32
Markus Kohm	06-00-2
Rolf Niepraschk	06-00-25, 06-00-29, 06-00-30, ??, 06-00-34, 06-00-42, 06-00-43, 06-00-45
Heiko Oberdiek	05-01-4
Bernd Raichle	05-01-1
Axel Reichert	06-00-9, 06-00-10, 06-00-11, 06-00-12, 06-00-13, 06-00-14, 06-00-15, 06-00-14, 06-00-15, 06-00-16, 06-00-17, 06-00-18, 06-00-19, 06-00-20, 06-00-21, 06-00-22, 03-03-5, 06-00-36, 06-00-37
Christian Tellechea	06-00-39, 06-00-40
Uwe Ziegenhagen	06-00-46

```
\usepackage{array,ragged2e,booktabs,capt-of}
\newcolumntype{C}[1]{>{\Centering}b{#1}}

\begin{tabular}{@{}l C{2cm} C{2.7cm} C{1.8cm}@{}}\toprule
\bfseries Pratiques & \bfseries Nombre de dossiers
  & \bfseries Cas où le gouvernement a eu gain de cause
  & \bfseries Cessions ordonnées \\\midrule
                                  & \itshape\bfseries 1890-1939  \\\midrule
\bfseries Concentrations          & 57 & 46 & 20 \\
\quad Marché national             & 33 & 25 & 12 \\
\quad Marché régional ou local & 24 & 21 &  9 \\
\bfseries Pratiques antitrust  & \bfseries97 & \bfseries79 & \bfseries8 \\
\quad Marché national             & 54 & 43 &  5 \\
\quad Marché régional ou local & 43 & 36 &  3 \\
\emph{Total}                      &154 &125 &\textbf{28} \\\midrule
                                  & \itshape\bfseries 1940-1999 \\\midrule
\bfseries Concentrations          & 28 & 25 &  9 \\
\quad Marché national             & 14 & 12 &  4 \\
\quad Marché régional ou local & 14 & 13 &  5 \\
\bfseries Pratiques antitrust  & \bfseries91 & \bfseries75 & \bfseries7 \\
\quad Marché national             & 52 & 42 &  2 \\
\quad Marché régional ou local & 39 & 33 &  5 \\
\emph{Total}                      &119 &100 &\textbf{16} \\\bottomrule
\multicolumn{4}{@{}l}{\scriptsize\emph{Source}: adapté de Posner (2001,p. 106).}
\end{tabular}
```

06-00-1

Pratiques	**Nombre de dossiers**	**Cas où le gouvernement a eu gain de cause**	**Cessions ordonnées**
	1890-1939		
Concentrations	57	46	20
Marché national	33	25	12
Marché régional ou local	24	21	9
Pratiques antitrust	**97**	**79**	**8**
Marché national	54	43	5
Marché régional ou local	43	36	3
Total	154	125	**28**
	1940-1999		
Concentrations	28	25	9
Marché national	14	12	4
Marché régional ou local	14	13	5
Pratiques antitrust	**91**	**75**	**7**
Marché national	52	42	2
Marché régional ou local	39	33	5
Total	119	100	**16**

Source : adapté de Posner (2001,p. 106).

```
\usepackage{tabularx,booktabs,ragged2e}
\newcommand\raggedcolumn{\RaggedRight\hspace{0pt}}
\newcommand\centercolumn{\Centering\hspace{0pt}}

\renewcommand*{\tabularxcolumn}[1]{b{#1}}%
\begin{tabularx}{\textwidth}{@{}*{3}{>{\raggedcolumn}X}*{3}
{>{\raggedcolumn}X}@{}}\toprule
header line 1 & header line 2 & header line 3 &
header line 4 & header line 5 & header line 6,
which is a bit longer as usual \\\midrule
foo & bar & baz & gg & gg & gg\\\midrule
foo & bar & baz & gg & gg & dd\\\bottomrule
\end{tabularx}
```

06-00-2

header line 1	header line 2	header line 3	header line 4	header line 5	header line 6, which is a bit longer as usual
foo	bar	baz	gg	gg	gg
foo	bar	baz	gg	gg	dd

```
\usepackage{array,booktabs}
\newcounter{Platz}

\begin{tabular}{@{}>{\ifnum\thePlatz>0 \thePlatz.\fi}r
  l rrr c@{ :}c c<{\stepcounter{Platz}} @{}}\\\toprule
\multicolumn{8}{c}{%
   \bfseries\rule[-2ex]{0pt}{5ex}German football league 1986/87.}\\ \midrule
\multicolumn{1}{@{}c}{}
 & club               &  S &  U &  N &\multicolumn{2}{c}{points}& comment\\\toprule
 & Bayern München     & 20 & 13 &  1 & 53 & 15 & champion\\
 & Hamburger SV       & 19 &  9 &  6 & 47 & 21 & cup winner\\
 & Bor. M'Gladbach    & 18 &  7 &  9 & 43 & 21 & starter\\
 & Bor. Dortmund      & 15 & 10 &  9 & 40 & 28 & in the\\
 & Werder Bremen      & 17 &  6 & 11 & 40 & 28 & UEFA cup\\
 & Bayer Leverkusen   & 16 &  7 & 11 & 39 & 29 & cup\\\midrule
 & 1.FC Kaiserslautern& 15 &  7 & 12 & 37 & 31 & \\
 & Bayer Uerdingen    & 12 & 11 & 11 & 35 & 33 & \\
 & 1.FC Nürnberg      & 12 & 11 & 11 & 35 & 33 & \\
 & 1.FC Köln          & 13 &  9 & 12 & 35 & 33 & \\
 & VfL Bochum         &  9 & 14 & 11 & 32 & 36 & mid field\\
 & VfB Stuttgart      & 13 &  6 & 15 & 32 & 36 & \\
 & Schalke 04         & 12 &  8 & 14 & 32 & 36 & \\
 & Waldhof Mannheim   & 10 &  8 & 16 & 28 & 40 & \\
 & Eintracht Frankfurt&  8 &  9 & 17 & 25 & 43 & \\\midrule
```

```
 & FC Homburg          &  6 &  9 & 19 & 21 & 47 & rel. St.Pauli\\\midrule
 & Fortuna Düsseldorf &  7 &  6 & 21 & 20 & 48 & \\
 & BW 90 Berlin        &  3 & 12 & 19 & 18 & 50
    & \raisebox{1.5ex}[-1.5ex]{relegated}\\\bottomrule
\end{tabular}
```

06-00-3

German football league 1986/87.

	club	S	U	N	points	comment
1.	Bayern München	20	13	1	53 :15	champion
2.	Hamburger SV	19	9	6	47 :21	cup winner
3.	Bor. M'Gladbach	18	7	9	43 :21	starter
4.	Bor. Dortmund	15	10	9	40 :28	in the
5.	Werder Bremen	17	6	11	40 :28	UEFA cup
6.	Bayer Leverkusen	16	7	11	39 :29	cup
7.	1.FC Kaiserslautern	15	7	12	37 :31	
8.	Bayer Uerdingen	12	11	11	35 :33	
9.	1.FC Nürnberg	12	11	11	35 :33	
10.	1.FC Köln	13	9	12	35 :33	
11.	VfL Bochum	9	14	11	32 :36	mid field
12.	VfB Stuttgart	13	6	15	32 :36	
13.	Schalke 04	12	8	14	32 :36	
14.	Waldhof Mannheim	10	8	16	28 :40	
15.	Eintracht Frankfurt	8	9	17	25 :43	
16.	FC Homburg	6	9	19	21 :47	rel. St.Pauli
17.	Fortuna Düsseldorf	7	6	21	20 :48	relegated
18.	BW 90 Berlin	3	12	19	18 :50	

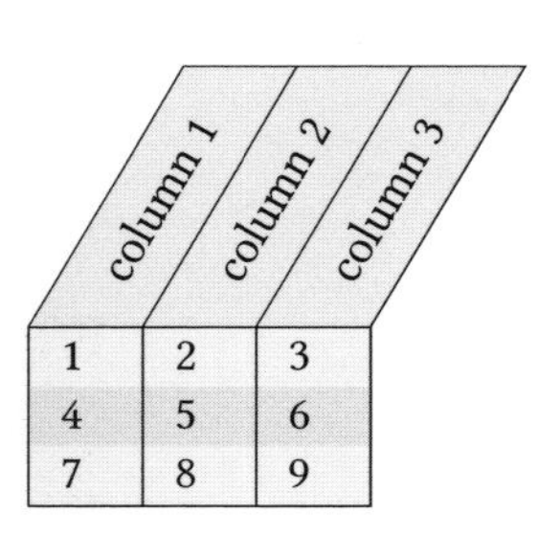

06-00-4

```
\usepackage[table]{pstricks}
\usepackage{pst-3d,pst-node}\SpecialCoor

\begin{tabular}{l}
\pstilt{60}{\begin{tabular}{|p{1em}|p{1em}|p{1em}|}\hline
  \rowcolor{magenta!10}\psrotateleft{\rnode{col1}{\hspace{2cm}}} &
  \psrotateleft{\rnode{col2}{\hspace{2cm}}} &
  \psrotateleft{\rnode{col3}{\hspace{2cm}}}
 \end{tabular}}\\% end head
\rput[t]{60}(col1){column 1}\rput[t]{60}(col2){column 2}%
\rput[t]{60}(col3){column 3}%
 \begin{tabular}{|p{1em}|p{1em}|p{1em}|}\hline
  \rowcolor{green!10} 1 & 2 & 3 \\\rowcolor{blue!10}  4 & 5 & 6 \\
  \rowcolor{green!10} 7 & 8 & 9 \\\hline
 \end{tabular}
\end{tabular}
```

```
\usepackage{pstricks}

\setlength\tabcolsep{2mm}\psset{xunit=12mm, yunit=\baselineskip}%
\pspolygon[linecolor=red,linewidth=2pt]
  (0,-3.3)(0,2.7)(2,2.7)(2,1.7)(4,1.7)(4,0.7)(6,0.7)(6,-1.3)(7,-1.3)
  (7,-2.3)(5,-2.3)(5,-3.3)(4,-3.3)(4,-2.3)(3,-2.3)(3,-3.3)
\begin{tabular}{*{8}{p{8mm}}}
H  &    &    &    &    &    &    & He\\  Li & Be & B  & C  & N  & O  & F  & Ne\\
Na & Mg & Al & Si & P  & S  & Cl & Ar\\  K  & Ca & Ga & Ge & As & Se & Br & Kr\\
Rb & Sr & In & Sn & Sb & Te & I  & Xe\\  Cs & Ba & Tl & Pb & Bi & Po & At & Rn\\
Fr & Ra & 112&    & 114&    &    &\\
\end{tabular}
```

06-00-5

H							He
Li	Be	B	C	N	O	F	Ne
Na	Mg	Al	Si	P	S	Cl	Ar
K	Ca	Ga	Ge	As	Se	Br	Kr
Rb	Sr	In	Sn	Sb	Te	I	Xe
Cs	Ba	Tl	Pb	Bi	Po	At	Rn
Fr	Ra	112		114			

```
\usepackage{pstricks}

\setlength\tabcolsep{2mm}\psset{xunit=12mm, yunit=\baselineskip}%
\pspolygon[fillcolor=lightgray,fillstyle=solid,linestyle=none](0,-3.3)(0,2.7)(2,2.7)
  (2,1.7)(4,1.7)(4,0.7)(6,0.7)(6,-1.3)(7,-1.3)(7,-2.3)(5,-2.3)(5,-3.3)(4,-3.3)
  (4,-2.3)(3,-2.3)(3,-3.3)
\begin{tabular}{*{8}{p{8mm}}}
H  &    &    &    &    &    &    & He\\  Li & Be & B  & C  & N  & O  & F  & Ne\\
Na & Mg & Al & Si & P  & S  & Cl & Ar\\  K  & Ca & Ga & Ge & As & Se & Br & Kr\\
Rb & Sr & In & Sn & Sb & Te & I  & Xe\\  Cs & Ba & Tl & Pb & Bi & Po & At & Rn\\
Fr & Ra & 112&    & 114&    &    &\\
\end{tabular}
```

06-00-6

H							He
Li	Be	B	C	N	O	F	Ne
Na	Mg	Al	Si	P	S	Cl	Ar
K	Ca	Ga	Ge	As	Se	Br	Kr
Rb	Sr	In	Sn	Sb	Te	I	Xe
Cs	Ba	Tl	Pb	Bi	Po	At	Rn
Fr	Ra	112		114			

```
\usepackage{pst-node}\SpecialCoor

\setlength\tabcolsep{2mm}
\begin{tabular}{*{8}{p{4mm}}}
  H  &    &    &    &    &\rnode{A}{~~}&& He\\  Li & Be & B  & C  & N  & O  & F  & Ne\\
```

```
  Na & Mg & Al & Si & P  & S  & Cl & Ar\\
  \rnode{B}{K}& Ca & Ga & Ge & As & Se & Br & \rnode{b}{Kr}\\
  Rb & Sr & In & Sn & Sb & Te & I  & Xe\\  Cs & Ba & Tl & Pb & Bi & Po & At & Rn\\
  Fr & Ra & 112&    & 114 & \rnode{a}{~~} &&
\end{tabular}
\psset{linecolor=red,linewidth=1.5pt,nodesep=-1em}\pcline(A)(a)\pcline(B)(b)
```

H							He
Li	Be	B	C	N	O	F	Ne
Na	Mg	Al	Si	P	S	Cl	Ar
K	Ca	Ga	Ge	As	Se	Br	Kr
Rb	Sr	In	Sn	Sb	Te	I	Xe
Cs	Ba	Tl	Pb	Bi	Po	At	Rn
Fr	Ra	112		114			

06-00-

text text	text text	text text

```
\usepackage{array}

\parbox[0cm][0.5ex][s]{0mm}{\makebox[42mm]{\dotfill}}%
\begin{tabular}{|b{9mm}|m{9mm}|p{9mm}|}\hline
text text & text text & text text \\\hline
\end{tabular}
```

06-00-

```
\usepackage{dcolumn,booktabs,ragged2e} \newcolumntype{d}[1]{D{.}{,}{#1}}
\newcolumntype{P}[1]{>{\scriptsize\Centering\hspace{0pt}}p{#1}}

\begin{tabular}{@{} l *{3}{d{7.0}} @{}}\toprule
\scriptsize city
 & \multicolumn{1}{P{6em}@{}}{total number of local and national calls}
 & \multicolumn{1}{P{6em}@{}}{calls from public telefons}
 & \multicolumn{1}{P{6em}@{}}{national and international calls from home} \\
      \cmidrule(r){1-1}\cmidrule(lr){2-2}\cmidrule(lr){3-3}\cmidrule(l){4-4}
London    & 723849  &  436322 &  287527 \\ Exeter   & 957365  &  593146 &  364219 \\
Newcastle& 1242212 & 1115321 & 1326861 \\ Dover    & 1641050 &  942316 &  698734 \\
Edinburgh & 1351204 &  651223 &  442747 \\ Glasgow & 1274714 &  394613 &  915853 \\
\bottomrule
\end{tabular}
```

city	total number of local and national calls	calls from public telefons	national and international calls from home
London	723849	436322	287527
Exeter	957365	593146	364219
Newcastle	1242212	1115321	1326861
Dover	1641050	942316	698734
Edinburgh	1351204	651223	442747
Glasgow	1274714	394613	915853

06-00-9

```
\usepackage{dcolumn,booktabs,tabularx}\let\addLS\addlinespace

\begin{tabularx}{0.85\linewidth}{@{} X l c D{.}{,}{2.2} @{}}\toprule
\small Schmelzeinsätze & \small Schalter & \small kg & \multicolumn{1}{c@{}}{\euro}\\
    \cmidrule(r){1-1}\cmidrule(lr){2-2}\cmidrule(lr){3-3}\cmidrule(l){4-4}\addLS
Pilzdruckknopf mit Rastung und Drehentriegelung & rot& 54 & 13.$---$\\\addLS
Pilzdruckknopf mit Rastung und Schloss     & rot     & 32 & 21.60\\\addLS
Schlüsselantrieb mit abziehbarem Schlüssel & schwarz & 43 & 15.10\\\addLS
Knebel mit 3~Schaltstellungen              & schwarz & 23 &  5.40\\\addLS\bottomrule
\end{tabularx}
```

06-00-10

Schmelzeinsätze	Schalter	kg	€
Pilzdruckknopf mit Rastung und Drehentriegelung	rot	54	13,–
Pilzdruckknopf mit Rastung und Schloss	rot	32	21,60
Schlüsselantrieb mit abziehbarem Schlüssel	schwarz	43	15,10
Knebel mit 3 Schaltstellungen	schwarz	23	5,40

```
\usepackage{dcolumn,booktabs,ragged2e} \newcolumntype{d}[1]{D{.}{,}{#1}}
\newcolumntype{P}[1]{>{\RaggedRight\hspace{0pt}}p{#1}}

\begin{tabular}{@{} P{12.5em} l c d{2.2} @{}}\toprule
\small Schmelzeinsätze & \small Schalter & \small kg & \multicolumn{1}{c}{\euro}\\
   \cmidrule(r){1-1}\cmidrule(lr){2-2}\cmidrule(lr){3-3}\cmidrule(l){4-4}
Pilzdruckknopf mit Rastung und Drehentriegelung & rot  & 54 & 13.$---$ \\
   \cmidrule(r){1-1}\cmidrule(lr){2-2}\cmidrule(lr){3-3}\cmidrule(l){4-4}
Pilzdruckknopf mit Rastung und Schloss         & rot     & 32 & 21.60 \\
   \cmidrule(r){1-1}\cmidrule(lr){2-2}\cmidrule(lr){3-3}\cmidrule(l){4-4}
Schlüsselantrieb mit abziehbarem Schlüssel     & schwarz & 43 & 15.10 \\
   \cmidrule(r){1-1}\cmidrule(lr){2-2}\cmidrule(lr){3-3}\cmidrule(l){4-4}
Knebel mit 3~Schaltstellungen                  & schwarz & 23 & 5.40\\\bottomrule
\end{tabular}
```

06-00-11

Schmelzeinsätze	Schalter	kg	€
Pilzdruckknopf mit Rastung und Drehentriegelung	rot	54	13,–
Pilzdruckknopf mit Rastung und Schloss	rot	32	21,60
Schlüsselantrieb mit abziehbarem Schlüssel	schwarz	43	15,10
Knebel mit 3 Schaltstellungen	schwarz	23	5,40

```
\usepackage{array,booktabs} \newcolumntype{C}{>{\small}c}

\begin{tabular}{@{}l *{4}{c} @{}}\toprule
\small month & \multicolumn{2}{C}{women} & \multicolumn{2}{C@{}}{men}\\
    \cmidrule(lr){2-3}\cmidrule(l){4-5}
 & \small 1967 & \small 1968 & \small 1967 & \small 1968\\
 \cmidrule(r){1-1}\cmidrule(lr){2-2}\cmidrule(lr){3-3}\cmidrule(lr){4-4}\cmidrule(l){5-5}
september& 2000 & 1700 & 2300 & 1900\\ october  & 1500 & 1800 & 1900 & 3000\\
november & 2500 & 2800 & 4700 & 3200\\ december & 2300 & 2000 & 3600 & 2700\\\bottomrule
\end{tabular}
```

month	women		men	
	1967	1968	1967	1968
september	2000	1700	2300	1900
october	1500	1800	1900	3000
november	2500	2800	4700	3200
december	2300	2000	3600	2700

06-00-12

```
\usepackage{array,booktabs,multirow,ragged2e,eurosym}
\renewcommand\multirowsetup{\RaggedRight\footnotesize}
\newcolumntype{N}{>{\footnotesize}l} \newcolumntype{C}{>{\footnotesize}c}
\newcommand\mc[3]{\multicolumn{#1}{#2}{#3}}

\begin{tabular}{@{} *{5}{l} @{}}\toprule
 &  & \mc{2}{N}{Ohne Sicherungen} & \multirow{3}{7em}{%
   Höchstzulässiger Erdungswider\-stand bei Berüh\-rungsspannung}\\\cmidrule(lr){3-4}
\mc{1}{C}{Reihe} & \mc{1}{C}{Spannung} & \mc{1}{C}{Type} & \mc{1}{C}{Preis} \\
 & \mc{1}{C}{V} & & \mc{1}{C}{\euro} \\\cmidrule(r){1-1}\cmidrule(lr){2-2}
   \cmidrule(lr){3-3}\cmidrule(lr){4-4}\cmidrule(l){5-5} \ldots \\\bottomrule
\end{tabular}
```

		Ohne Sicherungen		Höchstzulässiger Erdungswiderstand bei Berührungsspannung
Reihe	Spannung V	Type	Preis €	
...				

06-00-13

```
\usepackage{array,booktabs,ragged2e,rotating,eurosym}
\newcolumntype{N}{>{\small}l}   \newcommand\mc[1]{\multicolumn{1}{R{4.5em}}{#1}}
\newcolumntype{R}[1]{>{\begin{turn}{90}\begin{minipage}{#1}
  \footnotesize\RaggedRight\hspace{0pt}} l <{\end{minipage}\end{turn}}}

\begin{tabular}{@{} *{8}{l} @{}}\toprule
\small Typ&\multicolumn{6}{N}{Anlagen mit Freileitungen}&\small Preis\\\cmidrule(lr){2-7}
 & \mc{Betriebsspannung~kV} & \mc{Löschspannung~kV} & \mc{Wechselspannung~kV}
```

```
 & \mc{Ansprechspannung~kV} & \mc{Restspannung kV} & \mc{Nettogewicht~ kg}
 & \multicolumn{1}{c}{\small\euro}\\\cmidrule(r){1-1}\cmidrule(lr){2-2}\cmidrule(lr){3-3}
\cmidrule(lr){4-4}\cmidrule(lr){5-5}\cmidrule(lr){6-6}\cmidrule(lr){7-7}\cmidrule(l){8-8}
\ldots \\\bottomrule
\end{tabular}
```

06-00-14

Typ	Anlagen mit Freileitungen						Preis
	Betriebsspan-nung kV	Löschspan-nung kV	Wechselspan-nung kV	Ansprech-spannung kV	Restspannung kV	Nettoge-wicht kg	€
…							

```
\usepackage{array,booktabs,dcolumn,ragged2e,rotating}\newcolumntype{N}{>{\footnotesize}l}
\newcolumntype{P}[1]{>{\footnotesize\RaggedRight\hspace{0pt}}p{#1}}
\newcolumntype{d}[1]{D{.}{,}{#1}}  \newcommand\mc[2]{\multicolumn{1}{#1}{#2}}
\newcolumntype{R}[1]{>{\begin{turn}{90}\begin{minipage}{#1}
  \footnotesize\RaggedRight\hspace{0pt}} l <{\end{minipage}\end{turn}}}

\begin{tabular}{@{} l d{1.1} *{3}{d{1.2}} d{1.1} d{3.2} @{}}\toprule
&\multicolumn{5}{N}{Spannungsschutz für Netze}\\
&\multicolumn{5}{N}{Leiterspannung an der Einbaustelle}\\\cmidrule(lr){2-6}
&\multicolumn{2}{P{5em}}{Nicht geerdeter Sternpunkt}
&\multicolumn{2}{P{5em}}{Starr geerdeter Sternpunkt}\\\cmidrule(lr){2-3}\cmidrule(lr){4-5}
\mc{@{}N}{Typen-}  & \mc{R{4.5em}}{Normale Leiterspannung}
 & \mc{R{4.5em}}{Zulässiger Bereich} & \mc{R{4.5em}}{Normale Leiterspannung}
 & \mc{R{4.5em}}{Zulässiger Bereich} & \mc{R{4.5em}}{Nennspannung} &\mc{N}{Preis}\\[-2pt]
\mc{@{}N}{bezeichnung} & \mc{N}{kV} & \mc{N}{kV} & \mc{N}{kV} & \mc{N}{kV}
 & \mc{N}{kV} & \mc{N}{\euro}\\\cmidrule(r){1-1}\cmidrule(lr){2-2}\cmidrule(lr){3-3}
  \cmidrule(lr){4-4}\cmidrule(lr){5-5}\cmidrule(lr){6-6}\cmidrule(l){7-7}
H 484--1   & 1   & 1.15 & 1.25 & 1.45 & 1   & 220.$---$ \\  \ldots\\
H 484--3   & 3.5 & 3.5  & 3.8  & 4.3  & 3   & 264.$---$ \\\bottomrule
\end{tabular}
```

06-00-15

	Spannungsschutz für Netze Leiterspannung an der Einbaustelle					
	Nicht geerdeter Sternpunkt		Starr geerdeter Sternpunkt			
Typen-bezeichnung	Normale Lei-terspannung kV	Zulässiger Bereich kV	Normale Lei-terspannung kV	Zulässiger Bereich kV	Nennspan-nung kV	Preis €
H 484–1	1	1,15	1,25	1,45	1	220,–
…						
H 484–3	3,5	3,5	3,8	4,3	3	264,–

```
\usepackage{array,booktabs,dcolumn,ragged2e} \newcolumntype{N}{>{\footnotesize}l}
\newcolumntype{P}[1]{>{\footnotesize\RaggedRight\hspace{0pt}}p{#1}}
\newcolumntype{d}[1]{D{.}{,}{#1}}  \newcommand\mc[2]{\multicolumn{1}{#1}{#2}}

\begin{tabular}{@{}l *{6}{d{3.0}} @{}}\toprule
\mc{@{}N}{Zeit} & \multicolumn{2}{N}{Material von Drischel}
  & \multicolumn{2}{N}{Material von Bauer} & \multicolumn{2}{N@{}}{Eigenes Material}\\
    \cmidrule(lr){2-3}\cmidrule(lr){4-5}\cmidrule(l){6-7}
  & \mc{P{3.5em}}{Häufigster Wert} & \mc{P{3.5em}}{Extremwert}
  & \mc{P{3.5em}}{Häufigster Wert} & \mc{P{3.5em}}{Extremwert}
  & \mc{P{3.5em}}{Häufigster Wert} & \mc{P{3.5em}@{}}{Extremwert}\\
    \cmidrule(r){1-1}\cmidrule(lr){2-2}\cmidrule(lr){3-3}\cmidrule(lr){4-4}%
    \cmidrule(lr){5-5}\cmidrule(lr){6-6}\cmidrule(l){7-7}\addlinespace
Latenzzeit     & 220 & 330 & 245 & 325 & 235 & 320 \\
               &     & 150 &     & 155 &     & 160 \\\addlinespace
Halbwertszeit & 210 & 380 & 145 & 535 & 180 & 320 \\
des Abstiegs  &     &  90 &     &  95 &     &  70 \\\addlinespace
Gipfelzeit    & 485 & 700 & 375 & 535 & 420 & 600 \\
              &     & 260 &     & 315 &     & 290 \\\addlinespace
Halbwertszeit & 855 & 870 & 665 & 945 & 775 & 820 \\
des Abstiegs  &     & 590 &     & 575 &     & 490 \\\addlinespace\bottomrule
\end{tabular}
```

Zeit	Material von Drischel		Material von Bauer		Eigenes Material	
	Häufigster Wert	Extrem-wert	Häufigster Wert	Extrem-wert	Häufigster Wert	Extrem-wert
Latenzzeit	220	330	245	325	235	320
		150		155		160
Halbwertszeit	210	380	145	535	180	320
des Abstiegs		90		95		70
Gipfelzeit	485	700	375	535	420	600
		260		315		290
Halbwertszeit	855	870	665	945	775	820
des Abstiegs		590		575		490

06-00-1

```
\usepackage{booktabs,dcolumn,ragged2e,eurosym} \newcolumntype{N}{>{\footnotesize}l}
\newcolumntype{P}[1]{>{\footnotesize\RaggedRight}p{#1}}
\newcolumntype{d}[1]{D{.}{,}{#1}}  \newcommand\mc[2]{\multicolumn{1}{#1}{#2}}

\begin{tabular}{@{}l *{2}{d{3.0}d{2.2}} @{}}\toprule
\mc{@{}N}{Gegenstand} & \multicolumn{2}{N}{Vierleitersystem}
  & \multicolumn{2}{N@{}}{Fünf"|leitersystem}\\\cmidrule(lr){2-3}\cmidrule(l){4-5}
  & \mc{N}{Bestell-} & \mc{N}{Preis} & \mc{N}{Bestell} & \mc{N@{}}{Preis} \\[-2pt]
  & \mc{N}{Nr.} & \mc{P{2em}}{\euro} & \mc{N}{Nr.} & \mc{P{2.5em}@{}}{\euro}\\
 \cmidrule(r){1-1}\cmidrule(lr){2-2}\cmidrule(lr){3-3}\cmidrule(lr){4-4}\cmidrule(l){5-5}
```

```
Schienenkasten          & 103 & 70.$---$ & 107 & 83.$---$ \\
Schiene für Hauptleiter & 104 & 9.50     & 108 & 9.50     \\
Verbindungsklemme       & 105 & 1.25     & 109 & 1.25     \\
Schienenkastenöffnung   & 106 & 1.55     & 110 & 1.55     \\\bottomrule
\end{tabular}
```

06-00-17

Gegenstand	Vierleitersystem		Fünfleitersystem	
	Bestell-Nr.	Preis €	Bestell Nr.	Preis €
Schienenkasten	103	70,–	107	83,–
Schiene für Hauptleiter	104	9,50	108	9,50
Verbindungsklemme	105	1,25	109	1,25
Schienenkastenöffnung	106	1,55	110	1,55

```
\usepackage{booktabs,dcolumn,ragged2e} \newcolumntype{N}{>{\footnotesize}l}
\newcolumntype{P}[1]{>{\footnotesize\RaggedRight\hspace{0pt}}p{#1}}
\newcolumntype{d}[1]{D{.}{,}{#1}}  \newcommand\mc[2]{\multicolumn{1}{#1}{#2}}

\begin{tabular}{@{}lld{2.0}@{$\!$--}d{2.0}d{3.0}ld{1.0}@{$\!$--}d{2.0}d{3.0}l@{}}\toprule
  & \multicolumn{8}{N}{Zum Umsetzen} & \\\cmidrule(lr){2-9}
  & \multicolumn{4}{N}{von Frequenzen im} & \multicolumn{4}{N}{auf Frequenzen im} \\
      \cmidrule(lr){2-5}\cmidrule(lr){6-9}
\mc{@{}N}{Type} & \mc{P{3em}}{Fernsehbereich} & \multicolumn{2}{N}{Kanal} & \mc{N}{MHz}
  & \mc{P{3em}}{Fernsehbereich} & \multicolumn{2}{N}{Kanal} & \mc{N}{MHz}
  & \mc{P{2em}@{}}{Bauform}\\
    \cmidrule(r){1-1}\cmidrule(lr){2-2}\cmidrule(lr){3-4}\cmidrule(lr){5-5}
    \cmidrule(lr){6-6}\cmidrule(lr){7-8}\cmidrule(lr){9-9}\cmidrule(l){10-10}
SAFE 381 WK & F I   &  2 &  4 & 174 & F III & 5 & 12 & 174 & DO \\
SAFE 382 WK & F II  &  5 & 12 &  68 & F I   & 2 &  4 &  47 & DO \\
SAFE 383 WK & F III & 21 & 38 & 174 & F III & 5 & 12 & 174 & ES \\
SAFE 384 WK & F IV  & 42 & 48 &  47 & F III & 5 & 12 & 174 & ET \\\bottomrule
\end{tabular}
```

06-00-18

	Zum Umsetzen							
	von Frequenzen im			auf Frequenzen im				
Type	Fernseh-bereich	Kanal	MHz	Fernseh-bereich	Kanal	MHz	Bau-form
SAFE 381 WK	F I	2– 4	174	F III	5–12	174	DO
SAFE 382 WK	F II	5–12	68	F I	2– 4	47	DO
SAFE 383 WK	F III	21–38	174	F III	5–12	174	ES
SAFE 384 WK	F IV	42–48	47	F III	5–12	174	ET

```
\usepackage{dcolumn,booktabs,ragged2e,rotating,eurosym}
\newcolumntype{C}{>{\footnotesize}c}
\newcolumntype{N}{>{\footnotesize}l}
\newcolumntype{P}[1]{>{\footnotesize\RaggedRight\hspace{0pt}}p{#1}}
\newcolumntype{d}[1]{D{.}{,}{#1}}
\newcommand\mc[2]{\multicolumn{1}{#1}{#2}}
\newcommand\Rotate[1]{\begin{turn}{90}\rlap{#1}\end{turn}}

\begin{tabular}{@{}d{1.0}*{3}{d{3.0}}d{2.0}d{3.0}d{2.2}@{}}\toprule
  & \multicolumn{4}{N}{Leistungsaufnahme} & & \\\cmidrule(lr){2-5}
  & \multicolumn{2}{P{7em}}{kurzzeitig beim Ein"~~und Umschalten}
  & \multicolumn{2}{P{7em}}{nach dem Umschalten in die Dreieckstufe}
  & \mc{C}{\raisebox{-4em}{\Rotate{Spannung}}}
  & \mc{C@{}}{\raisebox{-4em}{\Rotate{Mehrpreis für}}
  \raisebox{-4em}{\Rotate{abweichende}} \raisebox{-4em}{\Rotate{Spannung}}}\\
    \cmidrule(lr){2-3}\cmidrule(lr){4-5}
\mc{@{}C}{\Rotate{Schaltergröße}}&\mc{C}{VA}&\mc{C}{W}&\mc{C}{VA}&\mc{C}{W}&\mc{C}{VA}
  & \mc{C}{\euro}\\\cmidrule(r){1-1}\cmidrule(lr){2-2}\cmidrule(lr){3-3}
    \cmidrule(lr){4-4}\cmidrule(lr){5-5}\cmidrule(lr){6-6}\cmidrule(l){7-7}
1& 120& 100& 16&  6&  24& 12.$---$\\ 2& 150& 100&  36& 12& 110& 15.$---$\\
4& 342& 210& 60& 18& 220& 19.$---$\\ 6& 733& 320& 100& 36& 220& 29.$---$\\\bottomrule
\end{tabular}
```

06-00-19

	Leistungsaufnahme					
	kurzzeitig beim Ein- und Umschalten		nach dem Umschalten in die Dreieckstufe		Spannung	Mehrpreis für abweichende Spannung
Schaltergröße	VA	W	VA	W	VA	€
1	120	100	16	6	24	12,–
2	150	100	36	12	110	15,–
4	342	210	60	18	220	19,–
6	733	320	100	36	220	29,–

```
\usepackage{dcolumn,booktabs,multirow,ragged2e}
\renewcommand\multirowsetup{\RaggedRight\footnotesize}
\newcolumntype{m}{>{$}l<{$}}
\newcolumntype{N}{>{\footnotesize}l}
\newcolumntype{d}[1]{D{.}{,}{#1}}
\newcommand\mc[2]{\multicolumn{1}{#1}{#2}}

\begin{tabular}{@{} *{3}{d{3.0}} d{2.0} *{3}{m} l@{}}\toprule
\multicolumn{3}{@{}N}{Listen-Nummer} & \mc{N}{Nennstrom} & \mc{N}{Polzahl}
  & \multicolumn{2}{N}{Anschluss bis mm$^2$} & \multirow{3}{3.5em}{Pg für Abgang oben}\\
    \cmidrule(r){1-3}\cmidrule(lr){6-7}
\mc{@{}N}{mit Bügel-} & \mc{N}{mit Mantel-} & \mc{N}{mit Block-}
  & & & \mc{N}{unten} & \mc{N}{oben} \\[-3pt]
```

```
\mc{@{}N}{klemme} & \mc{N}{klemme} & \mc{N}{klemme} & A & & & \\
  \cmidrule(r){1-1}\cmidrule(lr){2-2}\cmidrule(lr){3-3}\cmidrule(lr){4-4}%
  \cmidrule(lr){5-5}\cmidrule(lr){6-6}\cmidrule(lr){7-7}\cmidrule(l){8-8}\addlinespace
406 & 416 & 426 & 25 & 3+\mathrm{Mp}& 4\times16& 4\times16& Pg 21\\
407 & 417 & 427 &    &              &           &           & Pg 29\\\addlinespace
408 & 418 & 428 & 60 & 3+\mathrm{Mp}& 4\times35& 4\times16& Pg 29\\
409 & 419 & 429 &    &              &           &           & Pg 36\\ \addlinespace
456 & 466 & 476 & 90 & 3+\mathrm{Mp}& 4\times70& 4\times70& Pg 36\\
457 & 467 & 477 &    &              &           &           & Pg 42\\\addlinespace
                                                                   \bottomrule
\end{tabular}
```

06-00-20

Listen-Nummer			Nennstrom	Polzahl	Anschluss bis mm^2		Pg für Abgang oben
mit Bügel-klemme	mit Mantel-klemme	mit Block-klemme	*A*		unten	oben	
406	416	426	25	$3+\mathrm{Mp}$	4×16	4×16	Pg 21
407	417	427					Pg 29
408	418	428	60	$3+\mathrm{Mp}$	4×35	4×16	Pg 29
409	419	429					Pg 36
456	466	476	90	$3+\mathrm{Mp}$	4×70	4×70	Pg 36
457	467	477					Pg 42

```
\usepackage{dcolumn,booktabs,ragged2e,rotating}
\newcommand\Rotate[1]{\raisebox{-3ex}{\begin{turn}{90}\rlap{#1}\end{turn}}}
\newcolumntype{C}{>{\footnotesize}c}
\newcolumntype{N}{>{\footnotesize}l}
\newcolumntype{P}[1]{>{\footnotesize\RaggedRight\hspace{0pt}}p{#1}}
\newcommand\mc[2]{\multicolumn{1}{#1}{#2}}

\begin{tabular}{@{}l *{5}{r} c@{}}\toprule
\mc{@{}N}{Heilanstalten} & \multicolumn{6}{N}{Ärzte} \\\cmidrule(l){2-7}
  & \multicolumn{2}{N}{insgesamt} & \multicolumn{4}{N@{}}{davon}\\
    \cmidrule(lr){2-3}\cmidrule(l){4-7}
  & & & & \multicolumn{3}{N@{}}{nachgeordnete Ärzte} \\\cmidrule(l){5-7}
  & & & & & \multicolumn{2}{C}{davon}\\\cmidrule(l){6-7}
  & \mc{C}{\Rotate{zusammen}} & \mc{C}{\Rotate{davon weiblich}}
  & \mc{C}{\Rotate{leitende Ärzte}} &  \mc{C}{\Rotate{insgesamt}}
  & \mc{P{2em}@{}}{Ober"-ärzte} & \mc{P{3.5em}@{}}{Assistenz"-ärzte} \\
    \cmidrule(r){1-1}\cmidrule(lr){2-2}\cmidrule(lr){3-3}\cmidrule(lr){4-4}%
    \cmidrule(lr){5-5}\cmidrule(lr){6-6}\cmidrule(l){7-7}
Josefsstift, Bad Brückenau & 90 & 24 & 11 & 79 & 15 & 64 \\
Tannenheim, Schlüchtern    & 37 & 12 &  8 & 27 &  7 & 22 \\
Waldfrieden, Selters       & 24 &  8 &  2 & 22 &  6 & 22 \\
Habichtshöhe, Lauterbach   & 36 & 13 &  3 & 33 &  8 & 25 \\\bottomrule
\end{tabular}
```

Heilanstalten	Ärzte					
	insgesamt		davon			
	zusammen	davon weiblich	leitende Ärzte	nachgeordnete Ärzte		
				insgesamt	davon	
					Ober-ärzte	Assistenz-ärzte
Josefsstift, Bad Brückenau	90	24	11	79	15	64
Tannenheim, Schlüchtern	37	12	8	27	7	22
Waldfrieden, Selters	24	8	2	22	6	22
Habichtshöhe, Lauterbach	36	13	3	33	8	25

06-00-2

```
\usepackage{dcolumn,booktabs,ragged2e,rotating,nicefrac}
\newcolumntype{C}{>{\footnotesize}c}
\newcolumntype{N}{>{\footnotesize}l}
\makeatletter\newcolumntype{B}[1]{>{\boldmath\DC@{.}{,}{#1}} c <{\DC@end}}\makeatother
\newcolumntype{P}[1]{>{\footnotesize\RaggedRight\hspace{0pt}}p{#1}}
\newcolumntype{d}[1]{D{.}{,}{#1}}
\newcommand\mc[2]{\multicolumn{1}{#1}{#2}}

\begin{tabular}{@{} d{4.0} d{2.0} d{2.1} B{2} d{2.1} @{\,\,} l@{}}\toprule
\mc{@{}N}{Capacity} & \mc{N}{Power}
  & \mc{P{4.5em}}{Acceleration 0\,\nicefrac{km}{h} to 100\,\nicefrac{km}{h}}
  & \mc{>{\bfseries}P{4em}}{Maximum speed}
  & \multicolumn{2}{P{4em}@{}}{Fuel consumption per 100\,km}\\
\mc{@{}C}{cm$^3$} & \mc{C}{kW} & \mc{C}{s} & \mc{>{\bfseries}C}{\nicefrac{km}{h}}
  & \multicolumn{2}{C@{}}{l}\\\cmidrule(r){1-1}\cmidrule(lr){2-2}\cmidrule(lr){3-3}
                          \cmidrule(lr){4-4}\cmidrule(l){5-6}
1288 & 37 & 22.7 & 133 & 8.6          \\ 1488 & 44 & 18.8 & 140 & 8.7 \\
1688 & 55 & 13.7 & 155 & 9.4  & Super\\ 1985 & 66 & 11.7 & 165 & 9.9  & Super \\
2274 & 80 &  9.8 & 178 & 10.1 & Super\\\bottomrule
\end{tabular}
```

Capacity	Power	Acceleration 0 km/h to 100 km/h	**Maximum speed**	Fuel consumption per 100 km	
cm^3	kW	s	**km/h**	l	
1288	37	22,7	**133**	8,6	
1488	44	18,8	**140**	8,7	
1688	55	13,7	**155**	9,4	Super
1985	66	11,7	**165**	9,9	Super
2274	80	9,8	**178**	10,1	Super

06-00-22

06-00-23

first column	second column
~~second line~~	~~more text~~
third line	lower right

```
\begin{tabular}{ll}
 first column & second column\\
 second line  & more text
 \\[-.5\normalbaselineskip]\hline\noalign{\vspace{1ex}}
 third line   & lower right
\end{tabular}
```

06-00-24

u_n \ v_n	ℓ	$+\infty$	$-\infty$
ℓ'	$\ell+\ell'$	$+\infty$	$-\infty$
$+\infty$	$+\infty$	$+\infty$	F.I.
$-\infty$	$-\infty$	F.I.	$-\infty$

```
\usepackage{array,slashbox,ragged2e}

\renewcommand\arraystretch{1.6}
\begin{tabular}{|*{4}{>{%
  \Centering$}m{12mm}<{$}|}}\hline
\multicolumn{1}{|c|}{%
  \backslashbox{$v_n$}{$u_n$}}
  & \ell&+\infty&-\infty\\\hline
\ell'  &\ell+\ell'&+\infty&-\infty\\\hline
+\infty&+\infty&+\infty&$F.I.$\\\hline
-\infty&-\infty&$F.I.$&-\infty\\\hline
\end{tabular}
```

06-00-25

2	Tu		Seminar
3	We		
4	Th		
5	Fr		
6	Sa	round table	Weekend
7	So		
8	Mo		
9	Tu		

```
\usepackage{tabularx,longtable,amsmath}
\usepackage[table]{xcolor}
\newcommand*\RMarker{.}
\newcommand*\SeminarOn[1][Weekend]{%
  \def\RMarker{\rbrace\text{#1}}}
\newcommand*\SeminarOff{\def\RMarker{.}}
\newcommand*\SA{\rowcolor{black!20}}
\newcommand*\SO{\rowcolor{black!30}}

\begin{longtable}{>{$\left.}l<{\right\RMarker$}}
\SeminarOn[Seminar]
\begin{tabularx}{.6\linewidth}{rlX}
  2 & Tu & \\ 3 & We & \\
  4 & Th & \\ 5 & Fr & \\
\end{tabularx} \\\SeminarOn
\begin{tabularx}{.6\linewidth}{rlX}
\SA 6 & Sa & round table\\
\SO 7 & So & \\
\end{tabularx} \\\SeminarOff
\begin{tabularx}{.6\linewidth}{rlX}
    8 & Mo &\\  9 & Tu &
\end{tabularx}
\end{longtable}
```

The following two figures show two floating environments, which appear on pages that face each other. To make the two tables start at the same height, a `\phantom` instruction is used for the right table. They can also be moved towards the centre to emphasize their connection.

The source code for this example was omitted for space reasons; it can be found as `06-00-26.ltx` on CTAN.

06-00-26

1 DOUBLEPAGE

1 A Section title, which is a bit longer to make it go over two lines in the heading.

	1972	1973	1974	1975	1976	1977	1978	1979	1980
Zeile 1	1	3	1	1	1	0	1	1	0
Zeile 2	1	1	3	1	0	0	0	0	0
Zeile 3	2	1	2	1	0	0	0	0	0
Zeile 4	1	0	5	1	2	0	0	0	0
Zeile 6	2	1	1	0	0	0	0	0	0
Zeile 5	0	0	4	2	1	2	2	1	0
Zeile 8	0	1	1	0	0	0	1	1	0
Zeile 9	0	0	0	0	0	1	2	1	0
Zeile10	0	1	3	0	1	0	1	0	0
Zeile11	0	2	2	1	1	0	1	0	0
Zeile12	2	0	2	4	1	0	4	0	0
Lärm	2	3	0	0	0	0	0	0	0
Zeile13	0	1	0	0	1	0	3	0	0
Zeile14	0	1	0	0	0	0	0	0	0
Zeile15	0	0	0	0	0	0	0	0	0
Zeile16	0	0	0	0	0	1	0	0	0
Artikel gesamt	2	6	13	8	4	3	5	4	0

(a)

Table 1: Table caption, part I.

1

1 DOUBLEPAGE

	1981	1982	1983	1984	1985	1986	1987	1988
Z 1	0	0	0	20	0	2	2	2
Z 2	0	2	1	3	4	4	6	4
Z 3	0	0	1	5	3	1	7	7
Z 4	2	1	0	1	0	3	7	2
Z 6	1	2	0	5	2	2	5	4
Z 5	0	0	1	1	0	2	5	4
Z 8	3	2	1	2	1	3	5	3
Z 9	0	0	0	4	2	1	4	5
Z10	1	1	0	1	1	1	4	4
Z11	0	0	2	6	1	0	2	1
Z12	0	0	0	0	0	0	1	0
Lärm	0	1	0	2	0	0	2	2
Z13	0	0	0	2	0	1	3	0
Z14	0	0	0	3	3	2	1	1
Z15	1	0	0	4	0	0	3	1
Z16	0	0	0	0	0	3	5	0
Artikel gesamt	6	3	5	23	10	8	15	13

(b)

Table 1: Table caption, part II.

2

```
\usepackage{tabularx}

\begin{tabularx}{\linewidth}{@{}X|p{2mm}@{}|}\cline{2-2}
DANTE, Deutschsprachige Anwendervereinigung \TeX\ e.\,V., has been founded on April 14,
1989 in Heidelberg, Germany. The principal aim of the association is to encourage advice
and cooperation among German language TeX users. This includes consulting via WWW,
electronic mail, and usual letter mail concerning purchase, implementation, and \ldots
  & \rule{2mm}{0pt}\\\cline{2-2}
\end{tabularx}
```

06-00-27

DANTE, Deutschsprachige Anwendervereinigung TeX e. V., has been founded on April 14, 1989 in Heidelberg, Germany. The principal aim of the association is to encourage advice and cooperation among German language TeX users. This includes consulting via WWW, electronic mail, and usual letter mail concerning purchase, implementation, and . . .

Autor	Fläche	Airgap	Empfindl.	Frequenz	Rauschen	Materialien Membran, Elektrode	Quellen	Aufbauart
	mm^2	µm	mV/Pa	Hz-kHz	dBA SPL			
Schellin	1		0,3	–		Poly-Si, Poly-Si	[6,7,9]	1 Chip
van der Donk							[12]	1 Chip
Bernstein	0,57	2,2	10,77	-20	–	Nitrid, Gold	[13]	1 Chip
Chen	–	2	40	50–15	–	Poly-Si, Mono-Si	[17,18]	1 Chip
Dehé	∅1.2	1	3,2	100–10	30	Poly-Si, Epi-Poly	[19,10]	1 Chip
Hsu	2	4	–	200–10		Poly-Si, Mono-Si	[7]	1 Chip
Kronast	2	1,3	11	300–20	–	Nitrid+Alu, Mono-Si	[20,21,22]	1 Chip
Li	1	–	9,6	100–19	–	Poly-Si, Poly-Si	[1,24]	1 Chip
Pedersen	4,84	3,6	–	100–15	60	Gold, Polymid	[2,6]	1 Chip
Rombach	1	0,9	14	20–10	22,5	Poly-Si, Poly-Si	[17,18]	1 Chip
Kovács	0,25	1,5	–	–	–	Poly-Si, Poly-Si	[25,26]	1 Chip
Torkkeli	1	1,3	2	10–12	35	Poly-Si, Poly-Si	[26]	1 Chip
Bay	4	0,4	27				[26,27,28,30]	2 Chip
Füldner								2 Chip
Tajima	4	15	7	75–24	–	Oxid, Mono-Si	[29]	2 Chip
Kressmann	1	1	2,9	100–10	39	Oxid+Nitrid, Poly-Si	[11,12]	Elektret
Thielemann							[8]	Elektret
Hsieh	64	4,5	40	100–10	60	Nitrid, Nitrid	[1,2,4]	Elektret
Murphy	–	–	8	100–15	–	Al + Nitrid, Mono-Si	[3]	Elektret
Zou	1	2,6	14,2	9–16	–	Poly-Si , Mono-Si	[7]	Elektret

```
\usepackage{tabularx}
\makeatletter\newcolumntype{M}{>{\@minipagetrue}X}\makeatother

\begin{tabularx}{\linewidth}{|X|M|}\hline
left & right\\\hline
The right list now starts at the same height as this column.
 & \begin{itemize} \item a \item b \item c \end{itemize}\\\hline
\begin{itemize} \item a \item b \item c \end{itemize}
 & The left column is not an M-column now and therefore has vertical space at the
   beginning.\\\hline
\end{tabularx}
```

left	right
The right list now starts at the same height as this column.	• a • b • c
• a • b • c	The left column is not an M-column now and therefore has vertical space at the beginning.

06-00-29

Table 1: Automatic counting of lines in a table.

No. animal
1 gelse
2 chamois
3 skunk
4 anteater
5 armadillo

See line 2 or alternatively line 5 in Table 1 on page 1.

06-00-30

```
\usepackage{array}
\newcounter{tabline}
\newcolumntype{n}{>{%
  \refstepcounter{tabline}\thetabline\enspace}l}

\begin{table}
\centering
\caption{Automatic counting of lines
  in a table.}\label{BAZ}
\begin{tabular}{n}\hline
\multicolumn{1}{l}{\emph{No. animal}}\\\hline
gelse                                  \\
chamois \label{FOO}                    \\
skunk                                  \\
anteater                               \\
armadillo \label{BAR}                  \\\hline
\end{tabular}
\end{table}

\medskip
See line~\ref{FOO} or alternatively
line~\ref{BAR} in Table~\ref{BAZ}
on page~\pageref{BAR}.
```

```
\usepackage{array,booktabs,ragged2e} \def\xstrut{\rule{0pt}{3ex}}
\newcolumntype{P}[1]{>{\RaggedRight}p{#1}}

\begin{tabular}{@{}ccc@{\qquad}rrrr@{}}\toprule
\multicolumn{1}{@{}P{1.25cm}}{Tipo de avi\'on}
 & \multicolumn{1}{P{1.75cm}}{Capacidad (pasajeros)}
 & \multicolumn{1}{P{1.75cm}}{N\'umero de aviones}
 & \multicolumn{4}{@{}p{4cm}@{}}{%
     \xstrut N\'umero de viajes diarios en la ruta}\\\cmidrule{4-7}
\xstrut &     &    & 1  & 2 & 3 & 4 \\\midrule
   1    & 50  & 5  & 3  & 2 & 2 & 1 \\
   2    & 30  & 8  & 4  & 3 & 3 & 2 \\
   3    & 20  & 10 & 5  & 5 & 4 & 2 \\ \midrule
   4    & 10  & 18 & 3  & 1 & -- & 1 \\
   5    & 5   & 8  & 2  & 1 & -- & 6 \\
   6    & 1   & 80 & 6  & 5 & 12 & 4 \\\midrule
\multicolumn{3}{@{}l}{%
  N\'umero de clientes diarios} & 1000 & 2000 & 900 & 1200 \\\bottomrule
\end{tabular}
```

06-00-31

Tipo de avión	Capacidad (pasajeros)	Número de aviones	Número de viajes diarios en la ruta			
			1	2	3	4
1	50	5	3	2	2	1
2	30	8	4	3	3	2
3	20	10	5	5	4	2
4	10	18	3	1	–	1
5	5	8	2	1	–	6
6	1	80	6	5	12	4
Número de clientes diarios			1000	2000	900	1200

The following example shows how to add columns automatically with intermediate sums. For space reasons, the whole preamble was moved into the non-visible part here.

```
\usepackage{longtable}

\resetintsum
\begin{longtable}{p{0.7\linewidth}r}
  left & right
\endfirsthead
  carry & \\
\endhead
  intermediate sum: & \MarkIntSumPos \\
\endfoot
  sum: &\MarkIntSumPos \\
\endlastfoot
```

```
  An arbitrary introductory text at the start of the column\ldots.
    & \Val{1,00} \\
  b & \Val{2,1}  \\
  c & \Val{3,4}  \\
  d & \Val{4,5}  \\
  e & \Val{5,6}  \\
  f & \Val{6,7}  \\
  g & \Val{7,8}  \\
  h & \Val{8,9}  \\
  i & \Val{9,42} \\
  j & \Val{10,88}\\
  k & \Val{15,76}
\end{longtable}
```

left	right
An arbitrary introductory text at the start of the column....	1.—
b	2.10
c	3.40
d	4.50
e	5.60
f	6.70
g	7.80
h	8.90
intermediate sum:	40.— €

carry	40.— €
i	9.42
j	10.88
k	15.76
sum:	76.06 €

06-00-32

```
\usepackage{ragged2e,array,graphicx}

\renewcommand\arraystretch{1.3}
\begin{tabular}{@{}cc@{}}\small
\begin{tabular}{@{}c l l >{\RaggedRight}m{3.0cm}@{}}\hline
\emph{pin} & \emph{color} & \emph{at encoder} & \emph{description}\\\hline
1   & ---    & ---        & $\langle empty \rangle$          \\
2   & yellow & 8 (gray)   & Encoder channel B                \\
3   & white  & 7 (violet) & Encoder channel $\overline{B}$  \\
4   & blue   & 6 (blue)   & Encoder channel A                \\
5   & green  & 5 (green)  & Encoder channel $\overline{A}$  \\
6   & ---    & ---        & $\langle empty \rangle$          \\
7   & red    & 2 (red)    & Encoder power supply (+5V)       \\
8   & black  & 3 (orange) & GND                              \\ \hline
```

```
\end{tabular}
  & % right column for the image
\raisebox{-0.5\height}{\includegraphics[width=3cm]{images/din8}}
\end{tabular}
```

06-00-33

pin	*color*	*at encoder*	*description*
1	–	–	⟨*empty*⟩
2	yellow	8 (gray)	Encoder channel B
3	white	7 (violet)	Encoder channel $\overline{B}$
4	blue	6 (blue)	Encoder channel A
5	green	5 (green)	Encoder channel $\overline{A}$
6	–	–	⟨*empty*⟩
7	red	2 (red)	Encoder power supply (+5V)
8	black	3 (orange)	GND

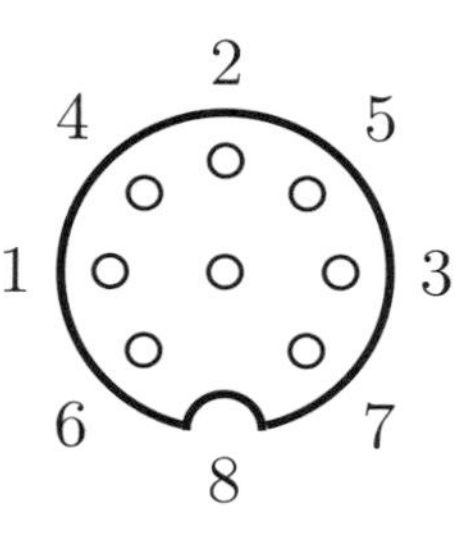


```
\usepackage{array,booktabs,arydshln,eurosym,graphicx}
\usepackage[table]{xcolor}

\resizebox{0.9\textwidth}{!}{\renewcommand\arraystretch{1.25}%
\begin{tabular}{@{}l c rr | rr@{}}\toprule
\textit{TEST 1} & & \multicolumn{2}{c}{1. Jahr} & \multicolumn{2}{c}{ab 2. Jahr}\\
\textit{TEST 2} & & Monat & Jahr & Monat & Jahr \\\midrule
\textit{Werkzeugkosten je Automat} && \textit{8.000} & \textit{96.000}
  & \textit{8.000} & \textit{96.000} \\
Anzahl Bestellungen für Werkzeuge       &    & 8   & 96     & 8     & 96 \\
Prozesskosten pro Beschaffungsprozess   & 40 &   &   &   & \\
Kosten für Stammdatenpflege             &    & 10  & 120 & 10 & 120 \\
\rowcolor[gray]{0.92}[\tabcolsep]
  Bestellkosten                           &    & 330 & 3.960 & 330 & 3.960 \\
 % \midrule
Durchschnittlicher Lagerwert (2 Monate)& & & 16.000 & & 16.000 \\\cline{3-6}
Gebundenes Kapital pro Jahr             & 6\% & 80 & 960 & 80 & 960 \\
Lagerabwertung vom Lagerwert pro Jahr   & 5\% & 67 & 800 & 67 & 800 \\
\rowcolor[gray]{0.92}[\tabcolsep]
  Lagerkosten                             &     & 147 & 1.760 & 147 & 1.760 \\
Personalkosten Werkzeugausgabe \euro/h & 30 &  &  &  & \\
Einsparung Werkzeugausgabe pro Tag in h & 2 & 1.200 & 14.400 & 1.200 & 14.400 \\
Werkzeugschwund                          & 1\% & 80 & 960 & 80 & 960 \\
\textit{Stillstand aufgrund fehlendem Werkzeug} & \textit{0,03h/Tag} & \textit{53}
    & \textit{636} & \textit{53} & \textit{636} \\
Anzahl Maschinen                       & 5    & 265 & 3.180 & 265 & 3.180 \\
Weniger Verbrauch durch Kontrolle      & 5\%  & 400 & 4.800 & 400 & 4.800 \\
Weniger Schwarzbestände im 1.Jahr      & 10\% & 800 & 9.600 &  &  \\
\rowcolor[gray]{0.92}[\tabcolsep]
  Verbrauch- und Personalkosten          &      & 2.745 & 32.940 & 1.945 & 23.340 \\
```

```
\rowcolor[gray]{0.88}[\tabcolsep]
  Einsparungen                          &      & 3.222 & 38.660 & 2.422 & 29.060 \\
\rowcolor[gray]{0.99}\multicolumn{4}{c|}{Abzüglich zusätzliche Kosten:}    \\
Miete                  & & 200 & 2.400 & 200 & 2.400 \\
Installation und Wartung& & 142 & 1.700 & 42  & 500   \\
Sonstige Kosten        & & 83  & 1.000 & 83  & 1.000 \\
\rowcolor[gray]{0.88}[\tabcolsep]Tatsächliche Einsparungen&&2.797&33.560&2.097&25.160\\
 & & \multicolumn{2}{c|}{$\stackrel{\wedge}{=}35\%$}
  & \multicolumn{2}{c@{}}{$\stackrel{\wedge}{=} 26\%$}\\
    \cmidrule{3-6}\morecmidrules\cmidrule{3-6}
\end{tabular}}
```

06-00-34

TEST 1		1. Jahr		ab 2. Jahr	
TEST 2		Monat	Jahr	Monat	Jahr
Werkzeugkosten je Automat		*8.000*	*96.000*	*8.000*	*96.000*
Anzahl Bestellungen für Werkzeuge		8	96	8	96
Prozesskosten pro Beschaffungsprozess	40				
Kosten für Stammdatenpflege		10	120	10	120
Bestellkosten		330	3.960	330	3.960
Durchschnittlicher Lagerwert (2 Monate)			16.000		16.000
Gebundenes Kapital pro Jahr	6%	80	960	80	960
Lagerabwertung vom Lagerwert pro Jahr	5%	67	800	67	800
Lagerkosten		147	1.760	147	1.760
Personalkosten Werkzeugausgabe €/h	30				
Einsparung Werkzeugausgabe pro Tag in h	2	1.200	14.400	1.200	14.400
Werkzeugschwund	1%	80	960	80	960
Stillstand aufgrund fehlendem Werkzeug	*0,03h/Tag*	*53*	*636*	*53*	*636*
Anzahl Maschinen	5	265	3.180	265	3.180
Weniger Verbrauch durch Kontrolle	5%	400	4.800	400	4.800
Weniger Schwarzbestände im 1.Jahr	10%	800	9.600		
Verbrauch- und Personalkosten		2.745	32.940	1.945	23.340
Einsparungen		3.222	38.660	2.422	29.060
Abzüglich zusätzliche Kosten:					
Miete		200	2.400	200	2.400
Installation und Wartung		142	1.700	42	500
Sonstige Kosten		83	1.000	83	1.000
Tatsächliche Einsparungen		2.797	33.560	2.097	25.160
		$\stackrel{\wedge}{=} 35\%$		$\stackrel{\wedge}{=} 26\%$	

You can control the row spacing in a table relatively easily, by using either the `tabls` package or altering the value of `\arraystretch`, which defaults to 1. Alternatively, you can insert an invisible line (`\rule`) with a depth *and* height. This example also shows how to use nested tables.

06-00-35

Vertical spacing in a table.

Default baseline height

1	An extremely long line of text in a m-column
2	An extremely long line of text in a m-column
3	An extremely long line of text in a m-column

`\renewcommand\arraystrech{1.5}`

1	An extremely long line of text in a m-column
2	An extremely long line of text in a m-column
3	An extremely long line of text in a m-column

`\rule[-3ex]{0pt}{7ex}` in first column

1	An extremely long line of text in a m-column
2	An extremely long line of text in a m-column
3	An extremely long line of text in a m-column

```
\usepackage{array,ragged2e}

\begin{center}
Vertical spacing in a table.\\[5pt]

Default baseline height\\[2pt]
\begin{tabular}{@{}c
  >{\RaggedRight}m{4cm}@{}}\hline
1 & An extremely long line of text
    in a m-column\\\hline
2 & An extremely long line of text
    in a m-column\\\hline
3 & An extremely long line of text
    in a m-column\\\hline
\end{tabular}

\bigskip
\renewcommand\arraystretch{1.5}
\verb=\renewcommand\arraystrech{1.5}=\\[2pt]
\begin{tabular}{@{}c
  >{\RaggedRight}m{4cm}@{}}\hline
1 & An extremely long line of text
    in a m-column\\\hline
2 & An extremely long line of text
    in a m-column\\\hline
3 & An extremely long line of text
    in a m-column\\\hline
\end{tabular}

\bigskip
\verb=\rule[-3ex]{0pt}{7ex}= in
  first column\\[2pt]
\begin{tabular}{@{}
  >{\rule[-3ex]{0pt}{7ex}}c
  >{\RaggedRight}m{4cm}@{}}\hline
1 & An extremely long line of text
    in a m-column\\\hline
2 & An extremely long line of text
    in a m-column\\\hline
3 & An extremely long line of text
    in a m-column\\\hline
\end{tabular}
\end{center}
```

The following two tables have been rotated through `sidewaystable` and `\rotatebox`. In the first case, the option `twoside` of the example document class is taken into account and rotated accordingly, while in the second case the table is simply rotated counter-clockwise.

```
\usepackage{array,booktabs,rotating,units}
\newcolumntype{N}{>{\scriptsize}l}

\begin{sidewaystable}
\caption{The following table has been rotated automatically with \texttt{sidewaystable}.}
\begin{center}
\begin{tabular}{@{}NN*{5}{l}@{}}\toprule
capacity  & $\unit{cm^3}$ & 1288 & 1488 & 1688 & 1985 & 2274 \\\midrule
power & \unit{kW} & 37 & 44 & 55  & 66 & 80 \\\midrule
acceleration \unitfrac[0]{km}{h} to \unitfrac[100]{km}{h} & \unit{s} & 22,7
  & 18,8 & 13,7 & 11,7 & 9,8 \\\midrule
\textbf{maximum speed}
  & \textbf{\unitfrac{km}{h}}
  & \textbf{133} & \textbf{140} & \textbf{155}
  & \textbf{165} & \textbf{178} \\\midrule
fuel consumption per \unit[100]{km} & \unit{l} & 8,6 & 8,7 & 9,4 (super)
  & 9,9 (super) & 10,1 (super) \\\bottomrule
\end{tabular}
\end{center}
\end{sidewaystable}
```

06-00-3

Table 1: The following table has been rotated automatically with `sidewaystable`.

capacity	cm^3	1288	1488	1688	1985	2274
power	kW	37	44	55	66	80
acceleration 0 km/h to 100 km/h	s	22,7	18,8	13,7	11,7	9,8
maximum speed	**km/h**	**133**	**140**	**155**	**165**	**178**
fuel consumption per 100 km	l	8,6	8,7	9,4 (super)	9,9 (super)	10,1 (super)

1

In contrast to the `sidewaystable` environment, the `\rotatebox` command can rotate the table without it appearing on a separate page. This means that text of the normal alignment can be placed next to the rotated table.

```
\usepackage{array,tabularx,booktabs,rotating,units,caption}
\newcolumntype{N}{>{\scriptsize}l}
\newsavebox\TBox

\savebox\TBox{\parbox{\linewidth}{%
\captionof{table}{The following table was rotated with \texttt{rotatebox}.}
\begin{tabular}{@{}NN*{5}{l}@{}}\toprule
capacity  & $\unit{cm^3}$ & 1288 & 1488 & 1688 & 1985 & 2274 \\\midrule
power & \unit{kW}      &   37 &   44 &   55 &   66 &   80 \\\midrule
acceleration \unitfrac[0]{km}{h} to \unitfrac[100]{km}{h}
        & \unit{s}       & 22,7 & 18,8 & 13,7 & 11,7 &  9,8 \\\midrule
\textbf{maximum speed} & \textbf{\unitfrac{km}{h}} & \textbf{133}
  & \textbf{140} & \textbf{155} & \textbf{165} & \textbf{178} \\\midrule
fuel consumption per \unit[100]{km}
        & \unit{l} & 8,6 & 8,7 & 9,4 (super)& 9,9 (super)& 10,1 (super) \\\bottomrule
\end{tabular}}}
\begin{tabularx}\linewidth{@{} l X @{}}
\raisebox{-1.3\height}{\rotatebox{90}{\usebox\TBox}} & \blindtext
\end{tabularx}
```

5-00-37

Table 1: The following table was rotated with rotatebox.

capacity	cm^3	1288	1488	1688	1985	2274
power	kW	37	44	55	66	80
acceleration 0 km/h to 100 km/h	s	22,7	18,8	13,7	11,7	9,8
maximum speed	**km/h**	**133**	**140**	**155**	**165**	**178**
fuel consumption per 100 km	l	8,6	8,7	9,4 (super)	9,9 (super)	10,1 (super)

Hello, here is some text without a meaning. This text should show, how a printed text will look like at this place. If you read this text, you will get no information. Really? Is there no information? Is there a difference between this text and some nonsense like »Huardest gefburn«. Kjift – Never mind! A blind text like this gives you information about the selected font, how the letters are written and the impression of the look. This text should contain all letters of the alphabet and it should be written in of the original language. There is no need for a special contents, but the length of words should match to the language.

1

```
\usepackage{pst-node,pst-tree,graphicx,geometry}
\def\GraphTabLine#1(#2,#3,#4,#5){%
  #1 & \rnode{A}{#2} & \checkSpace(#2,#3){B}{#3}
     & \checkSpace(#2,#4){C}{#4} & \checkSpace(#2,#5){D}{#5}
  \ncline{A}{B}\ncline{B}{C}\ncline{C}{D}}
\newlength\Vspace
\def\checkSpace(#1,#2)#3#4{%
  \Vspace=#1pt \advance\Vspace by -#2pt
  \raisebox{-3\Vspace}{\rnode{#3}{#4}}}

\psset{nodesep=2pt,arrows=->}
\resizebox{!}{0.5\textheight}{%
\begin{tabular}{@{}l*4{p{2cm}}@{}}
 & 5 year & 10 year & 15 year & 20 year\\
 \GraphTabLine{Prostate}                (99,95,87,81)\\
 \GraphTabLine{Thyroid}                 (96,96,94,95)\\
 \GraphTabLine{Testis}                  (95,94,91,88)\\[-15pt]
 \GraphTabLine{Melanomas}               (89,87,84,82)\\[-15pt]
 \GraphTabLine{Breast}                  (86,78,71,65)\\[-45pt]
 \GraphTabLine{Hodgkin's disease}       (85,80,74,67)\\[-10pt]
 \GraphTabLine{Corpus uteri, uterus}    (84,83,81,79)\\[-10pt]
 \GraphTabLine{Urinar bladder}          (82,76,70,67)\\[-27pt]
 \GraphTabLine{Cervix uteri}            (71,64,63,60)\\[-25pt]
 \GraphTabLine{Larynx}                  (69,57,46,37)\\[-35pt]
 \GraphTabLine{Rectum}                  (63,55,52,49)\\[-35pt]
 \GraphTabLine{Kidney, renal pelvis}    (62,54,50,47)\\[-25pt]
 \GraphTabLine{Colon}                   (62,55,54,52)\\[-20pt]
 \GraphTabLine{Non-Hodgkin's}           (58,46,38,34)\\[-63pt]
 \GraphTabLine{Oral cavity, pharynx}    (57,44,38,33)\\[-10pt]
 \GraphTabLine{Ovary}                   (55,49,50,50)\\[-10pt]
 \GraphTabLine{Leukaemias}              (43,32,29,26)\\[-10pt]
 \GraphTabLine{Brain, nervous system}(32,29,27,26)\\[-10pt]
 \GraphTabLine{Multiple myeloma}        (30,13, 7, 5)\\[-15pt]
 \GraphTabLine{Stomach}                 (24,19,19,15)\\[-20pt]
 \GraphTabLine{Lung and bronchus}       (15,11, 8, 6)\\[-20pt]
 \GraphTabLine{Esophagus}               (14, 8, 8, 5)\\[ 30pt]
 \GraphTabLine{Liver, bile duct}        ( 8, 6, 6, 8)\\
 \GraphTabLine{Pancreas}                ( 4, 3, 3, 3)
\end{tabular}}
```

6-00-38

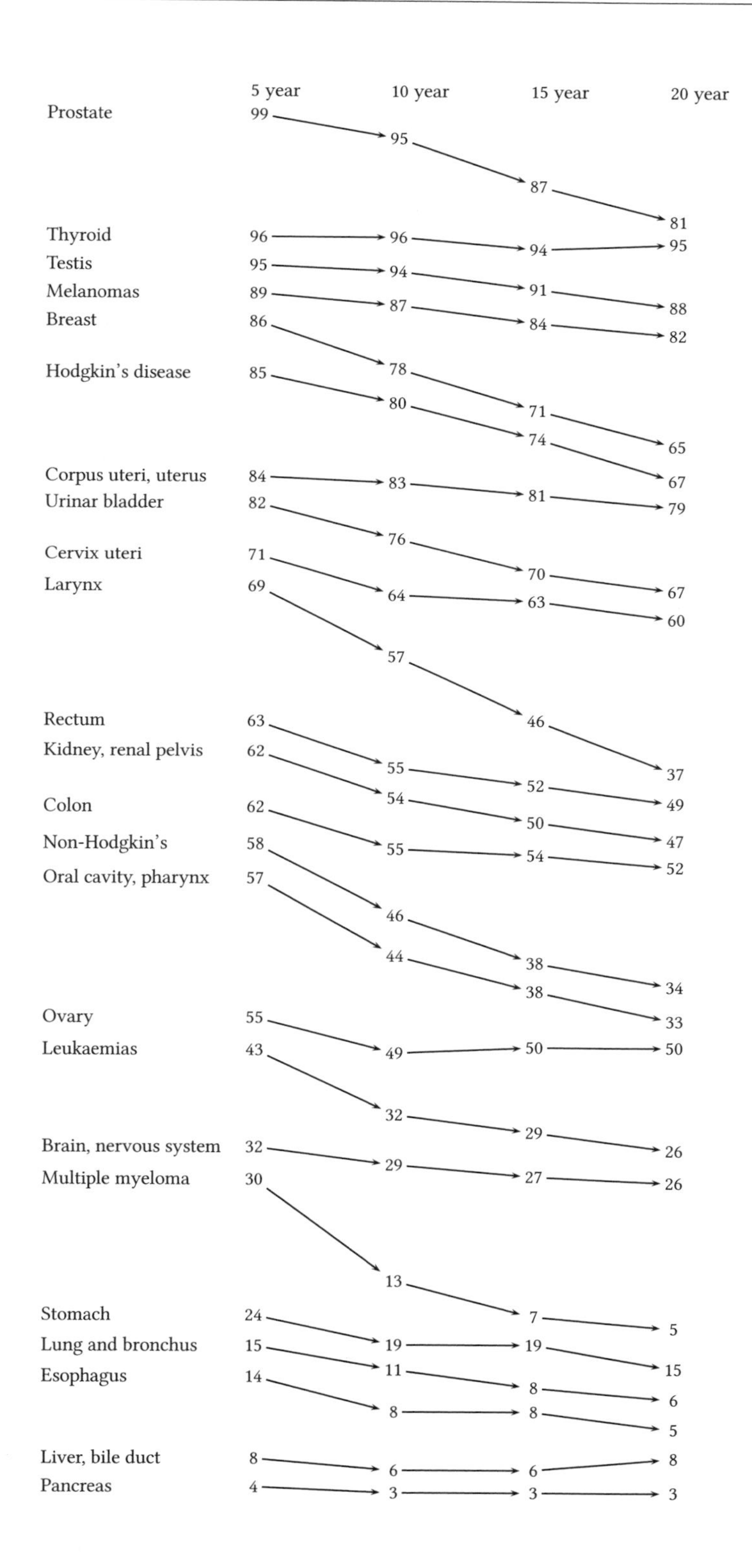
5 year
10 year
15 year
20 year
Prostate 99 95 87 81
Thyroid 96 96 94 95
Testis 95 94 91 88
Melanomas 89 87 84 82
Breast 86 78 71 65
Hodgkin's disease 85 80 74 67
Corpus uteri, uterus 84 83 81 79
Urinar bladder 82 76 70 67
Cervix uteri 71 64 63 60
Larynx 69 57 46 37
Rectum 63 55 52 49
Kidney, renal pelvis 62 54 50 47
Colon 62 55 54 52
Non-Hodgkin's 58 46 38 34
Oral cavity, pharynx 57 44 38 33
Ovary 55 49 50 50
Leukaemias 43 32 29 26
Brain, nervous system 32 29 27 26
Multiple myeloma 30 13 7 5
Stomach 24 19 19 15
Lung and bronchus 15 11 8 6
Esophagus 14 8 8 5
Liver, bile duct 8 6 6 8
Pancreas 4 3 3 3

```
\usepackage{numprint,spreadtab}

\begin{minipage}[t]{0.45\linewidth}\vspace{0pt}
\[\forall x\in \mathbf{R}\qquad e^x=\sum_{k=0}^\infty\frac{x^k}{k!}\]
The adjacent table shows the convergence for $x=0.5$.
\end{minipage}\hfill
\begin{minipage}[t]{0.45\linewidth}\vspace{0pt}
\STautoround{15}
\begin{spreadtab}[\STsavecell\xvalue{a1}]{{tabular}{cN{2}{15}}}
\multicolumn{2}{c}{convergence for $x={\numprint{:={0.5}}}$}\\[1.5ex]
@$n$       & e^a1\SThidecol & {@
  $\displaystyle e^{\numprint\xvalue}-\sum_{k=0}^n
   \frac{\numprint\xvalue^k}{k!}$}\\[3ex]\hline
  0        & a1^[-1,0]/fact([-1,0])          & b2-[-1,0] \\
 [0,-1]+1 & a1^[-1,0]/fact([-1,0])+[0,-1] & b2-[-1,0] \\
 [0,-1]+1 & a1^[-1,0]/fact([-1,0])+[0,-1] & b2-[-1,0] \\
 [0,-1]+1 & a1^[-1,0]/fact([-1,0])+[0,-1] & b2-[-1,0] \\
 [0,-1]+1 & a1^[-1,0]/fact([-1,0])+[0,-1] & b2-[-1,0] \\
 [0,-1]+1 & a1^[-1,0]/fact([-1,0])+[0,-1] & b2-[-1,0] \\
 [0,-1]+1 & a1^[-1,0]/fact([-1,0])+[0,-1] & b2-[-1,0] \\
 [0,-1]+1 & a1^[-1,0]/fact([-1,0])+[0,-1] & b2-[-1,0] \\
 [0,-1]+1 & a1^[-1,0]/fact([-1,0])+[0,-1] & b2-[-1,0] \\
 [0,-1]+1 & a1^[-1,0]/fact([-1,0])+[0,-1] & b2-[-1,0] \\\hline
\end{spreadtab}
\end{minipage}
```

$$\forall x \in \mathbf{R} \qquad e^x = \sum_{k=0}^{\infty} \frac{x^k}{k!}$$

The adjacent table shows the convergence for $x = 0.5$.

convergence for $x = 0{,}5$

n	$e^{0,5} - \sum_{k=0}^{n} \frac{0,5^k}{k!}$
0	0,648 721 270 700 128
1	0,148 721 270 700 128
2	0,023 721 270 700 128
3	0,002 887 937 366 795
4	0,000 283 770 700 128
5	0,000 023 354 033 461
6	0,000 001 652 644 572
7	0,000 000 102 545 366
8	0,000 000 005 664 166
9	0,000 000 000 281 877

06-00-

```
\usepackage{tabularx,numprint,spreadtab}

\nprounddigits2
\begin{spreadtab}{{tabularx}{0.8\linewidth}{|
  >{\rule[-1.2ex]{0pt}{4ex}}X >{{\bfseries}}N42
  >{\bfseries}c N42 >{\bfseries}c N42|}}\hline
@Pos. & @\multicolumn{1}{c}{price/unit} & @\multicolumn{1}{c}{number} &
```

```
@\multicolumn{1}{c}{price} & @\multicolumn{1}{c}{rebate} & @\textbf{net}\\\hline
@1 & 5.99 & 20 & [-2,0]*[-1,0] & $-:={20}\%$ & [-2,0]*(1-[-1,0]/100)\\
@2 & 12   & 7  & [-2,0]*[-1,0] & $-:={10}\%$ & [-2,0]*(1-[-1,0]/100)\\
@3 & 4.50 & 40 & [-2,0]*[-1,0] & $-:={35}\%$ & [-2,0]*(1-[-1,0]/100)\\
@4 & 650  & 2  & [-2,0]*[-1,0] & $-:={15}\%$ & [-2,0]*(1-[-1,0]/100)\\\hline
@\multicolumn{6}{c}{\vspace{-1.5ex}}\\\cline{4-6}
@\multicolumn{1}{c}{\rule[-1.2ex]{0pt}{4ex}} &
@\multicolumn{2}{r|}{sum} & sum(d2:[0,-2])
  & \multicolumn{1}{c}{$:={round(([1,0]/[-1,0]-1)*100,0)}\%$}
  & {\bfseries}:={sum(f2:[0,-2])}\\\cline{4-6}
@\multicolumn{3}{r|}{} & @\multicolumn{1}{r}{\textbf{VAT}} & @ 19\%
  & {\bfseries}:={[0,-1]*0.19}\\\cline{4-6}
@\multicolumn{3}{r|}{} &
@\multicolumn{2}{r}{\textbf{final sum}} & {\bfseries}:={[0,-2]+[0,-1]}\\\cline{4-6}
\end{spreadtab}
```

-00-40

Pos.	price/unit	number	price	rebate	**net**
1	**5,99**	**20**	119,80	−20%	95,84
2	**12,00**	7	84,00	−10%	75,60
3	**4,50**	**40**	180,00	−35%	117,00
4	**650,00**	2	1 300,00	−15%	1 105,00
		sum	1 683,80	−17%	**1 393,44**
			VAT	**19%**	**264,75**
				final sum	**1 658,19**

```
\usepackage{booktabs,paralist,dcolumn,ragged2e}
\newenvironment{Vorteile}
  {\hbox{}\vspace{-\baselineskip}\begin{compactitem}[$\oplus$]}
  {\hbox{}\vspace{-\baselineskip}\end{compactitem}}
\newenvironment{Nachteile}
  {\hbox{}\vspace{-\baselineskip}\begin{compactitem}[$\ominus$]}
  {\hbox{}\vspace{-\baselineskip}\end{compactitem}}
\newcolumntype{v}[1]{>{\RaggedRight\hspace{0pt}}p{#1}}

\sffamily\footnotesize
\begin{tabular}{@{}v{1.4cm}*{2}{v{6.9cm}}@{}}\toprule
Material & Vorteile & Nachteile \\\cmidrule(r){1-1}\cmidrule(rl){2-2}\cmidrule(l){3-3}
Edelstahl
  & \begin{Vorteile}
    \item robust \item preisgünstig \item leicht zu verarbeiten
    \item unterschiedliche Durchmesser und Längen im Handel erhältlich
    \end{Vorteile}
  & \begin{Nachteile}
    \item nur inert bei geringen Temperaturen in Verbindung mit bestimmten Substanzen
    \item Oxidationen der Oberfläche führen zu unsymmetrischen Peaks
```

```
    \item Zersetzung durch Verunreinigungen der Legierungsform
    \end{Nachteile} \tabularnewline\cmidrule(r){1-1}\cmidrule(rl){2-2}\cmidrule(l){3-3}
Glas
  & \begin{Vorteile}%
    \item fast vollständig inert
    \item durchsichtig, bessere Kontrolle der Packung auf Gleichmäßigkeit
    \end{Vorteile}%
  & \begin{Nachteile}%
    \item aufwendige Reinigung der Säule
    \item keine Analyse von aggressiver Fluoride möglich
    \item leicht zerbrechlich
    \item Knallgasexplosion beim Zerbrechen bei erhitzter Kapillare und
          Wasserstoff als Trägergas
    \end{Nachteile} \tabularnewline\cmidrule(r){1-1}\cmidrule(rl){2-2}\cmidrule(l){3-3}
Nickel
  & \begin{Vorteile}%
    \item stabil
    \item Analyse von empfindlichen Substanzen möglich, z\,.B. Steroide, Analgetica
          und Barbiturate
    \end{Vorteile}%
  & \begin{Nachteile}%
    \item nicht so inert wie Glassäulen
    \end{Nachteile} \tabularnewline\cmidrule(r){1-1}\cmidrule(rl){2-2}\cmidrule(l){3-3}
Kupfer
  & \begin{Vorteile}%
    \item leicht zu verarbeiten
    \end{Vorteile}%
  & \begin{Nachteile}
    \item Oberfläche ist autoxydabel
    \item Kupferoxid oxidiert organische Stoffe
    \item ungeeignet wenn Sauerstoff im Trägergas vorhanden ist
    \item aufwendiges Herstellungsverfahren
    \end{Nachteile} \tabularnewline\cmidrule(r){1-1}\cmidrule(rl){2-2}\cmidrule(l){3-3}
Teflon
  & \begin{Vorteile}
    \item vollständig inert
    \item Analyse von aggressiven Substanzen möglich
    \end{Vorteile}
  & \begin{Nachteile}
    \item Material kann mikroporös sein, Spurenelemente der Außenluft rufen negative
          Effekte bei der Analyse hervor
    \end{Nachteile} \tabularnewline\cmidrule(r){1-1}\cmidrule(rl){2-2}\cmidrule(l){3-3}
Silizium
  & \begin{Vorteile}
    \item fast vollständig inert
    \item nahezu unbegrenzte Rohstoffreserven
    \item autoxydable Bildung von nativen Siliziumdioxiden
    \end{Vorteile}
  & \begin{Nachteile}
    \item zerbrechlicher als Metalle
```

```
  \end{Nachteile} \tabularnewline\addlinespace\bottomrule
\end{tabular}
```

6-00-41

Material	Vorteile	Nachteile
Edelstahl	⊕ robust ⊕ preisgünstig ⊕ leicht zu verarbeiten ⊕ unterschiedliche Durchmesser und Längen im Handel erhältlich	⊖ nur inert bei geringen Temperaturen in Verbindung mit bestimmten Substanzen ⊖ Oxidationen der Oberfläche führen zu unsymmetrischen Peaks ⊖ Zersetzung durch Verunreinigungen der Legierungsform
Glas	⊕ fast vollständig inert ⊕ durchsichtig, bessere Kontrolle der Packung auf Gleichmäßigkeit	⊖ aufwendige Reinigung der Säule ⊖ keine Analyse von aggressiver Fluoride möglich ⊖ leicht zerbrechlich ⊖ Knallgasexplosion beim Zerbrechen bei erhitzter Kapillare und Wasserstoff als Trägergas
Nickel	⊕ stabil ⊕ Analyse von empfindlichen Substanzen möglich, z.B. Steroide, Analgetica und Barbiturate	⊖ nicht so inert wie Glassäulen
Kupfer	⊕ leicht zu verarbeiten	⊖ Oberfläche ist autoxydabel ⊖ Kupferoxid oxidiert organische Stoffe ⊖ ungeeignet wenn Sauerstoff im Trägergas vorhanden ist ⊖ aufwendiges Herstellungsverfahren
Teflon	⊕ vollständig inert ⊕ Analyse von aggressiven Substanzen möglich	⊖ Material kann mikroporös sein, Spurenelemente der Außenluft rufen negative Effekte bei der Analyse hervor
Silizium	⊕ fast vollständig inert ⊕ nahezu unbegrenzte Rohstoffreserven ⊕ autoxydable Bildung von nativen Siliziumdioxiden	⊖ zerbrechlicher als Metalle

The solution shown below lets us format the content of the table cell almost arbitrarily. It is based on a special environment that can be defined with the help of the environ package by Will Robertson. In contrast to the usual LaTeX environments, the text between \begin{...} and \end{...} is not output immediately, but saved in a command. Afterwards, the content of the command can be processed in many ways before actually outputting it. In the following example, the mentioned environment is used to define a new column modificator C. In addition to centring, the content is mirrored vertically.

U	Λ	W
LaTeX	LaTeX (mirrored)	LaTeX
X	⅄	Z

06-00

```
\usepackage{array,environ,graphicx}
\NewEnviron{collectC}{%
  \mbox{}\scalebox{1}[-1]{%
    \raisebox{-\height}{\BODY}}}
\newcolumntype{C}{>{\begin{collectC}} c
                   <{\end{collectC}}}

\begin{tabular}{|l C r|}        \hline
    U      & V      & W      \\
    \LaTeX & \LaTeX & \LaTeX \\
    X      & Y      & Z      \\\hline
\end{tabular}
```

Creating tables with a loop command is not always easy – creating a table in LaTeX can be a somewhat complex process.

```
\usepackage{ltablex,ragged2e}
\keepXColumns
\newcolumntype{C}{>{\Centering}X}
\newcolumntype{P}[1]{>{\Centering}p{#1}}
%----------- After a suggestion by David Kastrup ------------
\newcommand\replicate[2]{\ifnum#1>0 #2%
  \expandafter\replicate\expandafter{\number\numexpr#1-1}{#2}\fi}
\newcommand*\NumberLines{79} \newcounter{N}
\newcommand*\Space{\rule[-1.8mm]{0pt}{6mm}}

\begin{tabularx}{\linewidth}{|r|c|P{3cm}|C|P{3cm}|} \hline
\textbf{No} & \textbf{first name} & \textbf{last name}
  & \textbf{address} & \textbf{signature} \Space \\ \hline
\endhead
%
\replicate{\NumberLines}{\stepcounter{N}\theN &&&& \Space \\ \hline}
%
\end{tabularx}
```

5-00-43

A survey

No	first name	last name	address	signature
1				
2				
3				
4				
5				
6				
7				
8				
9				
10				
11				
12				
13				
14				
15				
16				
17				
18				
19				
20				
21				
22				
23				
24				
25				
26				

1

A survey

No	first name	last name	address	signature
27				
28				
29				
30				
31				
32				
33				
34				
35				
36				
37				
38				
39				
40				
41				
42				
43				
44				
45				
46				
47				
48				
49				
50				
51				
52				

2

```
\usepackage{booktabs}
\usepackage{dcolumn}
\newcommand\mc[1]{\multicolumn{1}{@{}c@{}}{#1}}
\newcolumntype{x}{D{.}{.}{3.2}@{\kern1pt\%\kern10pt}}
\newcolumntype{y}{D{.}{.}{3.1}@{\%\kern10pt}}

\begin{tabular}{@{} r @{\kern2pt} yyy x y x yyy @{}}\toprule
 &\mc{CSY} &\mc{Ezaki}  &\mc{Holz}&\mc{Maddison}&\mc{Wong}    &\mc{Chow}  &\mc{Wang}
   &\mc{Scheibe}&\mc{IMF} \\
 &\mc{}    &\mc{and Sun}&\mc{}    &\mc{}        &\mc{and Chan}&\mc{and Li}&\mc{and Yao}
   &\mc{}       & \mc{}\\
 &\mc{2006}&\mc{1999}   &\mc{2005}&\mc{2007}    &\mc{2003}    &\mc{2002}  &\mc{2003}
   &\mc{2003}   & \mc{}\\\midrule
1978 & 11.7 &\mc{} & 11.7 &  7.71 &\mc{} &  7.60 &  7.6 &  7.6 &\mc{} \\
1979 &  7.6 &\mc{} &  7.6 &  3.37 &\mc{} &  7.81 &  7.8 &  7.6 &\mc{} \\
1980 &  7.8 &\mc{} &  7.8 &  5.98 &\mc{} &  5.26 &  5.2 &  5.2 &  7.9 \\
1981 &  5.2 &  5.2 &  5.2 &  7.52 &  5.3 &  9.01 &  9.1 &  9.1 &  4.7 \\
1982 &  9.1 &  9.3 &  9.1 &  8.48 & 12.1 & 10.89 & 10.9 & 10.9 &  9.1 \\
1983 & 10.9 & 11.2 & 10.9 & 12.45 &  9.6 & 15.18 & 15.2 & 15.2 & 10.9 \\\bottomrule
% \mc{} in empty cells to prevent output of the % character
\end{tabular}
```

	CSY 2006	Ezaki and Sun 1999	Holz 2005	Maddison 2007	Wong and Chan 2003	Chow and Li 2002	Wang and Yao 2003	Scheibe 2003	IMF
1978	11.7%		11.7%	7.71%		7.60%	7.6%	7.6%	
1979	7.6%		7.6%	3.37%		7.81%	7.8%	7.6%	
1980	7.8%		7.8%	5.98%		5.26%	5.2%	5.2%	7.9%
1981	5.2%	5.2%	5.2%	7.52%	5.3%	9.01%	9.1%	9.1%	4.7%
1982	9.1%	9.3%	9.1%	8.48%	12.1%	10.89%	10.9%	10.9%	9.1%
1983	10.9%	11.2%	10.9%	12.45%	9.6%	15.18%	15.2%	15.2%	10.9%

06-00-

```
\usepackage{tabto}

\begin{testArea}% see preamble of the example -> CTAN
  \NumTabs{4}
  duck \tab goose \tab turkey \tab coot   \par
       \tab       \tab        \tab grouse
\end{testArea}

\bigskip
\begin{testArea}
  \TabPositions{1.5cm,5cm,8cm}
  duck \tab goose \tab turkey \tab coot   \par
       \tab       \tab        \tab grouse
\end{testArea}

\bigskip
\begin{testArea}
  duck      \tabto{1.5cm} goose  \tabto{5cm}  turkey \tabto{8cm}
  coot \par \tabto{8cm}   grouse \tabto*{4cm} pelican
\end{testArea}
```

06-00-

0 1 2 3 4 5 6 7 8 9 10 11 12 13

duck *goose* *turkey* *coot*
grouse

0 1 2 3 4 5 6 7 8 9 10 11 12 13

duck *goose* *turkey* *coot*
grouse

0 1 2 3 4 5 6 7 8 9 10 11 12 13

duck *goose* *turkey* *coot*
pelican *grouse*

The data file for the following example is a typical comma-separated list, which contains one data set per line and can be created from all database programs through the appropriate export option.

```
firstname;lastname;street;city;topay;paid
Nicole;Müller;Schillerplatz 61;18419 Vogelow;100,0;100,0
Tom;Lehmann;Nachtigallgasse 11;29098 Altaue;100,0;100,0
Tim;Wagner;Amselplatz 92;46917 Langenhausen;100,0;0,0
Moritz;Müller;Waldallee 71;55348 Kirchstein;100,0;0,0
Susi;Mayer;Sonnenweg 27a;83675 Heidehausen;100,0;100,0
Ines;Mayer;Wasserallee 83a;26118 Kirchfurt;100,0;100,0
Uwe;Meier;Sonnenplatz 7;07514 Vogelburg;100,0;0,0
Mandy;Berger;Goetheweg 25;03783 Wolfental;100,0;100,0
Tim;Grönwald;Wiesenplatz 9a;90778 Moosow;100,0;50,0
Jenny;Köster;Finkenallee 29c;53522 Wiesenow;100,0;100,0
Marko;Mayer;Amselweg 11c;32108 Grünstein;100,0;100,0
Jenny;Berger;Wiesenallee 82;72044 Moosaue;0,0;0,0
```

```
\usepackage{datatool}
\usepackage{eurosym,booktabs}
\DTLsetseparator{;}
\DTLsetnumberchars{}{,}
\DTLsetdefaultcurrency{\texteuro~}
\DTLloaddb{list}{data/data2d.csv}
\DTLsort{lastname,firstname}{list}
\DTLsumforkeys{list}{topay}{\debit}
\DTLsumforkeys{list}{paid}{\credit}

\small\addtolength\tabcolsep{-1pt}
\begin{tabular}{@{} r llll rr @{}}\toprule
ID & first name & last name & street & city & to pay & paid \\\midrule
\DTLforeach{list}{% defined list elements
 \first=firstname,\last=lastname,\address=street,
 \town=city,\fee=topay,\paid=paid}{%
   \\ \theDTLrowi & \first & \last & \address & \town & \euro\, %
      \DTLifcurrency {\fee} % if \fee is a currency
        {\DTLconverttodecimal{\fee}{\fee} % then convert to decimal
                                          % and save the converted value in
                                          % \fee
         {\fee}} % output the value of \fee
        {\fee}    % if no currency, then only output
  & \euro\, \DTLifcurrency{\paid}% if \paid is a currency
    {\DTLconverttodecimal{\paid}{\paid}{\paid}} % then convert
    {\paid}} \\\midrule                         % else output \paid
& & & & & \DTLdecimaltocurrency{\debit}{\debit}\euro\,\debit& %
\DTLdecimaltocurrency{\credit}{\credit}\euro\,\credit \\\bottomrule
\end{tabular}
```

ID	Vorname	Nachname	Straße	Ort	zu zahlen	bezahlt
1	Jenny	Berger	Wiesenallee 82	72044 Moosaue	€ 0,0	€ 0,0
2	Mandy	Berger	Goetheweg 25	03783 Wolfental	€ 100,0	€ 100,0
3	Tim	Grönwald	Wiesenplatz 9a	90778 Moosow	€ 100,0	€ 50,0
4	Jenny	Köster	Finkenallee 29c	53522 Wiesenow	€ 100,0	€ 100,0
5	Tom	Lehmann	Nachtigallgasse 11	29098 Altaue	€ 100,0	€ 100,0
6	Ines	Mayer	Wasserallee 83a	26118 Kirchfurt	€ 100,0	€ 100,0
7	Marko	Mayer	Amselweg 11c	32108 Grünstein	€ 100,0	€ 100,0
8	Susi	Mayer	Sonnenweg 27a	83675 Heidehausen	€ 100,0	€ 100,0
9	Uwe	Meier	Sonnenplatz 7	07514 Vogelburg	€ 100,0	€ 0,0
10	Moritz	Müller	Waldallee 71	55348 Kirchstein	€ 100,0	€ 0,0
11	Nicole	Müller	Schillerplatz 61	18419 Vogelow	€ 100,0	€ 100,0
12	Tim	Wagner	Amselplatz 92	46917 Langenhausen	€ 100,0	€ 0,0
					€ 1100,00	€ 750,00

06-00-4

Chapter 7

Questions and answers

7.1 Documentation

Apart from a few exceptions, each package comes with its own documentation, which is part of the TEX distribution just like the style or class file. You can consult this documentation at any time using the texdoc command. Depending on the operating system, the appropriate program is started to show the file. Figure 7.2 on the next page shows the result of the command "`texdoc tabularx`" in Linux. Alternatively, you can use the graphical texdoctk environment (Figure 7.1), though the list of packages available in it is somewhat dated. An example of the output is shown in Figure 7.3 on the next page.

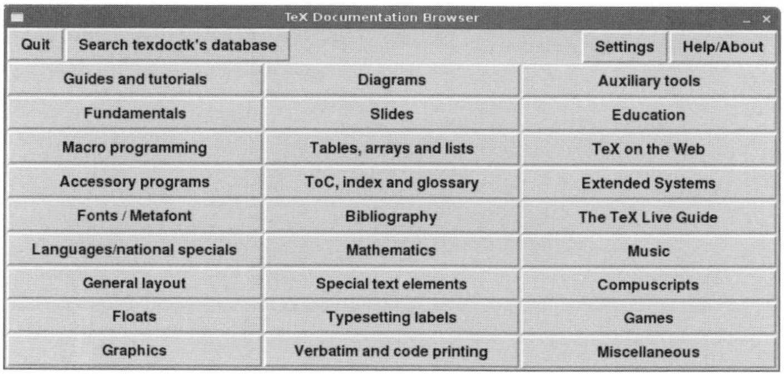

gure 7.1: The graphical environment the auxiliary program texdoctk.

Some authors don't provide self-contained documentation, but give hints in the package file itself, for example the `threeparttable` package. If there is an appropriate link to the

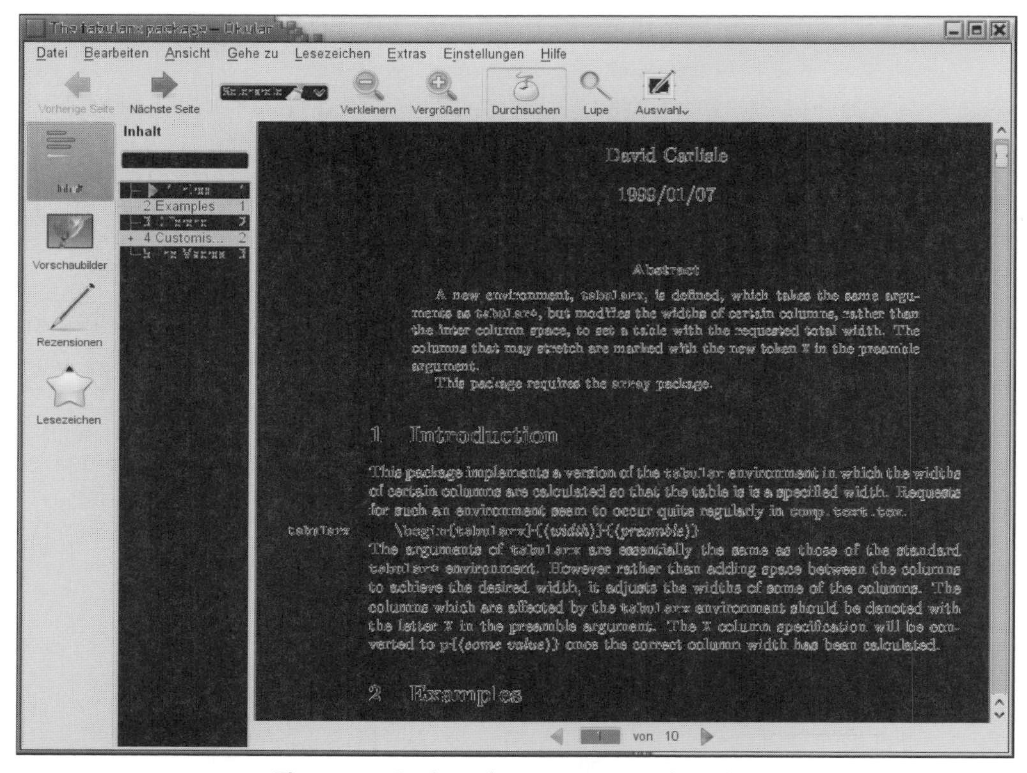

Figure 7.2: Package documentation with texdoc.

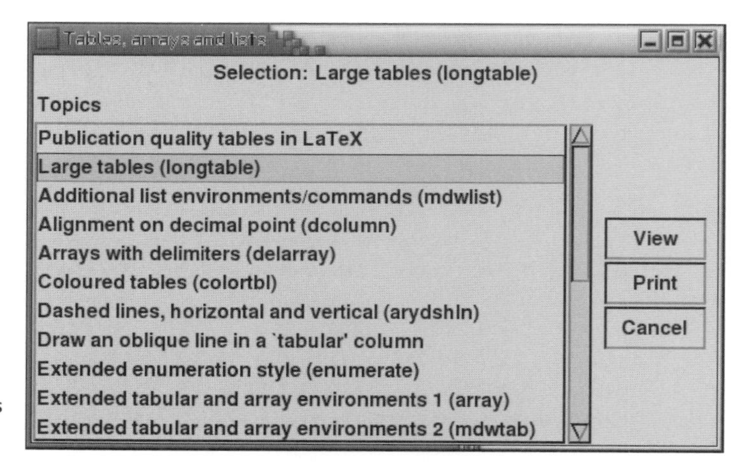

Figure 7.3: Selection menu for tables and lists.

package, texdoc will show this file as well. The location of a package can be found through the command kpsewhich `<file>`, which yields the result in Figure 7.4 on the facing page for the Windows command line. Now the file can be loaded and the description read with a normal editor. If there is no output, the package is either not installed or you have spelt the name of the package incorrectly.

Figure 7.4: Use of the program kpsewhich on the Windows command line.

TeX sources

Very often, the TeX sources of the documentation can be of help, letting you see at once how certain things were achieved. All source files for TeX Live can be found at `$TEXMF/texmf-dist/source/latex/` and for MiKTeX in the directory `...\MiKTeX 2.8\source`.[1]

7.2 Tables as floating objects

A table of type `longtable` internally increments the counter `table`, even if the table itself does not have a `\caption` command. This can lead to wrong counter values if there is another environment of type `table` *after* the `longtable`. In the following example, the floating environment is put in front of the `longtable` by TeX, but still has the wrong number.

07-02-1

\caption demo

Table 2: A table caption with the wrong number.

A normal table.

A `longtable` without `\caption`.

page 1

```
\usepackage{longtable}

\begin{longtable}{|c|}\hline
A \texttt{longtable} without
\texttt{\textbackslash caption}.\\\hline
\end{longtable}

\begin{table}
\centering
\caption{A table caption with
  the wrong number.}
\begin{tabular}{|c|}\hline
A normal table.\\\hline
\end{tabular}
\end{table}
```

[1] Adapt this path accordingly for versions of MiKTeX other than 2.8.

The problem can be fixed by decrementing the table counter `table` after a `longtable` *without* caption.

`\caption` demo

Table 1: A table caption with the correct number.

A normal table.

A `longtable` without `\caption`.

page 1

```
\usepackage{longtable}

\begin{longtable}{|c|}\hline
A \texttt{longtable} without
\texttt{\textbackslash caption}.\\\hline
\end{longtable}
\addtocounter{table}{-1}%%%%%

\begin{table}
\centering
\caption{A table caption with the correct number.}
\begin{tabular}{|c|}\hline
A normal table.\\\hline
\end{tabular}
\end{table}
```

07-02-2

Bibliography

[1] Paul W. Abrahams, Karl Berry und Kathryn Hargreaves. TeX for the Impatient, 2003. CTAN: /info/impatient/book.pdf

[2] Hendri Adriaens. The xkeyval package, 2005. CTAN: /macros/latex/contrib/xkeyval/

[3] Hendri Adriaens und Uwe Kern. »xkeyval – new developments and mechanism in key handling«. *TUGboat*, 25(2):194–198, 2004.

[4] Donald Arseneau. The threeparttable package, 2003. Version 3.0. CTAN: /macros/latex/contrib/ltxmisc/

[5] Donald Arseneau. The tabls package, 2006. Version 3.5. CTAN: /macros/latex/contrib/ltxmisc/

[6] Donald Arseneau. The tabto package, 2006. Version 1.0. CTAN: /macros/latex/contrib/ltxmisc/

[7] Enrico Bertolazzi. The easytable package, 2001. Version 1.0. CTAN: /macros/latex/contrib/easy/

[8] Johannes Braams und Theo Jurriens. The supertabular package, 2004. Version 4.1e. CTAN: /macros/latex/contrib/supertabular/

[9] D. Carlisle und S. Rahtz. The keyval package, 2001. CTAN: /macros/latex/required/graphics/

[10] David Carlisle. The delarray package, 1994. Version 1.01. CTAN: /macros/latex/contrib/tools/

[11] David Carlisle. The hhline package, 1994. Version 2.03. CTAN: /macros/latex/contrib/carlisle/

[12] David Carlisle. The ltxtable package, 1995. Version 0.2.
CTAN: /macros/latex/contrib/carlisle/

[13] David Carlisle. The blkarray package, 1999. Version 0.05.
CTAN: /macros/latex/contrib/carlisle/blkarray/

[14] David Carlisle. The tabularx package, 1999. Version 2.07.
CTAN: /macros/latex/contrib/carlisle/

[15] David Carlisle. The colortbl package, 2001. Version 0.1j.
CTAN: /macros/latex/contrib/carlisle/

[16] David Carlisle. The dcolumn package, 2001. Version 1.06.
CTAN: /macros/latex/contrib/carlisle/

[17] David Carlisle. The longtable package, 2004. Version 4.11.
CTAN: /macros/latex/required/tools/longtable.pdf

[18] David Carlisle. The tabulary package, 2008. Version 0.9.
CTAN: /macros/latex/contrib/carlisle/

[19] Hans-Peter Dörr. The exceltex package, 2006. Version 0.51.
CTAN: /macros/latex/contrib/xtab/

[20] Wybo Dekker. The ctable package, 2009. Version 1.15.
CTAN: /macros/latex/contrib/ctable/

[21] Michael Downes. Short Math Guide for LaTeX. American Mathematical Society, 2002. http://www.ams.org/tex/short-math-guide.html

[22] Jean-Pierre Drucbert. The Tabbing package, 1997. Version 1.0.
CTAN: /macros/latex/contrib/Tabbing/

[23] Victor Eijkhout. TeX by Topic, 1992. http://www.eijkhout.net/tbt/

[24] Simon Fear. The booktabs package, 2005. Version 1.6183.
CTAN: /macros/latex/contrib/booktabs/

[25] Anil Goel. The ltablex package, 1995. Version 1.0.
CTAN: /macros/latex/contrib/ltablex/

[26] Michel Goossens, Frank Mittelbach, Sebastian Rahtz, Denis Roegel und Herbert Voß. The LaTeX Graphics Companion: Illustrating Documents with TeX and PostScript, Second Edition. Tools and Techniques for Computer Typesetting. Addison-Wesley, Reading, MA, 2007.

[27] Eckhart Guthöhrlein. The rccol package, 2005. Version 1.2c.
CTAN: /macros/latex/contrib/rccol/

[28] Alan Hoenig. TeX Unbound: LaTeX & TeX Strategies, Fonts, Graphics, and More. Oxford University Press, London, 1998.

[29] Uwe Kern. Color extensions with the xcolor package, 2007. Version 2.11.
CTAN: /macros/latex/contrib/xcolor/

[30] Donald E. Knuth. The TEXbook. Addison Wesley Professional, 21. Auflage, 1986.

[31] Markus Kohm. »Satzspiegelkonstruktionen im Vergleich«. *Die TEXnische Komödie*, 14(4):28–48, 2002. http://www.dante.de/dante/DTK/PDF/komoedie_2002_4.pdf

[32] Helmut Kopka. LATEX—Eine Einführung. Addison-Wesley Verlag, Bonn, Germany, 3. Auflage, 2000. ISBN 3-89319-338-3.

[33] Helmut Kopka und Patrick W. Daly. Guide to LATEX. Addison-Wesley, Reading, MA, 4. Auflage, 2004.

[34] Leslie Lamport. LATEX: A Document Preparation System: User's Guide and Reference Manual. Addison-Wesley, Reading, MA, 2. Auflage, 1994. ISBN 0-201-52983-1.

[35] Olga Lapko. The `makecell` package, 2009. Version 0.1e. CTAN: /macros/latex/contrib/makecell/

[36] Jerry Leichter und Piet van Oostrum. The `bigdelim` package, 1994. Version 1. CTAN: /macros/latex/contrib/multirow/

[37] Jerry Leichter und Piet van Oostrum. The `bigstrut` package, 1994. Version 1. CTAN: /macros/latex/contrib/multirow/

[38] Jerry Leichter und Piet van Oostrum. The `multirow` package, 2004. Version 1.6. CTAN: /macros/latex/contrib/multirow/

[39] Hubert Gäßlein und Rolf Niepraschk. The `pict2e` package, 2004. CTAN: /macros/latex/contrib/pict2e/

[40] Andres Löh. The `polytable` package, 2005. Version 0.8.2. CTAN: /macros/latex/contrib/polytable/

[41] Frank Mittelbach und David Carlisle. The `array` package, 2008. Version 2.4c. CTAN: /macros/latex/contrib/tools/

[42] Frank Mittelbach, Michel Goosens, David Carlisle und Johannes Brahms. The LATEX Companion. Pearson Education, Reading, MA, 2. Auflage, 2004. The general book to LATEX.

[43] Lapo Filippo Mori. »Tables in LATEX 2$_\varepsilon$: Packages and Methods«. *The PracTEX Journal*, (1):1–38, 2007.

[44] Hiroshi Nakashima. The `arydshln` package, 2004. Version 1.71. CTAN: /macros/latex/contrib/arydshln/

[45] Josselin Noirel. The `cellspace` package, 2009. Version 1.6. CTAN: /macros/latex/contrib/cellspace/

[46] Heiko Oberdiek. The `tabularkv` package, 2006. Version 1.1. CTAN: /macros/latex/contrib/oberdiek/

[47] Heiko Oberdiek. The `tabularht` package, 2007. Version 2.5. CTAN: /macros/latex/contrib/oberdiek/

[48] Scott Pakin. The Comprehensive LaTeX Symbol List. CTAN, 2009.
CTAN: /info/symbols/comprehensive/symbol-a4.pdf

[49] Hubert Partl. »German TeX«. *TUGBoat*, 9(1):70–72, 1988.

[50] Axel Reichert. Satz von Tabellen, 1999. CTAN: /info/german/tabsatz/tabsatz.pdf

[51] Wayne Rochester. The `warpcol` package, 2007. Version 1.0c.
CTAN: /macros/latex/contrib/warpcol/

[52] Sigitas Tolušis. The `stabular` package, 1998. CTAN: /macros/latex/contrib/sttools/

[53] Nicola Talbot. Databases and data manipulation, 2009. Version 2.03.
CTAN: /macros/latex/contrib/datatool/

[54] The LaTeX team. `clsguide` – documentation pf LaTeX class and package writing, 2003. CTAN: /macros/latex/base/clsguide.pdf

[55] Herbert Voß. PSTricks – Grafik mit PostScript für TeX und LaTeX. DANTE/LOB-media.de, Berlin, 5. Auflage, 2008.

[56] Herbert Voß. Mathematiksatz mit LaTeX. DANTE/LOB-media.de, Berlin, Heidelberg, 2009.

[57] Herbert Voß. LaTeX Referenz. DANTE/LOB-media.de, Berlin, Heidelberg, 2. Auflage, 2010.

[58] Michael Wiedmann. References for TeX and Friends, 2005.
http://www.miwie.org/tex-refs/

[59] Peter Wilson. The `xtab` package, 2008. Version 2.3c.
CTAN: /macros/latex/contrib/xtab/

[60] Mark Wooding. The `mdwtab` package, 1998. Version 1.9.
CTAN: /macros/latex/contrib/mdwtab/

[61] Joseph Wright. The `siunitx` package, 2009. Version 1.3c.
CTAN: /macros/latex/contrib/siunitx/

[62] Koichi Yasuoka. The `slashbox` package, 1993. CTAN: /macros/latex/contrib/slashbox/

Index of commands and concepts

To make it easier to use a command or concept, the entries are distinguished by their "type" and this is often indicated by one of the following "type words" at the beginning of an entry:

> boolean, counter, document class, env., file, file extension, font, font encoding, key value, keyword, length, option, package, program, rigid length, or syntax.

The absence of an explicit "type word" means that the "type" is either a TeX or LaTeX "command" or simply a "concept".

Use by, or in connection with, a particular package is indicated by adding the package name (in parentheses) to an entry.

An italic page number indicates that the command is demonstrated in a source code snippet or in an example on that page.

When there are several page numbers listed, **bold** face indicates a page containing important information about an entry.

Symbols

A

B

People

ALSO PUBLISHED BY UIT

Typesetting Mathematics with LaTeX

Herbert Voss

From a simple equation to a mathematical treatise, this practical guide offers an in-depth review of the mathematics typesetting aspects of the industry-leading typesetting software, LaTeX. Among the topics discussed in this manual are mathematics in line with normal text, the software's special mathematics mode, color in math expressions, and fonts and math.

Handy features include a list of mathematical symbols for quick-reference, a survey of a wide range of additional mathematics packages—with a particular emphasis on the American Mathematical Society package—and ready-to-run examples to enable users to get going quickly.

This book will:

▷ Save you time by quickly giving you the detailed command syntax you require.

▷ Improve your mathematical typesetting by providing a reference to all the available commands.

▷ Showing the advantages of the packages from the American MAthematical Society

▷ Show you how to choose suitable math fonts, using the convenient samples of font output.

Contents

1. Introduction
2. Math in inline mode with standard LaTeX
3. Math in display mode with standard LaTeX
4. Math elements from standard LaTeX
5. Colour in math expressions
6. AMS packages
7. Symbols
8. TeX and math
9. Other packages
10. Examples
11. Fonts and math
12. Bibliography

ISBN: 9781906860172
290 pages

ALSO PUBLISHED BY UIT

LaTeX quick reference

Herbert Voss

This book lists all LaTeX macros and environments in a comprehensive reference format. (The packages **array** and **graphicx** are included even though they are not part of standard LaTeX, because they are so widely used.) The book also lists examples of fonts for both plain text and math, making it a convenient graphical resource.

This book will:

- Save you time by quickly giving you the detailed command syntax you require.
- Improve your LaTeX by providing a quick-reference to all the available command options.
- Show you how to choose suitable fonts, using the convenient samples of font output.

Contents

1. The Standard Programs
2. Document Structure
3. Commands for Fine-Tuning your Typography
4. Command List
5. Lengths and Counters
6. Fonts
7. Packages
8. Bibliography

Praise for the German Edition

"An essential resource for LaTeX users"

ISBN: 9781906860219
160 pages

ALSO PUBLISHED BY UIT

PSTricks

Graphics and PostScript for LaTeX

Herbert Voss

A comprehensive guide to creating and including graphics in TeX and LaTeX documents. It is both a reference work and a tutorial guide.

PSTricks lets you produce very high-quality PostScript graphics, by programming rather than interactive drawing. For designers, data publishers, scientists and engineers, generating graphics from data or formulas instead of having to draw manually allows large data collections or complex graphics to be created consistently and reliably with the minimum of effort.

There are many special-purpose extensions, for visualizing data, and for drawing circuit diagrams, barcodes, graphs, trees, chemistry diagrams, etc.

Numerous examples with source code (freely downloadable) make it easy to create your own images and get you up to speed quickly.

Contents

1. Introduction **2.** Getting Started **3.** The Coordinate System **4.** Lines and Polygons **5.** Circles, Ellipses and Curves **6.** Points **7.** Filling **8.** Arrows **9.** Labels **10.** Boxes **11.** Custom styles and objects **12.** Coordinates **13.** Overlays **14.** Basics **15.** Plotting of Functions and Data **16.** Nodes and Connections **17.** Trees **18.** Manipulating Text and Characters **19.** Filling and Tiling **20.** Coils, Springs and Zigzag Lines **21.** Exporting PSTricks Environments **22.** Color Gradients and Shadows **23.** Three-Dimensional Figures **24.** Creating Circuit Diagrams **25.** Geographic Projections **26.** Barcodes **27.** Bar Charts **28.** Gantt Charts **29.** Mathematical Functions **30.** Euclidean Geometry **31.** Additional Features **32.** Chemistry Diagrams **33.** UML Diagrams **34.** Additional PSTricks Packages **35.** Specials **36.** PSTricks in Presentations **37.** Examples

Praise for the German Edition

"A nice Christmas present – for me!"

"A detailed current description of PSTricks and the huge variety of PSTricks packages that are available, and written by an experienced LaTeX package developer."

"Searching through loads of different pieces of documentation is a thing of the past. This single compendium is a quick reference to everything I need."

ISBN: 9781906860134
900 pages

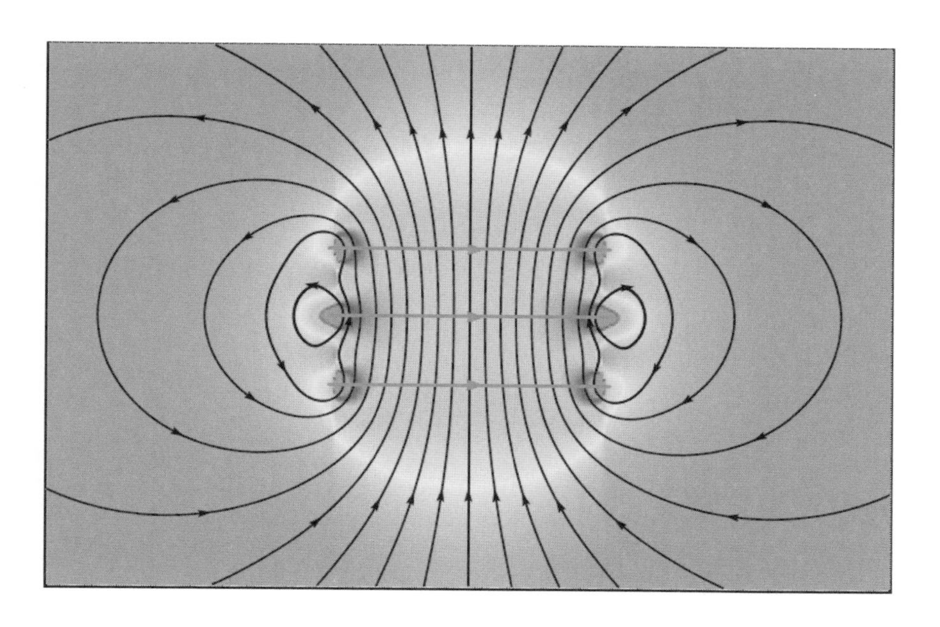

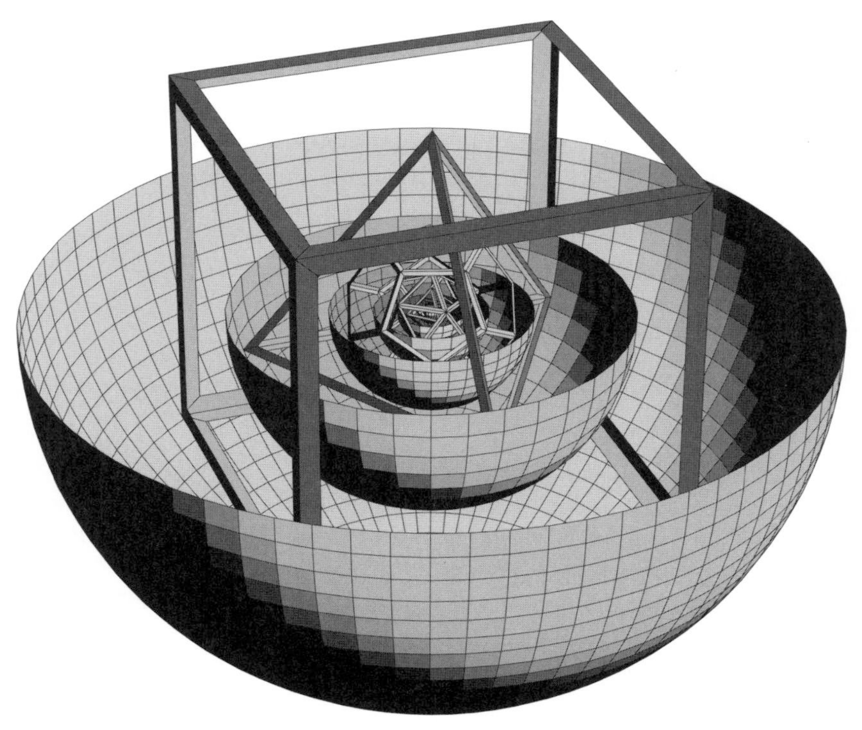

Example illustrations from PSTricks

ALSO PUBLISHED BY UIT

Practical TCP/IP

Designing, using, and troubleshooting TCP/IP networks on Linux and Windows

Niall Mansfield

Reprinted first edition

Key benefits

1. Explore, hands-on, how your network really works. Build small test networks in a few minutes, so you can try anything out without affecting your live network and servers.
2. Learn how to troubleshoot network problems, and how to use free packet sniffers to see what's happening.
3. Understand how the TCP/IP protocols map onto your day-to-day network operation – learn both theory and practice.

What readers have said about this book

"Before this book was released I was eagerly searching for a book that could be used for my Linux-based LAN-course. After the release of this book I stopped my searching immediately"
Torben Gregersen, Engineering College of Aarhus.

"Accuracy is superb – written by someone obviously knowledgable in the subject, and able to communicate this knowledge extremely effectively."

"You won't find a better TCP/IP book!"

"An excellent book for taking your computer networking career from mediocre to top notch."

"Covers TCP/IP, and networking in general, tremendously."

"This book has been touted as the 21st-century upgrade to the classic TCP/IP Illustrated (by Richard W. Stevens). These are big boots to fill, but Practical TCP/IP does an impressive job. In over 800 pages of well-organized and well-illustrated text, there is no fat, but rather a lean and – yes – practical treatment of every major TCP/IP networking concept."

"It's an ideal book for beginners, probably the only one needed for the first and second semesters of a university networking course. ... (But it is not a book just for beginners. ...)"

ISBN: 9781906860363
880 pages

ALSO PUBLISHED BY UIT

The Exim SMTP Mail Server

Official Guide for Release 4

Philip Hazel

Second edition

Email is one of the most widely used applications, and Exim is one of the most widely used mail servers, handling mail for tens of millions of users daily.

Exim is free software. It's easy to configure. It's scalable, running on single-user desktop systems as well as on ISP servers handling millions of users. (It's the default server on many Linux systems, and it's available for countless versions of UNIX.)

Exim is fast, flexible, and reliable. It is designed not to lose messages even if your server machine crashes. It can be used as a secure Internet-facing front-end to other, proprietary, mail systems used internally in your organization.

Exim supports lookups from LDAP servers, SQL databases, and other data sources, letting you automate maintenance and configuration. It can work in conjunction with other tools for virus-checking and spam-blocking, to reject unwanted emails before they even enter your site.

This book will help you deploy Exim as your SMTP email server throughout your organization, and to configure, tune, and secure your Exim systems.

Praise for the First Edition

"The book is simply amazing. I find the format/style/whatever 100 times better than [other documentation]."

"If there's even a whiff of a chance of you having to come into contact with Exim or its runtime configuration, then I can do nothing else but strongly recommend this book. The detail's there in spades, it reads very well, and is a fine complement to the reference manual."

"The book exceeds my expectations."

"Well presented and easy to follow"

"An excellent book that is very well written"

"So well written I learn new things every time I open it"

ISBN: 9780954452971
xviii + 622 pages

ALSO PUBLISHED BY UIT

The Joy of X

The architecture of the X window system

Niall Mansfield

This is a reprint of the 1993 classic, describing the architecture of the X window system – the de facto standard windowing system for Linux, UNIX and many other operating systems. The book has three sections:

1. X in a nutshell – a quick overview.
2. How X works, in detail, and how the user sees it.
3. Using the system, system administration, performance and programming.

The book is written in a clear, uncomplicated style, with over 200 illustrations. For maximum accessibility, it has a flexibile, modular structure that makes it easy to skip to the sections that interest you. The book has been widely recommended as a course text.

Niall Mansfield founded the European X window system User Group. He also wrote *The X window system: a user's guide*, and the widely-acclaimed *Practical TCP/IP*.

Praise for This Book

"User interfaces come and go, but X remains the standard window system across a range of operating systems. Niall's book, The Joy of X, still offers an excellent look into how X works and how to make it work better for you.

Keith Packard, X.org project leader

"If you are new to the X Window System environment, we strongly suggest picking up a book such as The Joy of X" **Eric Raymond, in the *Linux XFree86 HOWTO***

"a great little book called The Joy of X by Niall Mansfield that taught me much of what I know." **Jeff Duntemann's ContraPositive Diary**

"My personal touchstone when looking for a broad introduction to all things X is The Joy of X... by Niall Mansfield" **Peter Collinson**

ISBN: 9781906860004
xii + 372 pages

ALSO PUBLISHED BY UIT

OpenStreetMap

Using and enhancing the free map of the world

Frederik Ramm and Jochen Topf, with Steve Chilton

Second edition

OpenStreetMap is a map of the whole world that can be used and edited freely by everyone. In a Wikipedia-like open community process, thousands of contributors world-wide survey the planet and upload their results to the OpenStreetMap database. Unlike some other mapping systems on the Web, the tools and the data are free and open. You can use them and modify them as you require; you can even download all the map data and run your own private map server if you need to.

This book introduces you to the OpenStreetMap community, its data model, and the software used in the project. It shows you how to use the constantly-growing OSM data set and maps in your own projects.

The book also explains in detail how you can contribute to the project, collecting and processing data for OpenStreetMap. If you want to become an OpenStreetMap "mapper" then this is the book for you.

About the authors: Frederik Ramm and Jochen Topf both joined the OpenStreetMap project in 2006, when they were freelance developers. Since then they have made their hobby their profession – by founding Geofabrik, a company that provides services relating to OpenStreetMap and open geodata.

Praise for the First (German) Edition

> *"A must-have for OSM newcomers. The basics are presented well and are easy to understand, and you do not need to be an IT specialist to contribute your first data to OSM after a short time."*

> *"The book is very well written. It is obvious that the authors have a lot of knowledge and experience ..."*

> *"A very good OSM introduction. Getting up to speed with OpenStreetMap is much easier if you have read this book."*

ISBN: 9781906860110
352 pages + 32 pages of color plates

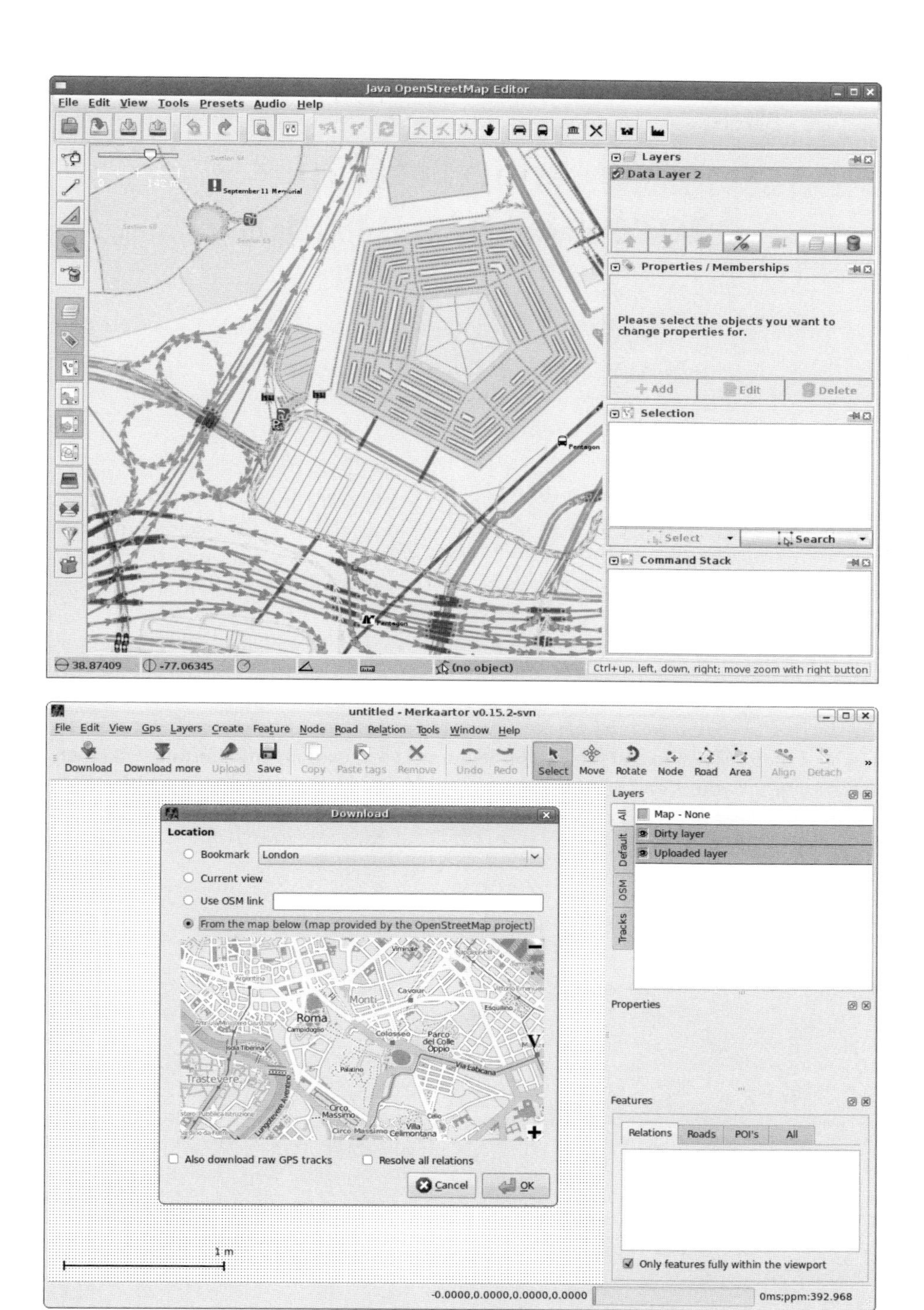

Example illustrations from OpenStreetMap

More about this book

Register your book: receive updates, notifications about author appearances, and announcements about new editions. ***www.uit.co.uk/register***

News: forthcoming titles, events, reviews, interviews, podcasts, etc. ***www.uit.co.uk/news***

Join our mailing lists: get email newsletters on topics of interest. ***www.uit.co.uk/subscribe***

How to order: get details of stockists and online bookstores. If you are a bookstore, find out about our distributors or contact us to discuss your particular requirements. ***www.uit.co.uk/order***

Send us a book proposal: if you want to write – even if you have just the kernel of an idea at present – we'd love to hear from you. We pride ourselves on supporting our authors and making the process of book-writing as satisfying and as easy as possible. ***www.uit.co.uk/for-authors***

UIT Cambridge Ltd.
PO Box 145
Cambridge
CB4 1GQ
England

Email: *inquiries@uit.co.uk*
Phone: **+44 1223 302 041**